The Politics of Injustice: Crime and Punishment in America

TITLES OF RELATED INTEREST FROM PINE FORGE PRESS

The Social Worlds of Higher Education: Handbook for Teaching
edited by Bernice Pescosolido and Ronald Aminzade

Adventures in Social Research: Data Analysis Using SPSS®
for Windows95/98™ Versions 7.5, 8.0, or Higher
by Earl Babbie and Fred Halley

Adventures in Criminal Justice Research, Revised Edition: Data Analysis
Using SPSS® for Windows95/98™ Versions 7.5, 8.0, or Higher
by George Dowdall, Kim Logio, Earl Babbie, and Fred Halley

Exploring Social Issues Using SPSS® for Windows 95/98™
Versions 7.5, 8.0, or Higher *by Joseph Healey, John Boli, Earl Babbie,
and Fred Halley*

The Pine Forge Press Series in Research Methods and Statistics
edited by Kathleen S. Crittenden

A Guide to Field Research *by Carol A. Bailey*

Designing Surveys: A Guide to Decisions and Procedures
by Ronald Czaja and Johnny Blair

Social Statistics for a Diverse Society, Updated Printing
by Chava Frankfort-Nachmias

Experimental Design and the Analysis of Variance *by Robert Leik*

How Sampling Works *by Richard Maisel and Caroline Hodges Persell*

Program Evaluation *by George McCall*

Investigating the Social World: The Process and Practice of Research,
Second Edition, *by Russell K. Schutt*

The Politics of Injustice: Crime and Punishment in America

Katherine Beckett
Theodore Sasson

Pine Forge Press
Thousand Oaks, California • London • New Delhi

For information, address:

Pine Forge Press
A Sage Publications Company
2455 Teller Road
Thousand Oaks, California 91320
(805) 499-4224
E-mail: sales@pfp.sagepub.com

SAGE Publications Ltd.
6 Bonhill Street
London EC2A 4PU
United Kingdom

SAGE Publications India Pvt. Ltd.
M-32 Market
Greater Kailash I
New Delhi 110 048 India

Production Editor: Wendy Westgate
Production Assistant: Karen Wiley
Typesetter/Designer: Danielle Dillahunt
Cover Designer: Ravi Balasuriya

Printed in the United States of America

00 01 02 03 04 05 10 7 6 5 4 3 2 1

Library of Congress Cataloging-in-Publication Data

Beckett, Katherine, 1964-
    The politics of injustice: Crime and punishment in America/by
Katherine Beckett and Theodore Sasson.
        p. cm.
    Includes bibliographical references and index.
    Contents: Criminal justice expansion—Crime in the United States—
Murder, American style—The politics of crime—Crime in the
news—Crime as entertainment—Crime and public opinion—
Activism and the politics of crime—Crime and public policy—
Alternatives.
    ISBN 0-7619-8639-1 (pbk: acid-free paper)
    ISBN 0-7619-8682-0 (cloth: acid-free paper)
    1. Crime—United States. 2. Crime prevention—United States.
3. Criminal justice. Administration of—United States. I. Sasson,
Theodore, 1965—   . III. Title.
Hv 6789.B38 2000
364.973—DC21   99-6712

About the Authors

Katherine Beckett, Ph.D., is Assistant Professor, Department of Criminal Justice, and Adjunct Assistant Professor, Department of Sociology, Indiana University. She teaches courses on violence, miscarriages of justice, drugs, and punishment. She is the author of "How Unregulated Is the U.S. Labor Market? The Dynamics of Jobs and Jails, 1980-1995," with Bruce Western (*American Journal of Sociology*, 1999), and *Making Crime Pay: Law and Order in Contemporary American Politics* (1997).

Theodore Sasson, Ph.D., is Assistant Professor of Sociology, Middlebury College, where he teaches courses in criminology, political sociology, social theory, and media studies. He has also taught sociology and criminology at Northeastern University, Boston College, and the University of Southern Maine. He is the author of *Crime Talk: How Citizens Construct a Social Problem* (1995), as well as numerous journal articles and book chapters.

About the Publisher

Pine Forge Press is an educational publisher, dedicated to publishing innovative books and software throughout the social sciences. On this and any other of our publications, we welcome your comments and suggestions.

Please call or write us at:

Pine Forge Press
A Sage Publications Company
2455 Teller Road
Thousand Oaks, CA 91320
(805) 499-4224
E-mail: sales@pfp.sagepub.com

Visit our World Wide Web site, your direct link to a multitude of online resources:
http://www.pineforge.com

For our children,

Jesse Beckett-Herbert
Kineret Grant-Sasson
Aryeh Grant-Sasson

Contents

Preface

❖❖❖ Over the past 30 years, crime has played an increasingly pivotal role in U.S. politics and culture. Politicians go to great lengths to define themselves as tough on criminals and drug addicts. Journalists cover crime more extensively than any other issue. Television networks launch new "reality-based" shows that glamorize law enforcement and blur the line between entertainment and news. And victims' rights activists clamor for more aggressive policing and harsher penalties. In this context, lawmakers have adopted a wide range of anticrime policies aimed at "getting tough" on offenders. The rate of incarceration in the United States is now among the highest in the world, and one out of three young black males is under the supervision of the criminal justice system.

Throughout this period, most criminologists have devoted their attention to investigating the causes of crime and criminal justice processes. At the margins of the discipline, however, a growing number of scholars have pursued a different line of inquiry, analyzing the role of the crime issue in U.S. politics and culture and the way in which the politicization of this issue has affected the policy-making process. In spite of widespread interest in these issues, almost none of this new work is discussed in standard sociology, criminology, and criminal justice texts.

The Politics of Injustice is the first book to communicate this new research to nonspecialists and specialists alike. We examine the U.S.

crime problem, crime as a political and cultural issue, and the policies that have resulted in the dramatic expansion of the penal system. In so doing, we draw on a wide range of scholarship, including research on crime, its representation in political discourse and the mass media, public opinion, crime-related activism, and public policy. Our review of these literatures is thorough yet focused on the development of our central argument: The punitive turn in crime policy is not primarily the result of a worsening crime problem or an increasingly fearful and vengeful public. Rather, above all else, growing punitiveness reflects efforts by national politicians to shift public policy on a variety of social problems—including crime, addiction, and poverty—toward harsher, more repressive solutions.

We hope the book will provide readers with a better understanding of the nature of crime and punishment in the United States, as well as the cultural and political contexts in which they occur.

ACKNOWLEDGMENTS

The book reflects our efforts over several years, together and separately, to understand the political and cultural determinants of crime policy. Parts of Chapter 4 appeared in Katherine's *Making Crime Pay* (1997). The case study in Chapter 5 originally appeared in our contribution to *The New War on Drugs*, edited by Eric Jensen and Jurg Gerber (1998). Material borrowed from these earlier publications has been revised and updated.

We would like to thank Northeastern University's Center for Criminal Justice Policy Research for providing office space and support for Ted during his 1997–1998 sabbatical. The center's director, Jack McDevitt, and its coordinator, Suzanne Bennett, were gracious and generous hosts. Middlebury College provided the sabbatical and additional research support through its Ada Howe Kent and faculty development funds.

Students in Ted's fall semester 1998 Sociology of Punishment seminar read drafts of several chapters and offered useful suggestions. Two Middlebury students, Alison Vratil and Grace Amao, helped edit the endnotes and prepare a final draft of the manuscript. Charlene Barrett, administrator of Middlebury's Sociology and Anthropology Department, helped Ted keep track of the duties of his day job in the final phase of writing. Our department colleagues at Middlebury College and Indiana University provided important insight and encouragement.

We are especially grateful to Steve Rutter, publisher of Pine Forge Press, for embracing the project and shepherding it to completion, and to Rebecca Smith, for making our writing as clear and accessible as possible. At the production end, we would like to thank Kate Chilton for copyediting, Jillaine Tyson for designing the book's many exhibits, and Wendy Westgate for unflappably knitting the various strands together. In addition, we are grateful to the following reviewers for reading early drafts of the book:

Gray Cavender, *Arizona State University*
Vincent F. Sacco, *Queens University*
Raymond Surette, *University of Central Florida*
David Forde, *University of Illinois, Chicago*

Last but always first, we want to thank our spouses, Steve Herbert and Deborah Grant, for their intellectual and emotional support, and for watching the kids while we worked.

Katherine Beckett
Theodore Sasson

1
◆ Criminal Justice
◆ Expansion

◆ ◆ ◆ Sabrina Branch, a 10-year-old Baltimore resident, sounds a lot like other children her age. She likes pizza and Cherry-Pepsi slushes, playing basketball, and reading "Goosebumps" mystery books. When she grows up, she would like to be lawyer or a basketball player. And like a growing number of children, Sabrina's life, described in a recent newspaper article, has been turned upside down by the dramatic growth of the U.S. criminal justice system.[1]

Sabrina and her three brothers live with their grandmother. Her father, an Army veteran, has been arrested and jailed several times for selling drugs. After his most recent release, he concealed his criminal record and tried to find work. Unsuccessful, he began using drugs again, then sought treatment for his drug habit unsuccessfully (Baltimore has treatment beds for 15,000 of its estimated 60,000 addicts). Arrested again for selling drugs, Vernon Branch is now locked away in the city jail, waiting to be sentenced to prison. Sabrina's mother, also addicted to drugs, has been locked up for petty theft. Sabrina's cousin Tony served 7 years for selling drugs and now wears an electronic monitor strapped to his ankle. One of Sabrina's aunts is serving 6 months for assault. Another aunt is nurturing a romantic relationship with a prison inmate.

Most of Sabrina's relatives have been incarcerated in the penal complex right down the street from her apartment. The complex—known as
"Eager Street University" to distinguish it from Johns Hopkins University a mile away—includes the city jail, two new high-security prisons,
and the state penitentiary that houses death row.

These institutions reach into the lives of Sabrina's schoolmates as
well. Seven of the 15 students gathered in Sabrina's math class one
afternoon had fathers who have been in prison. One boy's father died in
prison. A girl said she regularly visits the local jail with her older sister
to visit her boyfriend. Likewise, almost half of the players on a local
youth basketball team have a relative in prison, and several have served
time themselves:

> One hot afternoon, a 20-year-old shoots baskets on an outdoor court. He is
> wearing long pants so no one will see the monitoring device strapped to his
> ankle. An 11-year-old tossing lay-ups is wearing a t-shirt from Courtside Bail
> Bonds featuring a silhouette of a man behind bars.
>
> Upstairs in a meeting room, Harold Richard, 14, sits with some friends and
> calmly ticks off the people he knows who have served time. "My father," he
> begins in a soft monotone. "My mother. Both my uncles. My cousin." Around
> the table, other boys chime in: An 11 year old has an uncle just imprisoned for
> theft; another visited his mother in prison last week.
>
> Derrick Ross, 15, is waiting for his favorite uncle to be released in two
> weeks. His father and several cousins have also served time. Still, he declares,
> "I'm never going to prison." His twin brother, Eric, interrupts him: "Never
> say never."

On a trip to the courthouse with her grandmother to straighten out
administrative issues relating to her guardianship, Sabrina witnesses a
group of women prisoners being led away. "I saw all these women," she
later told the reporter. "They were walking through the hallway with
shackles. It made me think, is that going to be my mother? Or my aunt?
It could be any one of my relatives. Who will be next?"

Sabrina's concern is well-founded. In Baltimore and nearby Washington, DC, more than half of all African American men between the ages
of 18 and 35 are under the supervision of the justice system. The State of
Maryland recently assigned probation officers to Baltimore schools in
which as many as 4 out of 10 students have served time. Sadly, Baltimore
and Washington, DC, are not unique, but are the leading edge of a national
trend. Between 1980 and 1998, the number of people incarcerated grew

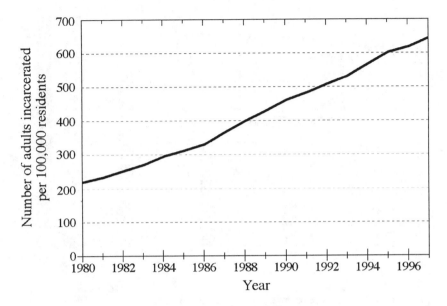

Exhibit 1.1. U.S. Incarceration Rate

SOURCE: Bureau of Justice Statistics, *Correctional Populations in the United States 1995*, Table 1.5, and Maguire and Pastore, *Sourcebook of Criminal Justice Statistics 1997*.

by over 300%, from half a million to over 1.8 million. The proportion of the population imprisoned has also grown rapidly, as Exhibit 1.1 shows, and over 3.8 million people are now on parole or probation. By 1998, nearly 6 million people—almost 3% of the adult population—were under some form of correctional supervision.[2]

These developments have disproportionately affected young African Americans and Latinos (see Exhibit 1.2). By 1994, one of every three Black males between the ages of 18 and 34 years was under some form of correctional supervision,[3] and the number of Hispanic prisoners had more than quintupled since 1980.[4] These developments have also had important consequences for criminal justice institutions. Since 1980, roughly 1,000 new jails and prisons have been built in the United States.[5] Despite this, at the end of 1997, state prisons were operating at between 15% and 25% above capacity, and federal prisons at 19% above their official limit.[6] In this context, resources for prisoner education, vocational training, and recreation have declined significantly.[7]

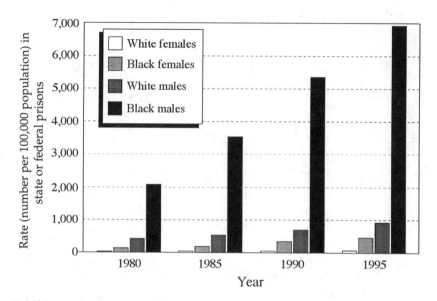

Exhibit 1.2. Incarceration Rate by Race and Sex

SOURCE: Bureau of Justice Statistics, *Correctional Populations in the United States 1990*, Table 1.7; *Correctional Populations in the United States 1995*, Table 1.7.

Apprehending, processing, and warehousing this many people is quite expensive. Annual expenditures on law enforcement, for example, have increased from $5 billion to $27 billion over the past two decades.[8] It costs approximately $30,000 to house a prisoner for a year—even with cuts in prison programs—so spending on correctional institutions has grown even more dramatically. By 1993, the annual public cost of such facilities was nearly $32 billion. As shown in Exhibit 1.3, the United States now spends over $100 billion annually fighting crime.[9]

In this book, we argue that the historically unprecedented expansion of the U.S. justice system is not the inevitable by-product of a rising or unusually high rate of serious crime. Rather, since the late 1960s, conservative politicians, together with the mass media and activists in the victim rights movement, have kept the issue of crime at the top of the nation's political agenda. Focusing on the most sensational and violent crimes, these actors have promoted policies aimed at "getting tough" and "cracking down." As a result, the criminal justice system has become more and more punitive, and its scope and expense are now unparalled

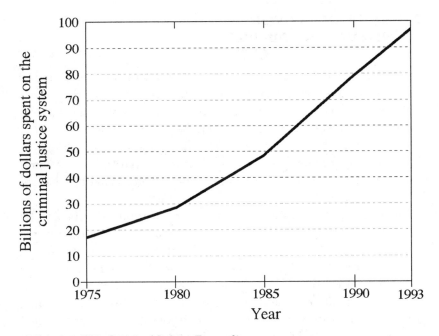

Exhibit 1.3. U.S. Criminal Justice Expenditures
SOURCE: Bureau of Justice Statistics, *Sourcebook of Criminal Justice Statistics 1980,* Table 1.3, and Bureau of Justice Statistics, *Sourcebook of Criminal Justice Statistics 1996,* Table 1.2.

among Western democracies. Yet there is little reason for optimism about the capacity of these harsh criminal justice practices to reduce the volume of crime in the society, and there is good reason to worry about their implications for social justice and democracy.

In developing this argument, we pursue two distinctive lines of inquiry. On the one hand, we examine representations of crime in political and media discourse and the relationship between these representations and public opinion, political activism, and public policy—this is the "constructionist" dimension of our analysis. On the other hand, we also examine the nature, extent, and causes of serious crime in the United States, as well as the merits of various public policies designed to deal with it—the "objectivist" dimension of our work. Perhaps surprisingly, some contemporary scholars regard these two lines of inquiry as altogether incompatible. Our analytical approach therefore merits a brief discussion.

BEYOND THE OBJECTIVIST-CONSTRUCTIONIST DIVIDE

Historically, sociologists analyzing social problems such as crime and drug abuse focused on the "objective conditions" that comprised those problems. Although these analysts did not deny that harmful behaviors or conditions must be defined as such to be recognized as social problems, their analyses concentrated on explaining the social conditions or behaviors that were understood to be harmful rather than on the processes by which those conditions were defined as problematic in the first place.

This approach to social problems has been roundly criticized by scholars now loosely referred to as "constructionist." Pointing out that many harmful conditions (such as the use of paint containing lead in public housing) are not defined as social problems—and that many conditions that are defined as problems may not be all that harmful—constructionists analyze the processes by which conditions are defined as problems or nonproblems and how those conditions that are defined as problems are framed or understood. In so doing, constructionists call attention to the socially constructed nature of social problems.[10]

The "crime issue" illustrates both the socially constructed nature of social problems and the significance of battles over how they are understood. Although the harm victims of crime suffer is very real, our understanding of the significance of crime as a social problem and our views on its causes and cures depend largely on the way in which the issue is represented in political discourse. Crime can be portrayed as a normal fact of life or as a crisis demanding immediate attention. Similarly, the "crime problem" can be understood in a variety of ways: as a consequence of criminal justice leniency, the decline of the traditional nuclear family, the corrosive effects of violence in the mass media, or socioeconomic inequality. Each of these interpretations (or "frames") has quite distinct policy implications.

In recent years, some scholars have argued that constructionist researchers should avoid evaluating the merits of the competing claims made by those involved in debates over social problems. According to these "strict constructionists," the researcher's goal should be confined to describing the rhetorical practices through which certain conditions are constituted as social problems.[11] In this view, social scientists do not have privileged access to the "truth" about social conditions and when we attempt to evaluate the validity of the competing claims we become "claims-makers" ourselves—participants in political debate rather than disinterested scholarly observers. [12] Strict constructionists also argue that researchers should not analyze why claims-makers frame certain problems in this way rather than that way, or how these efforts are related to larger social-historical circumstances. Indeed, the entire ensemble of social and political relationships that shape debates over social problems, they argue, are "outside" the claims-making process; consideration of these relationships is therefore theoretically and empirically unsound. In short, strict constructionists argue that students of social problems should analyze only the linguistic and rhetorical processes by which claims-makers frame social problems.

We disagree with this line of reasoning. Although we are interested in the rhetorical practices through which crime-related problems are constructed, we—along with other so-called contextual constructionists—believe that analyzing the social and historical context in which battles over social problems occur is both appropriate and useful. Furthermore, although it is true that social scientific knowledge about "objective conditions" (such as the rate of crime or drug use) is imperfect, we do not agree that social scientists should refrain from using data and research to evaluate the various claims that are made about those conditions. Indeed, in the chapters that follow, we base our arguments on what we consider to the most robust and reliable research findings in sociology and criminology. Although it is true that our discussion and use of these research findings—like all such discussions—reflect and support a particular perspective, these studies are nonetheless the soundest basis at our disposal for understanding and evaluating the crime problem, representations of it, and public policies aimed at reducing it. In the end, our readers will have to decide if we have done so in a way that is convincing.

EXPLAINING THE EXPANSION OF THE PENAL SYSTEM

We begin in Chapter 2 by showing that the expansion of the criminal justice system in recent decades is not a consequence of a rising or unusually high crime rate. On the contary, the best available data indicates that while the incarceration rate has soared, the U.S. crime rate has moved in both an upward and a downward direction. There is also evidence that levels of criminal victimization in the United States, although somewhat high, are comparable to those in other industrialized countries. There is one exception to this generalization: the United States is characterized by an exceptionally high rate of homicide. Indeed, despite recent declines in the murder rate, people in the United States are between 6 and 10 times more likely to be killed than in comparable countries. In Chapter 3, we analyze why this is the case and argue that the United States' unusually high homicide rate is due to the catastrophic interaction of a number of factors, including the ubiquity of guns, high rates of economic and racial inequality (especially in the form of concentrated urban poverty), the trade in illegal drugs, and the emergence of a "code of the streets" that encourages the use of violence. This understanding of the pervasiveness of lethal violence in America has important policy implications and helps us to understand the limited utility of the prevailing "lock-'em-up" strategy. But the fact that the United States has a higher homicide rate than comparable countries does not explain the growth in prison and jail populations: homicide is a relatively rare crime, and most of today's offenders are incarcerated for crimes that are far less serious than murder.

The best available evidence therefore casts doubt on the argument that prison populations are growing because crime rates are rising or exceptionally high. Instead, criminal justice expansion is the consequence of new policies and practices that target, prosecute, and punish offenders more aggressively than in the past. The number of police officers has increased significantly, for example, and although the police spend much of their time responding to citizen complaints, they are also increasingly aggressive in their efforts to detect and apprehend lawbreakers. The chances that an arrested person will end up in jail or prison have also grown steadily, while the chances that he or she will be funneled out of the system or placed on probation have declined.[15] For those who are sentenced to jail or prison, penalties have become more severe; indeed, longer sentences account for much of the growth of the prison population.[16] Finally, the number of juveniles tried and sentenced in the adult criminal justice system has sharply increased, as has the number of completed and impending executions.

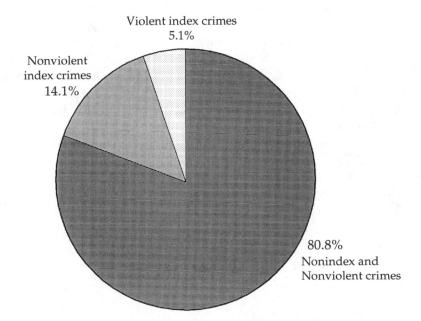

Exhibit 1.4. Arrests by Offense Type, 1996
SOURCE: Bureau of Justice Statistics, *Sourcebook of Criminal Justice Statistics 1997*, Table 4.6.

Nonviolent offenders have been especially affected by the growing harshness of the criminal justice system. The United States now arrests and incarcerates a much larger proportion of those accused of property, public order, or drug offenses than other industrialized countries, and it does so for significantly longer periods of time.[17] In some countries, persons guilty of public intoxication or drug possession are largely ignored or diverted into treatment programs. In the United States, they are more likely to be arrested and incarcerated. By 1996, nearly 5 million people were arrested annually for "consensual" or "victimless" crimes (crimes in which all parties are willingly involved), such as curfew violations, prostitution, gambling, drug possession, vagrancy, and public drunkenness.[18] Fewer than one in five of all arrests in that year involved persons accused of the more serious "index" crimes (for an explanation of index crimes, see Chapter 2). And as Exhibit 1.4 shows, only about one quarter of these more serious index crimes involved violence.

Increasingly, our prisons and jails are filled with people whose most serious violation is the possession or sale of illicit drugs. In state prisons, for example, the percentage of inmates convicted of nonviolent drug offenses increased from 9% in 1985 to 23% in 1996.[19] Among federal inmates, the percentage of inmates whose most serious offense was drug related jumped from 33% to 60%.[20] Most of those incarcerated for drug offenses are convicted of possession—rather than distribution—of drugs.[21]

In sum, the volume and nature of crime in the United States does not explain the dramatic growth of the criminal justice system. Rather, the expansion of the penal system is a consequence of the decision to "get tough" on criminal offenders—including those convicted of minor offenses that are not even tabulated in conventional crime statistics. This policy choice is, in turn, a consequence of the increased importance of "the crime issue" in U.S. political culture and the ascendance of certain ways of framing or understanding the crime problem.

THE POLITICS OF CRIME

The policies and practices that have contributed so significantly to the expansion of the U.S. penal system are numerous and diverse, but are similarly predicated on the view that "getting tough" and "waging war" is the best way to solve the crime problem. This perspective was initially promoted by the same actors who struggled to put the issue of crime on the national political agenda. In Chapter 4, we show that the politicization of crime began in earnest over three decades ago. In response to the civil rights movement and the expansion of the War on Poverty programs of the 1960s, conservative politicians highlighted the problem of "street crime" and argued that this problem was caused by an excessively lenient welfare and justice system that encouraged bad people to make bad choices.

By emphasizing the severity and pervasiveness of "street crime" and framing the problem in terms of immoral individuals rather than criminogenic social conditions, conservative politicians effectively redefined the poor—especially the minority poor—as dangerous and undeserving. In the process, these politicians attracted socially conservative voters to the ranks of the Republican Party and legitimated efforts to redirect state policy toward crime control rather than social welfare. This ideological campaign was so successful that Democrats are now nearly as likely as Republicans to support welfare spending cuts and draconian anticrime initiatives. The reorientation of state policy around social control rather than social welfare now enjoys widespread, bipartisan support.

The mass media were crucial to the success of these efforts to highlight crime-related problems—especially violent street crime—and frame them in ways that indicate the need for enhanced punishment. In Chapter 5, we examine the role of the news media, arguing that news coverage of crime and drugs has tended to amplify rather than challenge the claims of national politicians. Indeed, the volume of crime news coverage has increased (even during periods when the crime rate was dropping), and the problem has typically been framed in terms of the alleged unwillingness of the criminal justice system to truly get tough on criminal offenders. Crime news also tends to focus on the most sensational types of violent crime, ignoring the less frightening and far more petty offenses for which an increasing number of Americans are incarcerated.

Americans are drawn to fictional as well as news accounts of crime, and these also affect the way people think about the issue. In Chapter 6, we examine images and narratives of crime on television and in film. The rate of violence in these media has historically outstripped real-world rates, and this gap has grown wider in recent decades. Moreover, in film and television programming, police efforts to catch criminals are often thwarted by legal technicalities, liberal judges, and bureaucratic red tape. The thin blue line protecting citizens from criminals is therefore patrolled by heroic cops who must operate outside the boundaries of the law to get the job done. Like crime news stories, these programs echo conservative complaints about the alleged leniency of the criminal justice system. Tabloid television programs (*Hard Copy*, *48 Hours*) and reality-based police shows (*Cops*, *Real Stories of the Highway Patrol*) further amplify this theme and, by blurring the line between news and entertainment, do so in ways that are particularly dramatic.

Although the American public did not put the crime issue on the public agenda, many people have responded to political demands for a tougher justice system. In Chapter 7, we examine public opinion regarding crime and punishment and conclude that the tendency of most Americans to support the "get-tough" rhetoric of politicians—a tendency rooted deeply in American culture—has grown more pronounced. But this conclusion needs to be qualified in two important ways. First, we argue that the intensification of popular punitiveness is largely a consequence rather than a cause of political initiative on the crime issue; popular attitudes increasingly reflect the claims and narratives about crime that dominate political rhetoric and saturate the mass media. Second, we marshal evidence to show that although popular attitudes and beliefs have hardened, they remain ambivalent and contradictory. Despite the current get-tough mood, most Americans are still eager to see a greater emphasis placed on crime prevention and are willing to support a variety of alternatives to incarceration. There is therefore reason to suspect that politicians willing to challenge the prevailing get-tough approach to crime control might enjoy popular support for doing so.

In Chapter 8, we explore popular responses to crime, this time analyzing a range of crime-related, grassroots activities. These include neighborhood anticrime efforts, the victim rights movement, and human rights activism against the death penalty, mandatory drug sentences, and police brutality. Some of these movements have been able to influence the direction of crime control policy; others have not. In this chapter, we analyze why this is so and, in particular, explain why the victim rights movement has received more attention and more successfully affected policy than have groups that challenge the logic of the war on crime.

The initiatives of politicians, amplified through the mass media and resonant with many Americans, have resulted in many new laws and practices. In Chapter 9, we take a closer look at the policy changes that have contributed most directly to the growth of the criminal justice system, including harsh new mandatory minimum and "three strikes" sentencing laws, the restoration of the death penalty, and intensification of surveillance in the community. We argue that these and other get-tough policy initiatives have done little to suppress crime. In fact, by breaking up families and disrupting communities, reducing the job prospects of hundreds of thousands of ex-cons, and consuming resources that might otherwise be directed toward crime prevention, these new policies are increasingly important causes of contemporary urban problems, including crime. Furthermore, these policies are corrosive of democratic institutions and values and reflect a disturbing tendency to scapegoat and discard those citizens now considered to be part of an "urban underclass."

In Chapter 10, we suggest that political activism is needed to induce politicians to reconsider the policies associated with the war on crime.

In the hope of furthering this cause, we sketch out an alternative policy agenda. Our proposals emphasize the need to scale back the reach of the justice system and shift the balance in crime control from punishment to prevention. We therefore recommend decriminalizing drugs, reducing the number of guns in circulation, and improving the quality of life and opportunities for poor children.

2
❖ Crime in
❖ the United States

❖ ❖ ❖ The extraordinary expansion of the penal system—especially the prison and jail populations—demands explanation. According to conventional wisdom, the criminal justice system has grown so rapidly because the crime problem in the United States is unusually severe and/or getting worse. In this chapter, we evaluate this explanation in light of the available evidence. Is the crime rate really higher than ever? Is crime a more serious problem in the United States than in other industrialized countries? If so, the growth of the U.S. prison and jail populations may be understood as a response to a worsening or particularly severe crime problem. But if the U.S. crime rate is neither increasing nor unusually high, we will need to identify other factors that help to explain the unprecedented expansion of the penal system.

CRIME IN HISTORICAL PERSPECTIVE

Many people have the impression that crime is a much more serious problem than in the past. Indeed, many believe that the moral fabric of society is unraveling, and, as a result, crime rates are rising. By contrast, historical research suggests that modern, industrialized societies—including our own—are significantly safer than the predominantly rural societies of previous centuries. In Europe, for example, rates of crime and violence declined steadily from the 13th century through the mid-20th century. In fact, rates of homicide in medieval and early modern Europe were between 10 and 20 times higher than in the 20th century. In the United States, too, urbanization and industrialization were associated with declining levels of violence.[1] Contrary to popular perceptions, it appears that Western society has become less rather than more violent over time.

The incidence of violence continued to decline through the 1940s in most industrialized countries, although the U.S. homicide rate did increase under Prohibition in the 1920s.[2] After World War II, however, reported rates of crime in the United States (and most European countries) began an upward trend that continued for some time. Despite this upward trend, homicide was far less common in 1981 (a peak year for murder in the United States) than it had been at several points in the 19th century.[3]

Whether or not the incidence of crime has increased in the more recent past is hotly debated. The uncertainty stems from the fact that different data sources give us very different information about crime trends. For most of the 20th century, the Federal Bureau of Investigation's Uniform Crime Reports (UCR) have served as the main source of information about crime. The UCR measure the frequency of seven "index" crimes, including homicide, robbery, rape, assault, larceny, burglary, and arson. These reports are based on the number of crimes known to the police and reported by the police to the FBI. According to the UCR, both violent and property crime rates increased fairly steadily from the early 1960s, reaching high levels in the early 1990s. Although the UCR show a drop in serious crime in more recent years, the overall picture is that of an unprecedented crime problem (see Exhibit 2.1).

In the early 1970s, concern about the volume of crime not reported to police (and hence omitted from the UCR) led to the creation of the National Crime Survey (now called the National Crime Victimization Survey or NCVS). The results of the NCVS are based on interviews with a random sample of 100,000 noninstitutionalized U.S. residents 12 years old and older. NCVS respondents are asked by interviewers to describe their experience with different types of crime. Because many people do not report such experiences to the police but are willing to describe them to telephone interviewers, the NCVS data show a much higher level of criminal victimization than do the UCR. (Many people also do not report their experiences to telephone interviewers, and those most likely to be

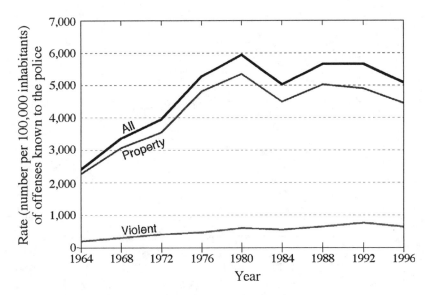

Exhibit 2.1. Crime Trends: Uniform Crime Report Data
SOURCE: Maguire and Pastore, *Sourcebook of Criminal Justice Statistics 1997,* Table 3.111.

victimized are less likely to be reached by telephone, so the victimization survey data still underestimate the incidence of criminal victimization).

Unlike the UCR data, the NCVS results show that rates of violent crime have not increased in recent decades (see Exhibit 2.2). Instead, the NCVS results indicate that crime rates have fluctuated over the past 25 years and that violent crime was less common in 1997 than it was in 1973. The NCVS data also suggest that rates of property crime declined sharply during this period.

Why do the UCR and NCVS provide contradictory information regarding trends in criminal victimization? Answering this question is a bit more complicated than it may seem. For one thing, the UCR and NCVS do not measure exactly the same crimes or cover the identical time period.[4] Comparisons of the two data sources must take this and other methodological differences into account. Most researchers attempting to sort these issues out have concluded that the increase in crime reported in the UCR is largely a consequence of two main developments:

◆ Members of the public have become more likely to report their victimization to the police.

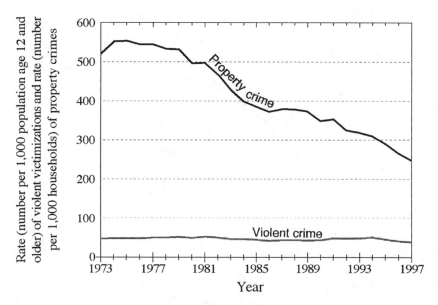

Exhibit 2.2. Crime Trends: National Criminal Victimization Survey Data
SOURCE: Bureau of Justice Statistics, *National Criminal Victimization Survey, Crime Trends, 1973-1997*.
NOTE: Data from 1976 to 1991 have been adjusted to make them comparable to data following the 1992 redesign.

◆ The police have become more likely to record these reports and to share their records with the FBI, the agency responsible for compiling the UCR.[5]

The fact that more victims of crime are choosing to report their victimization to the police appears to reflect growing awareness of and concern about crime.[6] Studies investigating the decision to report rape, for example, suggest that heightened awareness of violence against women has increased the likelihood that rape victims will report their victimization to the police.[7]

Growing police awareness of the prevalence and seriousness of rape has also increased the likelihood that police will "found" (judge to be reliable) reports of rape and include them in official records. In Indianapolis, for example, the number of rape reports founded and recorded by the police increased significantly following the establishment of a sex offender unit in that department.[8] Police recording of other types of crimes has also increased. For example, in 1973, about half of all of aggravated assaults reported in the NCVS were recorded by the police;

in 1988, an estimated 97% of all such reports were recorded by local law enforcement.[9]

This change occurred largely at the behest of the federal government. Between 1973 and 1988, the Justice Department began to aid local police departments with their record keeping, and officers on the beat were encouraged to spend more time on paperwork. Overall, although the number of victimizations reported to the police decreased 5% between 1973 and 1995, the number of crimes recorded by police during this period grew by 116%.[10] As one crime-trend analyst concluded, "the 20 year period from 1973 [through] 1992 was not a period of ever-increasing rates of violent crime. Instead it was a period of increasing police productivity in terms of the recording of crimes that occurred."[11]

One type of crime that is less affected by changes in public reporting and police recording practices is homicide. Unlike other types of crime, the desire of victims to conceal their victimization has no impact on whether this crime comes to the attention of the police. Friends and relatives are also much less likely to be able to cover up a murder, and the police rarely fail to record a crime as serious as homicide. Moreover, data from medical sources regarding the incidence of death by homicide closely parallel the homicide rate compiled by the FBI. For all of these reasons, UCR estimates of the murder rate are seen as fairly trustworthy.[12]

What do these data tell us about lethal violence in the United States? According to the UCR, the homicide rate doubled from the mid-1960s to the late 1970s and has fluctuated ever since (see Exhibit 2.3). The homicide rate reached very high levels in 1980 and 1991—and, as we shall see, homicide is a more serious problem in the United States than in other industrialized countries. But murder is not becoming an ever more frequent occurrence in the United States. In fact, in 1997, the murder rate reached its lowest level in 25 years.

In sum, the upward trend in the crime rate between 1960 and 1990 suggested by the UCR appears to be largely a consequence of increased reporting and improved police recording practices. Although also imperfect, most analysts regard the NCVS as a more reliable indicator of crime trends.[13] The results of this survey indicate that rates of property crime have dropped steadily over the past two decades and that violent crime is slightly less common in the mid-1990s than it was two decades ago. Finally, homicide data clearly indicate the severity of the problem of lethal violence in the United States but do not suggest that homicide has become ever more frequent in recent decades.

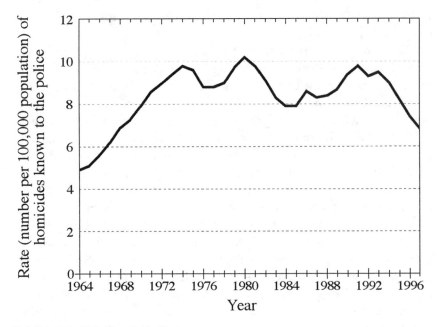

Exhibit 2.3. U.S. Homicide Rate
SOURCE: Federal Bureau of Investigation, *Uniform Crime Reports, 1964-1997.*

Together, these findings suggest that the expansion of prisons and jails is not simply a result of a worsening crime problem. Recent trends have made this even more evident. Since 1990, the state prison population has grown 7% annually—despite drops in the crime rate (shown by both the UCR and the NCVS) for seven consecutive years.[14]

CRIME IN COMPARATIVE PERSPECTIVE

Even if crime rates are stable or declining, it is possible that the crime problem is far worse in the United States than in other comparable countries. This difference, if it exists, could explain the United States' exceptionally high rate of incarceration. Indeed, many people believe that the United States has more crime than other industrialized countries. This impression is based largely on research that compares UCR data and European crime statistics. However, such comparisons are unsound, for a number of reasons:

◆ As discussed earlier, the UCR data appear to misrepresent crime trends in recent decades; comparisons that rely on them are therefore misleading.
◆ Some European crime statistics are based on the number of persons convicted, but the UCR data measure those crimes that are known to the police. Clearly, most crimes known to the police do not result in convictions. As a result, such comparisons overestimate the difference between crime rates in the United States and in other industrialized countries.[15]
◆ Cross-national comparisons have been hampered by the fact that countries may define crimes differently. For example, what would be considered pickpocketing in one country might be classified as robbery in another and larceny in yet a third.

Recognition of these problems led to the creation of the International Crime Surveys, first administered by the Dutch Ministry of Justice in 1988. These international surveys offer several advantages:

◆ Those administering the international survey use a single definition of each type of crime in every country in which the survey is conducted.
◆ Like the NCVS results, the findings of the international surveys do not depend on the actions of criminal justice officials but are based on the direct reports of surveyed individuals. (Although some survey respondents lie, we have no reason to suspect that Americans lie any more or any less than Belgians, Swedes, or Japanese).

The results of the International Crime Surveys cast doubt on the assumption that the United States is far more crime prone than other industrialized nations. The 1989 survey found that although rates of victimization in the United States were somewhat high, for no crime were the American rates the highest. For example, rates of auto theft were higher in England, Italy, Australia, New Zealand, and France than in the United States; burglary was more common in New Zealand and Australia than in the United States.[16] Surveys administered by the United Nations in 1991 also found that U.S. rates of property crime were fairly average and that the incidence of violent crime was on the high end, but not exceptionally so.[17]

The 1996 International Crime Survey provides even stronger evidence that U.S. crime rates are not exceptionally high. According to this survey, the overall victimization rate (weighted to reflect the seriousness

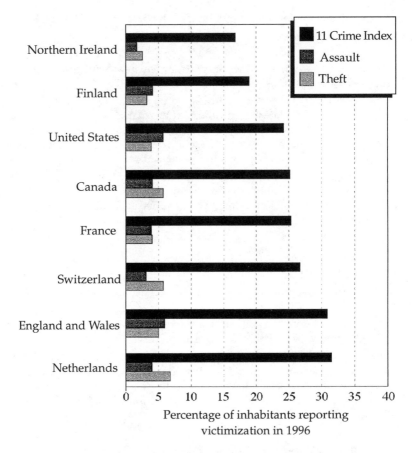

Exhibit 2.4. International Crime Victimization Survey Results
SOURCE: Mayhew and Van Dijk, *Criminal Victimization in Eleven Industrialized Countries.*

of offenses) was lower in the United States than in six other industrial-ized countries and was actually slightly below the norm (see Exhibit 2.4). Presumably, these more up-to-date data reflect the recent decline in violent crime in the United States.[18]

In sum, international survey data suggest that the United States does not have an unusually severe crime problem. Although historically the rates of violent crime in the United States have been at the high end of the international distribution, this fact alone cannot account for a U.S. incarceration rate that is *6 to 10 times greater* than that of other industri-

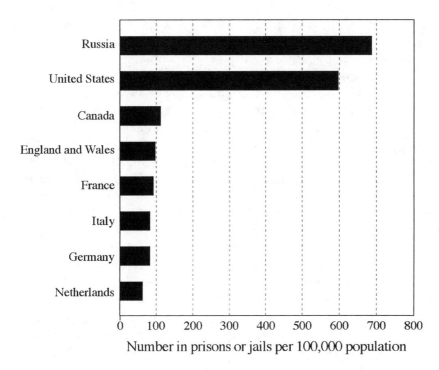

Exhibit 2.5. International Incarceration Rates, 1995
SOURCE: Mauer, *Americans Behind bars: U.S. and International Use of Incarceration, 1995.*

alized nations (see Exhibit 2.5). Furthermore, recent surveys suggest that the rate of violent crime is now actually lower in the United States than in many other countries.

Cross-national comparisons of crime that analyze all available data sources (police statistics as well as national and international survey data) reach similar conclusions. One such study sponsored by the National Institute of Justice found that England and Wales are, in general, more crime ridden than the United States.[19] Another study concluded that U.S. rates of nonlethal violence are roughly similar to those in other English-speaking countries but that rates of serious property crime are significantly lower than in many other industrialized countries, including Australia, Canada, Sweden, and the Netherlands. As the author of this study concludes, "the United States has higher levels of lethal violence than other nations but similar levels of minor [nonlethal] violence and property crime than other nations normally considered more civil."[20]

Indeed, lethal violence is a dramatic exception to the rule that U.S. crime rates are unexceptional. (Homicide is not measured in the International Crime Survey—or any other survey—because dead people cannot report their victimization.) According to police statistics, homicide is between 5 and 10 times more common in the United States than any other industrialized country, even after the recent decline.[21] Murder is thus a problem of enormous significance in the United States, the causes of which will be explored in the following chapter. However, the point we wish to stress here is that the high murder rate in the United States cannot explain why we have such large and growing prison and jail populations. Homicide convictions account for only a small proportion of those admitted to prison. In 1992, for example, only 4.1% of new court commitments to prison involved persons convicted of homicide.[22] By contrast, more than 70% of new court commitments involved persons convicted of drug, property, or public order offenses.[23] Jail inmates are even less likely to have been charged with homicide and are more likely to be minor offenders.[24] Most of those incarcerated in the United States are doing time for crimes much less serious than murder.

CONCLUSION

In this chapter, we have argued that the U.S. crime rate is neither rising nor (with the exception of homicide) unusually high in comparison to other industrialized countries. Thus it is clear that the prison boom in the United States is not a consequence of an exceptional crime problem.

These same data might be interpreted as suggesting that incarceration is an effective anticrime strategy. According to this argument, crime rates are dropping in the United States—both absolutely and relatively—because we have incarcerated so many people.[25] This seems plausible, but there are many reasons to doubt that the incarceration boom is responsible for declining crime rates. For example, cross-sectional research shows that states and countries that incarcerate at higher rates are not necessarily characterized by lower crime rates.[26] This issue will be addressed in greater detail in Chapter 9.

Although crime in the United States has diminished over the past decade and is roughly comparable to the level experienced in other industrialized countries, the U.S. homicide rate continues to be exceptionally high. In the next chapter, we examine why this is so.

3

◆ Murder,
◆ American Style

◆ ◆ ◆ The United States does not have an unusually severe crime problem, but it does have an exceptionally high rate of homicide. The frequency of murder in the United States does not explain our high rate of incarceration—the main focus of this book. Nevertheless, in this chapter, we analyze the problem of homicide to cast doubt on the popular explanations of violence that permeate public discourse about crime and influence the direction of criminal justice policy.

Some might object that by focusing on conventional, interpersonal homicide we are defining the concept of murder too narrowly. In the United States, thousands of people are killed every year by unsafe products, dangerous working conditions, and other irresponsible corporate practices such as illegal hazardous waste disposal. In addition, large numbers of people have been and continue to be victimized by state-sponsored acts of terror such as the slaughter of Central Americans by U.S.-backed armies in Guatemala, El Salvador, and Nicaragua in the 1980s.[1] By excluding these acts of corporate and state violence from our analysis, are we not reinforcing the erroneous impression that murder is something done mostly by the poor and powerless rather than by the rich and powerful? We are, for the most part, sympathetic to this argument. However, our aim in this chapter is to set the stage for our critique of political and media claims about violence and the policies that derive from them. These claims and policies ignore corporate and state-

27

sponsored violence, and so it is the problem of interpersonal homicide that we address in this chapter.

In what follows, we suggest that four interrelated factors underlie the unusually high rate of interpersonal homicide in the United States:

- The profusion of guns has made assaultive behavior much more likely to result in death than it would if guns were not so widely available.
- The high levels of economic and racial inequality that characterize the United States, particularly in the form of concentrated urban poverty, create an ecological context that encourages lethal violence.
- The illegal drug trade generates a significant amount of deadly violence in the form of battles over turf and drug deals gone bad.
- In the context of declining job opportunities, a "code of the streets" that prizes respect and regards violence as a necessary means of obtaining it has emerged in many poor, urban communities.

These four factors are intertwined in complex ways. For example, the drug trade and the code of the streets are both related to the social and economic organization of inner city neighborhoods, especially the growing concentration of poverty and increased family disruption. One dominant theme in our discussion of contemporary patterns of homicide will therefore be the significance of the social transformation of ghetto neighborhoods. More generally, we emphasize the way in which a number of social, political, and economic factors interact to produce high rates of deadly violence. Before presenting our argument, however, we critically assess two more popular explanations of lethal violence in America.

POPULAR EXPLANATIONS OF VIOLENCE

When politicians discuss the high U.S. murder rate, they often point an accusing finger at the criminal justice system. The courts and prisons let violent criminals off the hook too easily, they argue, sending the message that crime pays. This argument has been the main rationale for harsh new sentencing laws for adult and juvenile offenders, as well as for the increased use of the death penalty.

This explanation ignores the fact that homicide rates are much lower in other Western democracies that treat violent criminals less punitively than the United States. In the 1980s, before the introduction of harsh new sentencing laws in the United States, the murder rate in Canada was about one third of the U.S. rate; in England it was about one seventh. If the politicians are right, we would expect to find that these two countries kept their murder rates under control by treating violent crime more harshly than the United States—but this was not so. A cross-national comparison of criminal punishment practices in the 1980s shows that the average prison term served for homicide in the United States (50.5 months) was roughly the same as the average terms served in both Canada (57 months) and England (42.5 months). For robbery, the average term served in the United States (20.9 months) was similar to the average term served in Canada (23.6 months) and considerably longer than the average term served in England (15.8 months). The similarities end there, however. Less serious offenses—including property, drug, and public order offenses—were punished far more severely in the United States than in comparable countries.[2] Moreover, the United States was (and remains) the only Western democracy that imposed the death penalty on some of those convicted of murder.

If criminal justice leniency cannot explain the high U.S. homicide rate in the 1980s, it certainly cannot explain it in the 1990s. One study reports that persons convicted of homicide in the United States in 1992 will spend on average 110 months behind bars—if they are not executed.[3] In short, the United States is not more lenient—and is often more punitive—than comparable countries that have much lower levels of lethal violence.

Politicians and other opinion leaders are also quick to blame the mass media for high rates of lethal violence—apparently with good cause. By age 18, the average American adolescent has viewed about 200,000 acts of violence and 40,000 murders—on television alone. The average body count in 1980s action films such as *Die Hard*, *Rambo III*, and *Total Recall* was just under 60 per movie.[4] More recent films like *Scream* and *I Know What You Did Last Summer* depict comparable levels of mayhem. Quite plausibly, all this violent imagery encourages people to resort to violence in their own lives and desensitizes them to the real-life consequences of violence. Yet countries that have far lower rates of homicide than the United States, like Canada and Japan, have just as much (if not more) violence in their television programs and films.[5] The argument that U.S. violence is caused by violent media imagery thus implies that life imitates art only in the United States.

Images of violence in the mass media might, however, interact with factors peculiar to the United States to foster a relatively high U.S.

homicide rate.[6] In particular, more children in the United States grow up in a context characterized by poverty, neglect, and violence than in other industrialized democracies.[7] Such children might be especially vulnerable to images of violence in the mass media. Thus, although media violence is almost certainly not a direct cause of homicide, it might be one among many background factors. Unfortunately, there is little published research in the voluminous literature on mass media effects that convincingly tests this hypothesis.[8] In the sections that follow, we examine factors that we believe are more directly responsible for the high rate of lethal violence in the United States.

GUNS

A National Rifle Association bumper sticker states, "Guns don't kill people, people kill people." Strictly speaking, the slogan is incontrovertible. But so too is the observation that "people kill people" more frequently when guns are readily available. Gun assaults are far more likely to result in death than assaults with the next most deadly weapon, the knife.[9] And guns are the instrument of death in 7 out of 10 homicides in the United States, a figure that is unparalleled among industrial democracies.[10]

These facts help to explain the high rate of lethal violence in the United States. In 1992, assaults in New York were 11 times more likely to result in death than assaults in London. This difference is largely a consequence of the higher propensity of New Yorkers to attack one another with firearms. Whereas New York residents were as likely to attack one another with a gun as with a knife, Londoners were six times more likely to use a knife. If New Yorkers had assaulted one another with the same mix of weapons as Londoners, the number of deaths resulting from assault would have been about one third the actual death from the assault figure of 2,152.[11] The greater availability of guns in the United States also means that robberies are more likely to result in death. In 1992, the overall "death rate" for gun robberies in New York was 8.4 per 1,000, about 10 times greater than the death rate for non-gun robberies. If the 91,000 New York City robberies in that year had resulted in death at the non-gun death rate, 79 New Yorkers would have lost their lives in the course of a robbery. The actual number of deaths from robberies was 357.[12]

It is possible that the extraordinary propensity of Americans to use guns to commit crimes and settle disputes reflects a greater motivation to kill. This issue is far from settled, but researchers have accumulated a good deal of evidence suggesting that the choice of weapon—rather than a greater determination to kill—accounts for the higher rate of homicide in the United States. For example, one study found that 70% of all homicide victims were killed by a single gunshot wound and that attacks with guns and knives resulting in death were indistinguishable from attacks that did not cause death. On the basis of this evidence, this researcher concluded that "most homicides were the result of ambiguously motivated assaults, so that the offender would risk his victim's death, but usually did not press on until death was assured."[13] These findings are consistent with what convicted offenders say about their motives in discharging firearms. In interviews with 184 incarcerated persons who fired a gun in the course of committing the offense for which they were serving time, only about one third claimed to have shot with the intent to kill. Larger percentages claimed to have fired to "scare the victim" or "to protect myself." Moreover, more than three quarters of these men claimed that they did not intend to actually use their firearm prior to the situation in which they ultimately took aim and fired.[14]

International comparisons also suggest that the greater availability of guns is a crucial cause of the U.S. homicide problem. Comparisons of Seattle and Vancouver, two cities on opposite sides of the U.S.-Canadian border, show that these cities have similar socioeconomic and demographic characteristics as well as comparable burglary and assault rates. Nonetheless, Seattle, with relatively lax gun control laws, has a homicide rate 60% higher than Vancouver's and a gun homicide rate 400% higher.[15]

Gun availability is also implicated in the recent upsurge in juvenile homicide in the United States. Between 1984 and 1993, the homicide rate tripled for adolescents 13 through 17 years old and doubled for those 18 through 24. What is interesting about this trend is that the rate of non-gun homicides remained absolutely stable; only the rate of juvenile gun murders increased. The increase in juvenile homicide thus appears to be related to the spread of guns among youths.[16]

Skeptics might nevertheless object that something other than gun availability—such as the expanding role of youth in the drug market—is to blame. Later in this chapter we will argue that drug dealing is indeed an important source of lethal violence and that participation in the crack trade did spur many youths to arm themselves. However, the growing participation of youth in the drug trade does not account for all of the increase in gun-related homicide: The ratio of gun to non-gun killings by juveniles rose in all six categories of the F.B.I.'s *Supplementary Homicide Report,* which include killings among family members and intimates, killings in the course of felonies, killings in the course of brawls and arguments, and gang-related killings. A surge in the practice of keeping and carrying guns seems to be a reasonable explanation of the increase in gun homicides among youths.[17]

According to recent estimates, there are about 200 million guns, including 70 million handguns, in circulation in the United States. The proportion of households possessing a firearm has remained stable at about 50% over the past three decades, but the percentage of households with a handgun has increased from 13% in 1959 to about 25% today.[18] The United States now has more federally licensed gun dealers than gas stations.[19] Perhaps most disturbing is the extent to which guns have proliferated among young people. In a survey of 96 randomly selected elementary, middle, and high schools, "fifteen percent of students reported carrying a handgun in the past 30 days, and four percent reported taking a handgun to school during the year. Nine percent of the students reported shooting a gun at someone else, while eleven percent had been shot at during the past year."[20] The recent massacres of school children and their teachers by heavily armed classmates in Jonesboro, Arkansas, Littleton, Colorado, and elsewhere, are an especially stark reminder of how serious the crisis has become. In the United States, guns are quite literally everywhere, and their contribution to the country's extraordinary rate of killing is clear.

INEQUALITY AND HOMICIDE

Opponents of gun control often point out that widespread gun ownership is not associated with an elevated rate of lethal violence in a few countries (such as Israel and Switzerland).[21] Human intentions do matter. People do indeed kill people. In the rest of this chapter, we consider the social, political, and economic factors that encourage Americans to use violence and risk death in the course of settling their disputes.

We begin with economic and racial inequality. A meta-analysis of the research on this subject reports that there is a "consensus that the incidence of homicide is higher in countries with greater income inequal-

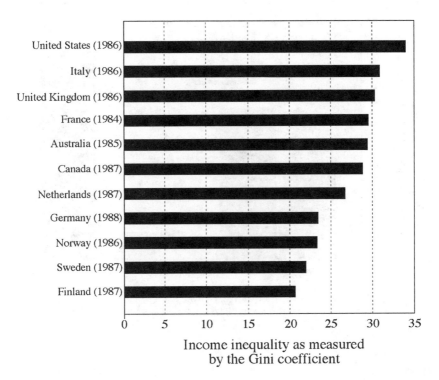

Exhibit 3.1. International Income Inequality
SOURCE: Atkinson, Rainwater, and Smeeding, *Income Distribution in OECD Countries.*

ity." In their analysis of 65 nations, these researchers found that the correlation between homicide rate and various measures of economic inequality is especially strong in democracies and wealthier countries.[22] A more recent study found an even stronger relationship between economic discrimination and the homicide rate: countries that practice "deliberate, invidious exclusion" on the basis of ascribed characteristics such as race have the highest rates of killing.[23]

These cross-national comparisons suggest that the elevated rate of homicide in the United States is a consequence of, at least in part, the country's pronounced disparities in wealth and its history of racial discrimination. Exhibit 3.1 shows that the income gap between the rich and poor is much higher in the United States than in other Western democracies.[24] Furthermore, as Exhibits 3.2 and 3.3 show, economic inequality in the United States is structured along racial and ethnic lines

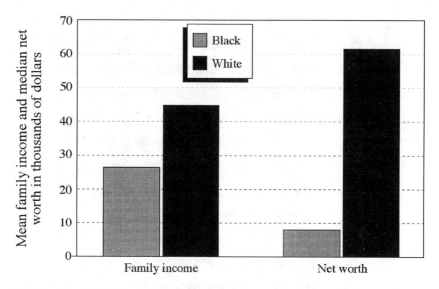

Exhibit 3.2. U.S. Economic Inequality, by Race
SOURCE: *Statistical Abstract of the United States,* 1998, Tables 51 and 55; and Wolff, "Recent Trends in the Size Distribution of Household Wealth, 1998."

and is especially devastating for children. The racial and ethnic nature of class inequality is striking whether we look at family income or family wealth. And, contrary to popular impressions, this sort of inequality is growing. Between 1970 and 1992, Black family income as a share of White family income actually dropped from 61% to 54%. Between 1975 and 1992, Hispanic family income as a share of White family income dropped from 66% to 63%.[25]

A rich sociological tradition helps to explain the relationship between inequality and elevated levels of violence. Roughly 100 years ago, French sociologist Emile Durkheim argued that elevated levels of both suicide and homicide reflect a societal breakdown in norms—"anomie," in the technical language of sociology—occasioned by a widening gap between the dreams and aspirations of the people, on the one hand, and their actual life experiences, on the other. When such a breakdown prevails, people experience bouts of frustration, despair, and outright anger and become more prone to destruction of both self and other.[26] In democracies, the promise of equal access to "the good life" is most vigorously advanced, and thus it is in democracies that arbitrary denial of opportunities is experienced as most painful. The fact that violence tends to get

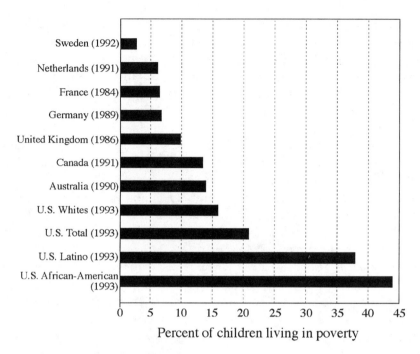

Exhibit 3.3. International Child Poverty
SOURCE: Donziger, *The Real War on Crime,* p. 29.

acted out among family members, acquaintances, and neighbors rather than against the rich and powerful does not challenge this argument. Rather, it suggests that people close at hand are simply "convenient targets" for pent-up anger.[27]

But it is not just the anger and frustration born of high levels of inequality that help to explain the connection between inequality and violence. Countries with higher levels of social and economic inequality are characterized by the ecological conditions that, as we will see, give rise to high levels of violence.

THE ECOLOGY OF URBAN VIOLENCE

There is a tendency, when thinking about the causes of violence, to focus on the characteristics of individuals and groups, such as family history, level of education, and household income. These personal characteristics are less helpful in explaining serious violence than are the qualities of residential neighborhoods. Indeed, because lethal violence is overwhelmingly concentrated in poor urban communities, understanding these neighborhood characteristics is crucial. In the suburban areas where most Americans live, rates of homicide are comparable to those in Finland. By contrast, half of all U.S. homicides occur in the 63 largest American cities—which house only 16% of the U.S. population.[28] Even within urban areas, the risk of homicide victimization is quite uneven: in areas of concentrated poverty, rates of homicide are 20 times the national average.[29] An ecological or community-level approach is best able to explain the concentration of violence in poor, urban communities.[30]

This type of explanation has a long pedigree in sociological accounts of crime and delinquency. More than five decades ago, in a landmark study, *Juvenile Delinquency and Urban Areas,* Clifford Shaw and Henry McKay reported that the distribution of delinquency across Chicago neighborhoods remained constant over many years despite population turnover. In other words, although the ethnic composition of these high-delinquency areas changed, the propensity of these neighborhoods to generate troublesome youths did not. To explain this pattern, these sociologists identified certain unchanging features of high-delinquency areas, especially their low economic status, ethnic heterogeneity, and high rates of residential mobility. These factors, they suggested, had the effect of undermining neighborhood social organization, especially the capacity of adults to exercise control over young people. In the absence of effective adult supervision and control, juvenile delinquency flourished.[31]

Taking their lead from Shaw and McKay, contemporary researchers have demonstrated that the most violent urban neighborhoods are characterized by a cluster of "social dislocations." These "dislocations" include racial segregation and high rates of poverty, joblessness, family disruption, and residential instability.[32] In his influential study of urban poverty, *The Truly Disadvantaged,* William Julius Wilson provides a portrait of one such neighborhood, a Chicago public-housing project:

> Cabrini-Green includes eighty-one high and low-rise buildings covering seventy acres on Chicago's Near North Side. In 1983, nearly 13,000 people, almost all black, were officially registered there. . . . Minors were 66 percent of the registered population; 90 percent of the families with children were [single-parent households] headed by women; 83 percent of the households were on

welfare (AFDC or General Assistance), and 81 percent of the families with children received AFDC in 1983. In a nine-week period beginning in early January 1981, ten Cabrini-Green residents were murdered; thirty-five were wounded by gunshots, including random sniping; and more than fifty fire-arms were confiscated, "the tip of an immense arsenal" according to the Chicago Police.[33]

In neighborhoods like Cabrini-Green, poor, young, and overwhelmed parents are often unable to exercise control over children and adolescents, especially teenage peer groups in public spaces.[34]

Like Shaw and McKay, contemporary scholars have demonstrated that it is not the racial or ethnic composition of places like Cabrini-Green that explains their extraordinary rates of homicide. A comparison of two Manhattan neighborhoods in the mid-1980s illustrates this point well. The Bowery, with an only average-size Black population but a high concentration of poor people, had a homicide rate among the highest of the city's neighborhoods. By comparison, Stuyvesant Town-Cooper Village, with an average-size Black population but a relatively low poverty rate, had a homicide rate well below the average. Quantitative analysis of the relationship between neighborhood characteristics and homicide rates across Manhattan neighborhoods reinforces the obvious conclusion: A neighborhood's poverty status, not its racial composition, best explains its homicide rate.[35]

The Relevance of Race

This is not to say, however, that race and ethnicity are irrelevant to the problem of lethal violence. In the first place, residents of "high poverty areas"—areas inhabited by high numbers of poor people—are overwhelmingly Black or Hispanic. In New York City, for example, 70% of the city's poor Black and Hispanic residents live in high-poverty neighborhoods, but 70% of the city's poor Whites live in non-poverty neighborhoods.[36] Nationwide, nearly 7 out of 8 persons living in a high-poverty urban area are members of a minority group. As one scholar put it, "American urban poverty is pre-eminently a racial poverty . . . rooted in the ghetto as a specific social form and mechanism of racial domination."[37]

Furthermore, both the number of high-poverty areas and the number of minority families that live in them are growing. Between 1970 and

1990, for example, the number of high-poverty census tracts in the nation's 100 largest cities more than doubled. During the 1980s alone, the number of African Americans living in high-poverty areas grew by more than one third to about 6 million. The proportion of all metropolitan-area Blacks living in such areas increased from 37% to 45% during this period.[38] In sum, Blacks and Hispanics in the United States are significantly more likely than Whites to be poor and, if poor, are more likely to live in areas of concentrated poverty.

Second, to understand the expansion of ghetto poverty, we must examine the interplay between economic changes and racial discrimination. The most significant economic development in this context is the process called *deindustrialization*. This restructuring of the economy began in the 1970s and entailed a massive loss of manufacturing jobs in central cities. New York City, for example, now has approximately 925,000 manufacturing jobs, down from 1.5 million in 1978.[39] The loss of manufacturing jobs in urban areas has not been fully offset by the expansion of the service sector, where wages for unskilled workers are markedly lower and where jobs are more likely to be temporary and less likely to provide benefits such as health insurance.

The sharp increase in joblessness among Black males that resulted from this economic restructuring reduced the pool of "marriagable men," which in turn contributed to the proliferation of single-parent households and intensification of inner city poverty. Meanwhile, middle class Blacks seized the opportunity created by new laws banning discrimination in housing and fled the ghetto. In their wake, they left neighborhoods composed mainly of jobless men and poor, female-headed, single-parent families.[40] Research examining the relationships among homicide rates, levels of poverty, and family structure suggests that the increase in single-parent families in these poor communities has had significant consequences. In Black communities, for example, the percentage of families headed by a single parent is the strongest predictor of the homicide rate and is in turn strongly associated with the rate of joblessness among men.[41]

Although deindustrialization was not motivated by racial considerations or intended to have racially disparate consequences, its effects have been particularly catastrophic for Black urban communities because of the prior existence of racial segregation. Had poor Blacks lived in racially integrated neighborhoods throughout metropolitan areas, deindustrialization would have driven up rates of Black poverty but would not have produced ghetto neighborhoods characterized by highly concentrated poverty.[42] Racial segregation is, of course, a product of racial discrimination. In the South and elsewhere, local ordinances once prevented Blacks from living in White neighborhoods. In the North, White property owners attached "restrictive covenants" to their properties to prevent transfer to Blacks (and Jews). In the 1960s, under the rubric of "urban renewal" (dubbed "Negro removal" by the literary critic James Baldwin), federal and municipal agencies destroyed about 20% of all central city housing occupied by Blacks.[43] The federal government did eventually extend mortgage assistance—long the ticket to home ownership for Whites—to African Americans, but only to subsidize home ownership within all-Black neighborhoods. New public housing was built but invariably located within the confines of the ghetto.[44]

Despite laws banning housing discrimination, the situation is not much improved today. Contemporary patterns of residential segregation cannot be explained by either the preferences of Blacks or their socioeconomic situation. Rather, ongoing housing discrimination and prejudice continue to keep many poor and working class Blacks in the ghetto.[45]

In sum, the relatively high rate of lethal violence among African Americans is not a consequence of any quality specific to this racial group. Instead, it is related to the ghetto poverty in which so many African Americans must struggle to make a life. Social inequality and racial discrimination, both past and ongoing, have played a central role in the formation of ghetto neighborhoods characterized by high rates of poverty, joblessness, and single-parent families. In what follows, we discuss two ways in which these social conditions give rise to high levels of serious interpersonal violence.

The Drug Trade

One connection between the ecological conditions of poor communities and lethal violence is the drug trade. The concentration of street-level drug dealing in ghetto neighborhoods is not new. Poor neighborhoods inhabited by ethnic minorities have long acted as "deviance service centers," providing illicit goods and services to surrounding communities.[46] In the context of deindustrialization, however, the drug trade emerged as an especially important source of employment. With urban manufacturing jobs increasingly scarce, many people have found the drug market to be a more attractive alternative than low-paying, unstable, and often degrading work in the expanding service sector. On average, selling drugs pays somewhat better than the available legal jobs. Moreover, the drug industry "offers hope, however illusory, of self-determination and economic independence, as contrasted with the petty humiliations and daily harassment faced in secondary service sector jobs."[47]

Unlike most legal work, however, drug dealing is highly dangerous. And it became dramatically more so with the advent of crack cocaine. For example, the percentage of New York City homicides in which drugs played a significant role increased from 24% in 1984 to an astounding 53% in 1988 (when the popularity of crack cocaine peaked).[48] Similarly, Washington, DC's homicide rate surged between 1986 and 1988 as the number of killings recorded as "drug related" climbed to 53%.[49]

These studies clearly show that drugs and violence are interrelated, but what is the nature of the relationship? Researchers have identified three types of drug-related homicide:

- ◆ "Psychopharmacological" killings are those caused by drug or alcohol intoxication, as when a person gets high and acts out in a violent fashion.
- ◆ "Economic compulsive" killings are those committed in the course of property crimes, such as robberies, motivated by the need for money to buy drugs.
- ◆ "Systemic" killings are the result of conducting business in an illegal market. Illegal markets are characterized by high profit margins and offer no recourse to the legal system to settle disputes.

Homicide records in New York City show that in 1988, only 15% of drug-related homicides were psychopharmacological in nature and just 4% fit the economic compulsive model. By contrast, nearly 80% of all drug-related homicides in 1988 were systemic in nature. Moreover, these systemic killings constituted nearly 40% of all homicides that year.[50] Contrary to popular impressions, then, it is not the chemical effects of crack cocaine but the nature of the illegal trade around it that appears to account for much drug-related violence.

Here are just three examples of the kinds of systemic conflicts generated by illegal drug markets:

[T]he victim in case #31 was a thirty-year-old male. He had been previously ousted from his drug sales location and had returned in an attempt to reassert his claim to the area. He was shot by a twenty-four-year-old male. Police report that this was not an isolated event, but part of a continuing turf war between two gangs. The perpetrator fled to Washington, DC, where he, in turn, was killed by associates of the victim.

In case #369 . . . the victim was a twenty-seven-year-old female crack user. The perpetrator was a twenty-two-year-old male who was both a crack user and a low-level crack dealer. He had lent her both money and crack, but she was not able to repay the debts. They engaged in an argument at a street crack sales location, which culminated in the woman being stabbed once in the chest.

In case #277, the victim was a thirty-two-year-old male. The perpetrator was a seventeen-year-old male. On a prior occasion, the victim had robbed the perpetrator of money and crack. The perpetrator subsequently shot the victim once in the abdomen in retaliation.[51]

All illegal drug markets tend to give rise to systemic violence, but the particular features of the crack trade and the socioeconomic context in which it emerged exacerbated this tendency. Crack was essentially a marketing innovation that made cocaine available in smaller and cheaper quantities to a broader segment of the public. The effects of crack cocaine are also extremely short lived. For both of these reasons, the crack market was, at its peak, characterized by a greater number of exchanges than is typically found in other drug markets. With an increase in the number of illicit exchanges comes an increase in the number of potential conflicts—and thus in the number of conflicts that can lead to murder. Finally, the fact that crack cocaine is relatively easy and cheap to make meant that people without much start-up capital could move into the trade, and the lack of legal alternatives enhanced their willingness to use and risk violence. The result was a high degree of instability in the market and intense competition over turf. For all these reasons, the crack trade in particular seems to have an especially strong link to lethal violence.

Ironically, the war on drugs contributes to the instability of the drug trade and thus to the problem of violence. Between 1980 and 1989, the number of African American men arrested for drug law violations more than tripled.[52] Between 1985 and 1987, 1 out of every 6 Black males born in Washington, DC, in 1967 was arrested for selling drugs.[53] Arresting so many (alleged) drug dealers disrupts turf arrangements and triggers violent struggles to establish control over newly available territory. The surge in drug arrests, coupled with harsh new sentencing laws for drug offenses, also filled the prisons with low-level drug offenders from ghetto neighborhoods.[54] Jailed men do not marry and raise their children; neither do men who cannot get a good job because of a criminal record. Indeed, research suggests that those who have experienced incarceration are significantly less likely to obtain employment than those sentenced to alternatives (such as probation).[55] By arresting and jailing such a large number of Black men, the war on drugs has perversely become a significant source of joblessness and family disruption, two social conditions that are strongly associated with high levels of homicide.

The Code of the Streets

Ghetto poverty generates cultural as well as economic adaptations, and these developments are also implicated in elevated rates of violence. Pervasive feelings of despair among the ghetto poor due to high rates of joblessness, widespread drug abuse, and severely limited opportunities have led to the emergence of an oppositional "code of the streets."[56] In this section, we discuss the emergence of this code, paying particular attention to its implications for the problem of lethal violence. However, we wish to emphasize that the attitudes and practices described below are linked to cultural patterns that extend far beyond American inner cities. To borrow a distinction from the scholar William Julius Wilson, these cultural developments are "ghetto-related" but not "ghetto-specific."[57] Those who articulate and live by the code are as American as apple pie.

At the heart of the code of the streets, according to sociologist Elijah Anderson, "is the issue of respect—loosely defined as being treated 'right,' or granted the deference one deserves."[58] Having respect means that one can avoid being bothered or menaced by others. This is especially important in violent areas, where vague slights can escalate into violent conflicts and where faith in the ability or willingness of the police to impose order is nonexistent. From a practical standpoint, "respect" is maintained through the projection of a menacing public presence: "one's bearing must send the unmistakable if sometimes subtle message to 'the next person' in public that one is capable of violence and mayhem when the situation requires it, that one can take care of oneself."[59] Anthropologist Philippe Bourgeois makes a similar point in his discussion of the "culture of terror": "Behavior that appears irrationally violent and self-destructive to middle class (and working class) observers can be more accurately interpreted according to the logic of the underground economy as judicious public relations, advertising, rapport building, and long-term investment in one's 'human capital.' "[60]

Because of its utility in deterring aggression, young people living in poor urban areas often project a menacing posture whether they are genuinely committed to the code of the streets or not. But for those young people most heavily invested in street culture, "respect" is about more than warding off unwanted aggression. Hard won and easily lost, it is an absolute precondition for dignity and self-respect. "Manhood and self respect are flip sides of the same coin; physical and psychological well-being are inseparable and both require a sense of control, of being in charge."[61]

On the streets, respect is often pursued through character contests involving displays of masculine "nerve":

> Nerve is shown when one takes another person's possessions (the more valuable the better), "messes with" someone's woman, throws the first punch, "gets in someone's face," or pulls a trigger. Its proper display helps on the spot to check others who would violate one's person and also helps to build a reputation that works to prevent future challenges. But because such a show of nerve is a forceful expression of disrespect toward the person on the receiving end, the victim may be greatly offended and seek to retaliate with equal or greater force. A display of nerve, therefore can easily provoke a life threatening response, and the background knowledge of that possibility has often been incorporated into the concept of nerve.[62]

The zero-sum nature of such character contests helps to explain why conflicts that from the outside seem petty can lead to violence and even murder. "True nerve exposes a lack of fear of dying. Many feel that it is acceptable to risk dying over the principle of respect. In fact, among the hard-core street oriented, the clear risk of violent death may be preferable to being 'dissed' by another."[63]

This emphasis on getting respect is not unique to the inner city. Neither is the notion that men must establish their masculinity by being "tough" in the face of challenges from other men. What is different is the context in which these displays of nerve and masculinity occur. Elsewhere in society, young men have multiple avenues for attaining status and demonstrating manhood. In the ghetto, however, most of the conventional avenues for doing so are dead ends. This is even more true in prisons, where the code of the streets is found in its purest form. Ironically, the massive expansion of incarceration in the 1980s and 1990s has exposed ever-increasing numbers of people to this environment and has thus strengthened the hold that the code of the street has on ghetto communities.[64]

CONCLUSION

In this chapter, we have argued that the distinctively high rate of homicide in the United States stems primarily from four interrelated factors: the prevalence of guns, comparatively high levels of social and racial inequality and the concentrated urban poverty with which they are associated, the drug trade, and a code of the streets that prizes "respect" and deference above all else. These deadly developments reinforce each other in complex ways. For example, the code of the streets has been strengthened by the spread of the drug trade and contributes to its lethal character. Both of these encourage the acquisition of firearms, even among those not directly involved in the drug trade. Inequality and racial discrimination facilitate violence by creating a sense of injustice and frustration and by contributing to the concentration of poverty in racially segregated neighborhoods. Concentrated poverty, in turn, encourages the code as well as the trade in drugs. No good purpose is achieved by trying to reduce this complexity to a simple causal argument.

The U.S. homicide rate has dropped by nearly a third since 1993. Despite politicians' claims to the contrary, this welcome development does not mean that the "get tough on crime" policies are working effectively. In fact, there is no clear relationship between penal severity and the volume of crime in society.[65] In the first half of the 1980s, for example, the homicide rate declined while the prison population expanded; in the second half of the 1980s, the homicide rate returned to its earlier level while the prison population continued its expansion.[66] Before abandoning these and other lessons of history, we ought to consider alternative explanations for the declining homicide rate.

The best alternative explanation concerns changes in the drug market. As we have seen, the spread of the drug trade stemming from the introduction of crack in the second half of the 1980s contributed to the rise in homicide in that period. In cities where the proportion of those arrested testing positive for cocaine is shrinking (a measure of the vitality of the crack trade), the homicide rate is also declining. In other words, the decline of the crack market appears to correspond to the decline in the incidence of lethal violence.[67] The impact of this development and other factors that have contributed to the recent drop in violent crime will be discussed in Chapter 9.

Although the U.S. homicide rate is indeed high relative to other Western democracies, this fact does not help to explain the country's rate of incarceration. Instead, understanding the breathtaking expansion of the criminal justice system requires that we delve into the areas of politics and culture. In the next chapter, we begin this inquiry by exploring the changing role of crime in political discourse.

4
◆ The Politics
◆ of Crime

◆ ◆ ◆ Over the past several decades, the United States has declared and waged vigorous wars against crime and drugs. Popular wisdom holds that the policy choices associated with these wars are a consequence of worsening crime and drug problems. However, as we saw in Chapter 2, the best available evidence suggests that crime has not increased significantly over the past several decades. Furthermore, although drug abuse is a serious problem for many individuals and communities, levels of illegal drug use have declined sharply since their peak in the late 1970s. The incidence of crime and drug use thus cannot account for the massive expansion of the criminal justice system. Instead, the growth of U.S. penal institutions is the result of policies aimed at "getting tough" with law breakers, especially drug offenders. In what follows, we suggest that these policy choices reflect a reframing of the crime problem in U.S. political discourse and culture.

Social problems like crime may be defined or framed in a number of different ways, and these different frames have quite distinct policy implications. For example, crime may be depicted as evidence of the breakdown of law and order, of the demise of the traditional two-parent family, or of social and economic inequality. Crime-related issues are thus socially and politically constructed: they acquire their meaning through struggles over their interpretation and representation. Social actors—

sometimes called "claims makers"[1]—compete for the public's attention and attempt to gain acceptance for the frames they prefer.[2]

The frames that come to dominate political and media discourse have a significant impact on policy. For example, to the extent that crime is seen as a consequence of lenience within the criminal justice system, policies that "get tough" with criminal offenders seem most appropriate. Conversely, frames that depict crime as a consequence of poverty, unemployment, or inequality suggest the need for policies that address these social and economic conditions. Debates over penal policy are less influenced by criminological research than by the way crime-related problems are framed in political discourse and popular receptivity to these frames.[3]

In this chapter, we suggest that today's "tough-on-crime" policies reflect the success of conservative efforts to frame crime as a consequence of excessive lenience or "permissiveness" in government policy and in society more generally. Conservative politicians have worked for decades to alter popular perceptions of problems such as crime, delinquency, addiction, and poverty and to promote policies that involve "getting tough" and "cracking down." Their claims-making activities have been part of a larger effort both to realign the electorate and to define social control rather than social welfare as the primary responsibility of the state.

Our analysis begins in the tumultuous decade of the 1960s, when southern officials first mobilized the discourse of law and order in an effort to discredit the civil rights movement. As the decade progressed, conservative opponents of the welfare state also used this rhetoric to attack President Lyndon Johnson's Great Society programs and the structural explanations of poverty with which these programs were associated. Conservatives offered two theories of the newly politicized crime problem:

- an individualistic theory, according to which both poverty and crime are freely chosen by dangerous and undeserving individuals who refuse to work for a living, and
- a cultural theory, according to which the "culture of welfare" is an important cause of a variety of social ills, including poverty, crime, delinquency, and drug addiction.

Although distinct in some ways, these individualistic and cultural theories both identify "permissiveness" as the underlying cause of crime and imply the need to strengthen the state's control apparatus. In the 1980s and 1990s, the ascendance of this frame has helped to legitimate the assault on the welfare state and the dramatic expansion of the penal system. As a rallying cry for Republicans, the permissiveness frame has also helped forge the party's new (but unstable) political majority. In short, the construction of the crime issue as a consequence of excessive permissiveness has been extraordinarily useful to conservative opponents of civil rights and the welfare state.

THE ORIGINS OF THE LAW AND ORDER DISCOURSE

In the years following the Supreme Court's 1954 *Brown v. Board of Education* decision, civil rights activists across the South used "direct action" tactics and civil disobedience to force reluctant southern states to desegregate public facilities. In an effort to sway public opinion against the civil rights movement, southern governors and law enforcement officials characterized its tactics as "criminal" and indicative of the breakdown of "law and order."[4] Calling for a crackdown on the "hoodlums," "agitators," "street mobs," and "lawbreakers" who challenged segregation and Black disenfranchisement, these officials made rhetoric about crime a key component of political discourse on race relations.

As the debate over civil rights moved to Washington, depictions of civil rights protest as criminal rather than political in nature reached the national stage. For example, after a reluctant President Kennedy finally expressed his willingness to press for the passage of civil rights legislation in 1963, Republicans and southern Democrats assailed him for "rewarding lawbreakers."[5] Later, retired Supreme Court Justice Charles Whittaker made the link between crime and protest more explicit when he attributed the spread of lawlessness and violence to

[t]he fact that some self-appointed Negro leaders who, while professing a philosophy of nonviolence, actually tell large groups of poor and uneducated Negroes. . . . whom they have harangued, aroused and inflamed to a high pitch of tensions, that they should go forth and force the whites to grant them their rights.[6]

Former Vice President Nixon also blamed civil rights leaders for the problem of crime and violence, arguing that "the deterioration of respect for the rule of law can be traced directly to the spread of the corrosive doctrine that every citizen possesses an inherent right to decide for himself which laws to obey and when to disobey them."[7]

The rhetoric of "law and order" became even more salient in 1964, when Republican presidential candidate Barry Goldwater announced that "The abuse of law and order in this country is going to be an issue [in this election]—at least I'm going to make it one because I think the responsibility has to start some place."[8] Despite the fact that crime did not even appear on the list of issues identified by the public as the nation's most important, Goldwater, a prominent civil rights opponent, made "law and order" the centerpiece of his campaign:

> Tonight there is violence in our streets, corruption in our highest offices, aimlessness among our youth, anxiety among our elderly. . . . Security from domestic violence, no less than from foreign aggression, is the most elementary form and fundamental purpose of any government, and a government that cannot fulfill this purpose is one that cannot command the loyalty of its citizens. History shows us that nothing prepares the way for tyranny more than the failure of public officials to keep the streets safe from bullies and marauders. We Republicans seek a government that attends to its fiscal climate, encouraging a free and a competitive economy and enforcing law and order.[9]

Striking the now familiar theme, Goldwater promised that, unlike President Johnson, he "would not support or invite any American to seek redress . . . through lawlessness, violence, and hurt of his fellow man or damage of his property."[10]

Initially, Goldwater's plea for a federal war on crime was controversial among conservatives and liberals alike. The United States Constitution allocates most crime control duties to local and state law enforcement. Some conservatives worried that a federally led anticrime initiative would impinge on state and local government authority. Furthermore, given that most southern conservatives opposed federal civil rights legislation on the basis of their commitment to "states' rights," calls for a federal war on crime struck many as highly inconsistent. Liberals also expressed concern, arguing that the proposed federal anticrime effort would compete for funds with the Great Society programs and therefore impede efforts to implement social and racial reform.

In sum, the introduction and construction of the crime issue in national political discourse in the 1960s reflects the claims-making activities of southern officials, presidential candidate Goldwater, and the other conservative politicians who followed his lead. Phrases like "crime in the streets" and "law and order" equated political dissent with crime and were used in an attempt to heighten opposition to the civil rights movement. Conservatives also identified the civil rights movement—and in particular, the philosophy of civil disobedience—as a leading cause of crime. Countering the trend toward lawlessness, they argued, would require holding criminals (including civil rights protesters) accountable for their actions through swift, certain, and severe punishment.

The racial subtext of these arguments was not lost on the public: Those most opposed to social and racial reform were also most receptive to calls for law and order.[11] Ironically, it was the success of the civil rights movement in discrediting more explicit expressions of racist sentiment that led politicians to attempt to appeal to the public with such "subliminally" racist messages.[12] In subsequent years, conservative politicians also found the crime issue—with its racial subtext now firmly in place—useful in their attempt to redefine poverty as the consequence of individual failure and to discredit welfare programs and their recipients.

FROM THE WAR ON POVERTY TO THE WAR ON CRIME

Throughout the 1960s, civil and welfare rights activists drew national attention to the issue of poverty. According to these activists, inequality of opportunity and racial discrimination ensured that poverty would remain widespread. To remedy this, they sought, among other things, to expand President Johnson's Great Society welfare programs. Largely as a result of their activism, the welfare rolls grew dramatically. In 1960, fewer than 600,000 families applied for Aid to Families with Dependent Children (AFDC) benefits; by 1972, more than three million Americans were receiving them.[13] Continued migration to northern cities from southern and rural areas meant that increasing numbers of those who received AFDC were African American women and their children.

During this period, liberals also argued that crime, like poverty, was a product of blocked opportunities. For example, early in his administration, President Johnson argued that programs that attacked social inequality were, in effect, anticrime programs: "There is something mighty wrong when a candidate for the highest office bemoans violence in the streets but votes against the war on poverty, votes against the Civil Rights Act, and votes against major educational bills that come before him as a legislator."[14] Initially, then, the Johnson administration stressed the need to address crime's "root causes" through initiatives of the welfare state.

The Conservative Attack on the Great Society

By contrast, conservative opponents of Johnson's social welfare initiatives argued that both poverty and crime were caused by a combination of bad people and excessive permissiveness. According to this argument, crime and related social problems originate in individual choice rather than in social conditions. "How long are we going to abdicate law and order—the backbone of any civilization—in favor of a soft social theory that the man who heaves a brick through your window is simply the misunderstood and underprivileged product of a broken home?" demanded House Leader Gerald Ford.[15] Later, independent presidential candidate George Wallace also ridiculed "soft social theories" that stress the social causes of crime:

> If a criminal knocks you over the head on your way home from work, he will be out of jail before you're out of the hospital and the policeman who arrested him will be on trial. But some psychologist will say, well, he's not to blame, society is to blame. His father didn't take him to see the Pittsburgh Pirates when he was a little boy.[16]

Discussions of crime and poverty were linked in other ways as well. Those who attributed poverty to the immorality of the impoverished often identified crime and delinquency as evidence of dysfunctional lifestyles. For example, Daniel Patrick Moynihan's much-discussed report on the Black family attributed Black poverty to the "subculture . . . of the American Negro":

> a community that allows large numbers of young men to grow up in broken families, dominated by women, never acquiring any stable relationships to male authority, never acquiring any set of rational expectations about the future—that community asks for and gets chaos. Crime, violence, unrest,

disorder, are not only to be expected, but they are very near to inevitable. And they are richly deserved.[17]

Although Moynihan (sometimes) identified unemployment as the cause of family disorganization, subsequent newspaper accounts and conservative reinterpretations of the report did not.

Highlighting the behavioral pathologies and, especially, the criminality of the poor was an important means of transforming their image from needy to undeserving. By emphasizing street crime and by framing that problem as the consequence of bad people making bad choices, conservatives made it much less likely that members of the public would empathize with the plight of the poor and support measures to assist them. As historian Michael Katz suggests, "when the poor seemed menacing they became the underclass."[18]

In a further attempt to marshal opposition to welfare programs, conservatives made the cultural argument that programs such as AFDC actually encouraged non-work-oriented lifestyles, thereby worsening the problems of poverty and crime. According to this argument, people will avoid work when possible and welfare programs reward this tendency. Furthermore, the mere existence of welfare encouraged people to think that they are entitled to that which they have not earned.

In this twist on the venerable "culture of poverty" thesis, conservatives argued that the "culture of welfare" undermines self-discipline and promotes "parasitism"—both legal (welfare dependency) and illegal (crime).[19] Goldwater gave expression to this view in the 1964 election campaign:

If it is entirely proper for the government to take away from some to give to others, then won't some be led to believe that they can rightfully take from anyone who has more than they? No wonder law and order has broken down, mob violence has engulfed great American cities, and our wives feel unsafe in the streets.[20]

In the mid-1960s, then, liberals and conservatives offered very different interpretations of poverty and crime-related problems. According to conservatives, social pressures such as racism, inadequate employment, lack of housing, low wages, and poor education do not cause crime. If they did, all poor people would be criminals. Instead, people are poor, criminal, or addicted to drugs because they made irresponsible or bad choices. Ironically, social programs aimed at helping the poor only encourage them to make these choices by fostering a culture of dependency and predation. By contrast, liberals argued that social conditions—especially racial inequality and limited opportunities for youth—were the "root causes" of crime, poverty, and addiction. It is only by addressing these social conditions, they argued, that we may begin to ameliorate the problems they cause.

Defection of the Liberals

By 1965, however, the liberal emphasis on the "root causes" of crime began to weaken. Only 4 months after his election, for example, President Johnson declared in an unprecedented special message to Congress his new determination to fight crime: "I hope that 1965 will be regarded as the year when this country began in earnest a thorough and effective war against crime."[21] Johnson presented his newly moderated analysis of the crime problem:

> The problem runs deep and will not yield easy and quick answers. We must identify and eliminate the causes of criminal activity whether they lie in the environment around us or in the nature of individual men. . . . crime will not wait until we pull it up by the roots. We must arrest and reverse the trend toward lawlessness.[22]

Toward that end, Johnson established the Law Enforcement Assistance Administration (LEAA), an agency with a mission to support local law enforcement. To coordinate law enforcement activities aimed at fighting drugs, he also created the Bureau of Narcotics and Dangerous Drugs (now called the Drug Enforcement Agency). These initiatives represented a shift away from the view that the most important crime-fighting weapons were civil rights legislation, War on Poverty programs, and other policies aimed at promoting inclusion and social reform. Although Johnson sometimes reiterated his earlier view that social and racial reform efforts would reduce crime, administration officials and other liberal politicians now tempered this argument with the claim that these "long-term" solutions must be balanced by the "short-term" need for increased law enforcement and more efficient administration of justice. Over time, the liberal commitment to assisting the poor also attenuated.

It is not entirely clear why the liberal emphasis on the "root causes" of crime weakened. According to public opinion polls taken at the time, there was no evidence that much of the public had abandoned the view that crime has environmental causes. Indeed, as we will see in Chapter 7, most members of the public continue to favor crime measures that address the social conditions that give rise to crime. Perhaps leaders in the Democratic party were worried about the views and sentiments of a particular segment of the public—those people who came to be known as "swing voters." As we shall see, analyses of voting patterns in the 1964 election revealed that these socially conservative White voters were shifting their loyalties to the Republicans. The liberal back-pedaling on crime was probably, at least in part, an attempt to woo these voters back to the Democratic Party.

The shift in liberal political discourse also occurred in the context of a growing chorus of criticism, from scholars and activists across the political spectrum, of "rehabilitation" as a primary justification for punishment.[23] Conservatives opposed rehabilitation on the grounds that punishment must be harsh and painful if it is to deter crime. Liberals also criticized policies associated with rehabilitation, arguing that the open-ended ("indeterminate") sentences designed to facilitate "correction" created the potential for the intrusive, discriminatory, and arbitrary exercise of power. Under the weight of these twin (if quite distinctive) critiques, the rehabilitative project was called into question. This development undoubtedly made it more difficult for liberal politicians to offer a clear alternative to the conservative calls to crack down on criminals and may therefore have facilitated the Democratic leap on to the law and order bandwagon.

The Republican Southern Strategy

In the 1968 presidential campaign, Republican candidate Richard Nixon rejected social explanations of crime, arguing that the lenience of the criminal justice system was in fact to blame. As he put it, the real cause of crime is not poverty or unemployment but "insufficient curbs on the appetites or impulses that naturally impel individuals towards criminal activities."[24] Nixon therefore concluded that the "solution to the crime problem is not the quadrupling of funds for any governmental war on poverty but more convictions."[25] The 1968 Republican Party platform concurred with Nixon's critique of liberal "permissiveness": "We must re-establish the principle that men are accountable for what they do, that criminals are responsible for their crime."[26]

Nixon's rhetorical emphasis on crime and other social issues was part of a political strategy aimed at weakening the electoral base of the Democratic Party—the New Deal coalition. This alliance of urban ethnic groups and the White South had dominated electoral politics from 1932 through the early 1960s. As a result of Black migration to the North, this alliance also included growing numbers of Blacks, a trend that created quite a dilemma for those interested in maintaining White southern allegiance to the party. In 1948, when President Harry Truman responded to the growing number of Black voters by pressing for a relatively strong civil rights platform, the first serious signs of strain in the Democratic partnership appeared. White southerners organized a states' rights party, and in the subsequent election, four Deep South states (Louisiana, South Carolina, Alabama, and Mississippi) delivered their electoral votes to this insurgent political force. In the 1952 and 1956 elections, Democrats attempted to placate these southern "Dixiecrat" delegates and pull in disaffected White southerners. The appeasement of southern racism was not without political costs, however, and the Republican share of the Black vote increased from 21% in 1952 to 39% in 1956.[27]

In 1957 and 1960, partisan competition for the Black vote led the Democratic Congress to pass the first civil rights measures of the 20th century. Convinced he could not resurrect White southern loyalty to the Democratic party, John F. Kennedy campaigned on a civil rights platform in 1960. Once in office, however, President Kennedy sought to minimize White southern resistance within the Democratic coalition. This ambivalence about the Democratic party's loss of the White South appears to account for Kennedy's weak and delayed support for civil rights legislation. Indeed, only under the extreme pressure generated by civil rights activists did Kennedy finally declare his allegiance to the civil rights cause.

By drawing significant public attention to the plight of Blacks in the South, civil rights activists forced the national Democratic party to choose between its southern White and northern Black constituencies. The high degree of support among nonsouthern Whites for the civil rights cause prior to 1965 and the increasing numbers of African American voters eventually led the Democratic party to cast its lot with Blacks and their sympathizers. This decision, however, alienated many of those traditionally loyal to the Democratic party, particularly White southerners. "Millions of voters, pried loose from their habitual loyalty to the Democratic party, were now a volatile force, surging through the electoral system without the channeling restraints of party attachment."[28] These voters were "available for courting," and the Republicans moved swiftly to seize the opportunity. Initially, the GOP targeted White southerners—voters who had formerly composed the Democrat's "solid South"—as potential swing voters. Although the 1964 presidential election was a landslide for Johnson, careful scrutiny of the returns indicated that the socioeconomic structure of the New Deal alliance could in fact be fractured by the issue of race. In the poorest White neighborhoods of Birmingham, for example, the Republican vote increased from 49% to 76%, and a similar trend was identified in other southern cities.[29]

Republican analysts began to argue that they might also find a responsive audience among White suburbanites, ethnic Catholics in the Northeast and Midwest, and White blue-collar workers and union members. Some conservative political strategists frankly admitted that appealing to racial fears and antagonisms was central to this strategy. For example, Kevin Phillips argued that a Republican victory and long-term realignment was possible primarily on the basis of racial issues and therefore suggested the use of coded anti-Black campaign rhetoric.[30] Similarly, John Ehrlichmann, Special Counsel to the President, described the Nixon administration's campaign strategy of 1968 in this way: "We'll go after the racists. That subliminal appeal to the anti-black voter was always present in Nixon's statements and speeches."[31]

New sets of Republican constituencies were thus courted through the use of racially charged "code words"—phrases and symbols that "refer indirectly to racial themes but do not directly challenge popular democratic or egalitarian ideals."[32] The "law and order" discourse is an excellent example of such coded language, and it allowed for the indirect expression of racially charged fears and antagonisms.[33] In the context of urban riots and reports that the crime rate was increasing, the capacity of conservatives to mobilize, shape, and express these racial fears and tensions became a particularly important political resource.

The "southern strategy," as this tactic came to be known, enabled the Republican party to replace the New Deal cleavage between the "haves" and the "have-nots" with a new division between some (overwhelmingly White) working and middle class voters and the traditional Republican elite, on the one hand, and "liberal elites" and the (disproportionately African American and Latino) poor on the other. As the traditional working class coalition that buttressed the Democratic party was ruptured along racial lines, race eclipsed class as the organizing principle of American politics. By 1972, attitudes on racial issues rather than socioeconomic status were the primary determinant of voter's political self-identification.[34]

Nixon's Federalist Dilemma

After assuming office, the Nixon administration was forced to contend with the fact that, campaign pledges to the contrary notwithstanding, the federal government has little authority to deal directly with "street crime" outside of Washington, DC. Dismayed Attorney General John Mitchell pointed out that "even if the federal government found an indirect way of intervening in the problem, the local government would get the credit for diminishing those classes of crime."[35] Administration insiders concluded that the only thing they could do was "exercise vigorous symbolic leadership." They therefore waged war on crime by adopting "tough-sounding rhetoric" and pressing for largely ineffectual but highly symbolic legislation.[36] Not fooled, journalists began to report that despite Nixon's tough talk, the crime rate was still rising.

Nixon administration officials attempted to resolve this dilemma in several ways. First, Nixon requested—and received—a massive increase in LEAA funds to support local law enforcement. Between 1970 and 1971, the budget of this agency increased from approximately $75 million to over $500 million.[37] Second, new statistical artifacts were created in the hope that these would permit a more flattering assessment of Nixon's capacities as a crime fighter. One of the more notorious of these showed that the rate of increase in the crime index was decreasing.[38] Most important, however, was the administration's identification of narcotics control—for which the federal government has significant responsibility—as a crucial anticrime weapon.[39]

To explain and legitimate this new antidrug strategy, administration officials argued that drug addicts commit the majority of street crimes to pay for their habits.[40] The evidence marshaled to support this claim was quite problematic. For example, in a well-publicized speech in 1971,

Nixon claimed that drug addicts steal over $2 billion worth of property per year. According to the FBI, however, the total value of all property stolen in the United States that year was $1.3 billion.[41] Despite these contradictions, fighting drugs became a crucial weapon in the war on crime and the resources of federal drug enforcement agencies increased from $65 million to $719 million between 1969 and 1975.[42]

The Assault on Defendants' Rights

The Nixon administration's argument that crime is a consequence of "permissiveness" had important implications for criminal and constitutional law. Indeed, many of the legal rights and protections previously extended to criminal defendants were undermined or abandoned altogether during the Nixon era.

Under the leadership of Justice Earl Warren, the Supreme Court strengthened the protections offered to criminal defendants throughout the 1960s. For example, in *Mapp v. Ohio* (1961), the court ruled that state police officers, like federal law enforcement agents, were under most circumstances obliged to obtain a search warrant before conducting a search or seizing evidence.[43] In *Gideon v. Wainwright* (1963), the Court ruled that all persons accused of a crime were guaranteed the right to counsel. In *Escobedo v. Illinois* (1964), coerced confessions were deemed inadmissible. And in *Miranda v. Arizona* (1966), the Court ordered that suspects must be informed of their legal rights upon arrest and that any illegally obtained evidence would be inadmissible in the courts. Finally, under the Warren Court, defendants were permitted to argue that they had been entrapped when the idea of the crime in question originated with the police or when police conduct "fell below standards for the proper use of governmental power."[44]

Some of the legislation sponsored by the Nixon administration directly undermined these legal protections. Title II of the 1968 Omnibus Crime Bill, for example, allowed for the use of confessions obtained "voluntarily" but without the use of Miranda warnings. And the Racketeer Influenced and Corrupt Organization Act (RICO) of 1970 allowed prosecutors, with a judge's permission, to seize an organization's assets before trial. This legislation also allowed federal law enforcement agents to seek and obtain "no-knock" search warrants permitting them to enter and search private homes without giving notice of the "authority and purpose" of these searches.[45]

By appointing several conservatives (including Warren Burger and William Rehnquist) to the Supreme Court, Nixon ensured that defendants' rights were further weakened. For example, in 1973, the Burger Court undermined the Warren Court's interpretation of the Fourth Amendment's prohibition against unwarranted searches and seizures by ruling that if an arrest is lawful, "a search incident to the arrest requires no additional justification."[46] Similarly, the Burger Court nearly eliminated the entrapment defense when it ruled that if a defendant is "predisposed" to committing a crime, he or she could not plead entrapment.[47] All of these efforts to undermine criminal defendants' rights were rooted in the notion that the excessive lenience of the criminal justice system was an important cause of crime. These changes in criminal and constitutional law did diminish defendants' rights, but they did not have a demonstrable affect on the rates of arrest, conviction, or incarceration.[48]

The Reagan Years

Despite the centrality of the law and order discourse to the GOP's electoral strategy, the salience of the crime and drug issues declined dramatically following President Nixon's departure from office. Neither (Republican) President Ford nor (Democratic) President Carter mentioned crime-related issues in their State of the Union addresses or took much legislative action on those issues.[49] For Ford, whose ascent into office was the consequence of criminal wrongdoing by his predecessor, emphasizing the Republican commitment to fighting crime would have been rather awkward. The Carter Administration also seems to have had little interest in the crime issue, although it did initially advocate decriminalization of marijuana. As a result of this inattention, both the crime and drug issues largely disappeared from national political discourse in the latter part of the 1970s.[50]

During and after the 1980 election campaign, however, the crime issue once again assumed a central place on the national political agenda. Candidate and President Ronald Reagan, following the trail first blazed by his conservative predecessors, lavished attention on the problem of "crime in the streets" and promised to enhance the federal government's role in combating it. Once in office, Reagan instructed the new Attorney

General, William French Smith, to establish a task force to recommend "ways in which the federal government can do more to combat violent crime."[51] Because state and local governments are largely responsible for identifying and prosecuting conventional street crime, however, the administration's desire to involve the federal government in combating violent crime was problematic. Nevertheless, the Reagan administration began to pressure federal law enforcement agencies to set aside their focus on white-collar offenses and shift their attention to street crime instead. By October 1981, less than 1 year into the new administration, the Justice Department announced its intention to cut the number of specialists assigned to identify and prosecute white-collar criminals in half. The Reagan administration's crackdown on crime also explicitly excluded domestic violence on the grounds that it was "not the kind of street violence about which the Task Force was organized."[52]

In the ensuing years, President Reagan frequently returned to the topic of crime, striking all the now familiar conservative themes. Time and again, for example, he rejected the notion that crime and related social ills have socioeconomic causes:

> Here in the richest nation in the world, where more crime is committed than in any other nation, we are told that the answer to this problem is to reduce our poverty. This isn't the answer. . . . Government's function is to protect society from the criminal, not the other way around."[53]

According to Reagan, "the American people have lost patience with liberal leniency and pseudointellectual apologies for crime."[54] Instead, Reagan argued, the new "political consensus" emphasized free will:

> Choosing a career in crime is not the result of poverty or of an unhappy childhood or of a misunderstood adolescence; it is the result of a conscious, willful choice made by some who consider themselves above the law, who seek to exploit the hard work and, sometimes, the very lives of their fellow citizens.[55]

Furthermore, he asserted, the reality of human nature is such that only the threat of punishment will deter criminal behavior:

> The crime epidemic threat has spread throughout our country, and it's no uncontrollable disease, much less an irreversible tide. Nor is it some inevitable sociological phenomenon. . . . It is, instead, and in large measure, a cumulative result of too much emphasis on the protection of the rights of the accused and

too little concern for our government's responsibility to protect the lives, homes, and rights of our law-abiding citizens. . . . the criminal element now calculates that crime really does pay.[56]

Reagan also echoed his conservative predecessors on the putative relationship between crime and welfare. The naive view that "blocked opportunities" cause crime, Reagan suggested, led liberals to believe that the "war on poverty" would solve the problem. In fact, it is the government's attempt to ameliorate poverty—not poverty itself—that causes crime:

By nearly every measure, the position of poor Americans worsened under the leadership of our opponents. Teenage drug use, out-of-wedlock births, and crime increased dramatically. Urban neighborhoods and schools deteriorated. Those whom the government intended to help discovered a cycle of dependency that could not be broken. Government became a drug, providing temporary relief, but addiction as well.[57]

President Reagan thus argued that welfare programs such as AFDC not only "keep the poor poor" but also accounted, along with lenient crime policies, for the rising crime rate. In fact, studies investigating the relationship of welfare and crime find that greater welfare spending is associated with lower—not higher—levels of crime.[58] Despite this, the argument that welfare causes crime was used, as it had been by welfare opponents in the 1960s, in an effort to legitimate reductions in welfare spending and the adoption of increasingly punitive crime and drug policies:

Our current welfare program, originally designed to raise people out of poverty, has become a crippling poverty trap, destroying families and condemning generations to a dependency. . . . Of course, one of the best things we can do for families is obliterate drug use in America. . . . [We must therefore make] society intolerant to drug use with stiff penalties and sure and swift punishment for offenders.[59]

Finally, President Reagan argued that the government's functions had been distorted by his liberal predecessors. The state would be on more legitimate constitutional grounds and would more effectively "help the poor," he suggested, by scaling back public assistance programs and expanding the criminal justice system and law enforcement:

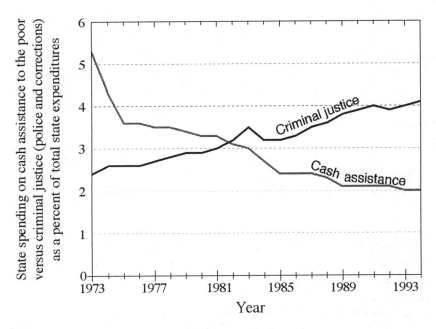

Exhibit 4.1. State Welfare and Criminal Justice Spending
SOURCE: U.S. Department of Commerce, *State Government Finances, 1973-1994.*

> [T]his is precisely what we're trying to do to the bloated Federal Government today: remove it from interfering in areas where it doesn't belong, but at the same time strengthen its ability to perform its constitutional and legitimate functions. . . . In the area of public order and law enforcement, for example, we're reversing a dangerous trend of the last decade. While crime was steadily increasing, the Federal commitment in terms of personnel was steadily shrinking.[60]

Reagan thus articulated the central premise of the conservative project of state reconstruction: Public assistance is an "illegitimate" state function; policing and social control constitute its real "constitutional" obligation. The conservative mobilization of crime-related issues was thus a key component of the effort to legitimate the shift from the "welfare state" to the "security state," a shift that is illustrated in Exhibit 4.1.

Political rhetoric notwithstanding, the view that crime had its origins in welfare dependence and humankind's propensity for evil was not widely supported. Instead, throughout the late 1970s and early 1980s, most Americans continued to attribute crime to socioeconomic conditions. In 1981, for example, a national poll found that most Americans believed that unemployment was the main cause of crime. Similarly, a 1982 ABC News Poll found that 58% of Americans saw unemployment and poverty as the most important causes of crime; only 12% identified "lenient courts" as the main source of this problem.[61] As we will see in Chapter 7, however, members of the public have become more likely to embrace the view that criminal justice lenience is an important cause of crime.

FROM THE WAR ON CRIME TO THE WAR ON DRUGS

When it came time to translate its harsh rhetoric into policy initiatives, the Reagan administration faced the same dilemma as the Nixon administration: in the United States, fighting conventional street crime is primarily the responsibility of state and local government. Once again, the identification of drugs as a crucial cause of crime partially resolved this dilemma. In 1981, FBI Director William Webster announced that "the drug problem has become so widespread that the FBI must assume a larger role in attacking the problem." In explaining his willingness to shift the agency's attention from white-collar crime to drugs, Webster argued that "when we attack the drug problem head on, it seems to me that we are going to make a major dent in attacking violent street crime."[62]

As a result of the Reagan administration's renewed interest in battling drugs, federal law enforcement agencies were able to stave off the General Accounting Office's proposed "across the board" budget cuts. For example, between 1980 and 1984, FBI antidrug monies increased from $8 million to $95 million, and the budget of the DEA increased from $215 to $321 million. Similarly, antidrug funds allocated to the Department of Defense more than doubled, from $33 to $79 million, during this period, and the Customs Department's allocation grew from $81 to $278 million.[63]

By contrast, funding for agencies with responsibility for drug treatment, prevention, and education was sharply curtailed. The budget of the National Institute on Drug Abuse, for example, was reduced from $274 million to $57 million between 1981 and 1984, and antidrug funds allocated to the Department of Education were cut from $14 million to $3 million. By 1985, 78% of the funds allocated to the drug problem went to law enforcement; only 22% went to drug treatment and prevention.[64]

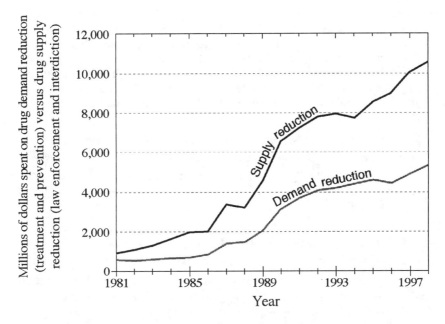

Exhibit 4.2. National Drug Demand and Supply Reduction Spending
SOURCE: *The National Drug Control Strategy, 1992*, pp. 216-219; (1998), Table 5; (1999), Table 5.

The only agencies that fared worse than those with drug treatment and prevention responsibilities in the 1982 budget were child nutrition (down 34%), urban development action grants (down 35%), and school milk programs (down 78%).[65] As is illustrated in Exhibit 4.2, the Reagan administration's early emphasis on the need for a "tough" approach to street crime and drugs gave a distinct advantage to law enforcement agencies in the bureaucratic scramble for funds.

Not all members of the Reagan administration were equally enthusiastic about increasing the responsibility (and budgets) of federal law enforcement. The Office of Management and Budget, for example, had a very different agenda. When OMB Director David Stockman advocated cutting the federal law enforcement budget in March 1981, he was met with fierce opposition from Attorney General Smith. As Stockman laments:

Attorney General William French Smith did not think his department was a place to start economizing. "The Justice Department is not a domestic agency" he said. "It is the internal arm of the nation's defense . . . " If anything, he said, the Reagan administration would have to spend more on law enforcement, rather than less. . . . Once the Attorney General had christened his agency an "Internal Defense Department" we would have lots of law enforcement at the federal level, even if we couldn't afford it. Justice's budget would grow and grow as the Attorney General came up with more and more schemes to show that the administration was "committed" to aggressive "internal defense."[66]

As Stockman indicates, Reagan sided with law enforcement in this dispute, reiterating the notion that social control (as opposed to social welfare) is a true governmental responsibility: "Bill is right. Law enforcement is something we have always said was a legitimate function of government."[67]

In sum, the Reagan administration's emphasis on the need for a tough approach to crime facilitated the emergence of the "war on drugs" and shaped the nature of that campaign. In particular, its analysis of the causes of the drug problem reflected the conservative emphasis on bad people rather than dangerous social conditions. "Narco-traffickers" and "drug pushers" were evil individuals motivated solely by greed. Drug users were also individually culpable:

> If this problem is to be solved, drug users can no longer excuse themselves by blaming society. As individuals, they're responsible. The rest of us must be clear that . . . we will no longer tolerate the illegal use of drugs by anyone.[68]

This belief in the importance of individual "accountability" also guided the recommendations made by the Department of Education under the leadership of (future drug czar) William Bennett. Students caught with drugs, Bennett argued, should be kicked out of school. Counseling these kids not only smacked of moral relativism but implied that drug abuse has "root causes" that are worth exploring.[69]

Although public opinion has not been irrelevant to the development of federal drug policy, the "get tough" approach to drugs was not primarily a response to public attitudes. As of 1981, only 3% of the American public believed that cutting the drug supply was the most important thing that could be done to reduce crime; 22% felt that reducing unemployment would be most effective. Furthermore, the percentage of poll respondents identifying drug abuse as the nation's most important problem had dropped from 20% in 1973 to 2% in 1974 and hovered between 0% and 2% until 1982. Thus, public opinion polls do

not indicate an upsurge in concern about drugs prior to Reagan's decla-
ration of war, nor is there evidence of widespread support for the idea
that fighting crime and drugs through tough law enforcement was the
best solution to these problems.[70]

The Escalation of the War on Drugs

Political and media attention to "the drug issue" intensified significantly in the summer of 1986. In part, this surge in attention to the drug
issue was a response to the cocaine-related deaths of athletes Len Bias
and Don Rogers and the increasing visibility of crack cocaine. The
claims-making activities of federal officials also played a key role.[71]

In October 1985, the DEA sent Robert Stutman to serve as Director of
its New York City office. Stutman made a concerted effort to draw
journalists' attention to the spread of crack. "The agents would hear me
give hundreds of presentations to the media as I attempted to call
attention to the drug scourge," Stutman wrote later. "I wasted no time in
pointing out [the DEA's] new accomplishments against the drug traffickers and using those cases to illustrate the full scope of the drug abuse
problem."[72] Stutman explains his strategy as follows:

> In order to convince Washington, I needed to make it [drugs] a national issue
> and quickly. I began a lobbying effort and I used the media. The media were
> only too willing to cooperate, because as far as the New York media was
> concerned, crack was the hottest combat reporting story to come along since
> the end of the Vietnam war.[73]

This campaign appears to have been quite effective. The number of
drug-related stories appearing in the *New York Times* increased from 43
in the latter half of 1985 to 220 in the second half of 1986.[74] Other media
outlets soon followed suit.

In an attempt to ensure that their party was perceived as taking action
on the drug issue, Democrats in the House began putting together
legislation calling for increased antidrug spending. Congressional Republicans warned Reagan that unless he came up with more specific
antidrug proposals—and quickly—they would be compelled to endorse
the $2 to $3 billion bill promoted by the Democratic leadership. And so
they were. In September 1986, the House passed legislation that allocated
$2 billion to the antidrug crusade for 1987, required the participation of

the military in narcotics control efforts, imposed severe penalties for possession of small amounts of crack cocaine, and allowed the death penalty for some drug-related crimes and the admission of some illegally obtained evidence in drug trials. Later that month, the Senate proposed even tougher antidrug legislation, and in October, President Reagan signed the Anti-Drug Abuse Act of 1986 into law. In addition to the House proposals described above, this legislation prescribed harsh mandatory minimum sentences for some drug offenses. These penalties were based on the type and volume of drugs seized and prohibited judges from considering other factors, such as the offender's role in the offense.[75]

Between 1986 and 1990, a period that bridged the administrations of Ronald Reagan and George Bush, drug use was one of the nation's most publicized issues. The 1988 Anti-Drug Abuse Act added more mandatory minimum sentencing statutes, including a 5-year minimum sentence for first-time offenders convicted of possessing five or more grams of crack cocaine.[76] Public concern about drugs reached its zenith immediately following President Bush's national address in 1989, in which he focused exclusively on the drug crisis. As Exhibit 4.3 indicates, federal funds allocated to the battle against drugs were greater under President Bush than under all presidents since Richard Nixon, combined.

The crime issue also enjoyed a high profile in the 1988 presidential campaign, in part as a result of George Bush's successful manipulation of what came to be known as the "Willie Horton" incident. Horton, a convicted murderer who had served most of his prison sentence, absconded from a Massachusetts furlough program while Michael Dukakis, Bush's Democratic rival, was governor. While on the loose, Horton kidnapped a couple in Maryland, tied up the husband, and raped the wife. During the 1988 campaign, Bush and his supporters used the incident in stump speeches and television commercials to mobilize outrage about crime and blame it on "liberal Democrats" like Dukakis. As one of Bush's political operatives explained, the incident was "a wonderful mix of liberalism and a big black rapist."[77]

The Triumph of Law and Order

The outbreak of the Persian Gulf war in early 1991 eclipsed all domestic issues, and President Bush largely ignored crime and drugs during the 1992 campaign season. This shift probably reflects the failure

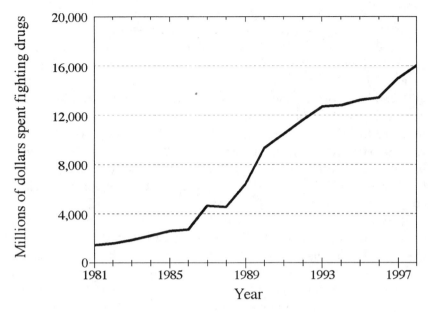

Exhibit 4.3. National Drug Control Spending
SOURCE: *The National Drug Control Strategy, 1992*, p. 219; (1999), Table 5.

of the war on drugs (as indicated by increases in drug-related emergency room visits and in the overall supply of cocaine and heroin within the United States), as well as candidate Clinton's relative invulnerability on these issues.

Like many "new" Democrats, 1992 presidential hopeful Bill Clinton was determined not to suffer the fate of the previous Democratic presidential candidate, Michael Dukakis, who was portrayed by the Bush administration as hopelessly "soft on crime." As both governor and presidential candidate, Clinton expressed strong support for expanded police efforts, more aggressive border interdiction programs, and tougher penalties for drug offenders. As a result, "there was little about Clinton's crime control record in Arkansas that Bush could taunt him about the way he mocked Dukakis as a patsy for every dark-skinned murderer in Massachusetts."[78] The 1992 Democratic platform also embraced the idea that levels of crime and drug use are a direct function of crime control efforts: "The simplest and most direct way to restore order in our cities is to put more police on the streets."[79]

Despite his record as governor and his relatively tough talk during the election campaign, some speculated that on ascension to office, Bill Clinton would create space for alternatives to the "get tough" approach. His record and campaign rhetoric were somewhat ambiguous in this regard. On the one hand, Clinton emphasized the need for greater law enforcement efforts and boot camps for juvenile offenders and touted his record on capital punishment. (Perhaps to make the point, Clinton returned to Arkansas in the midst of the 1992 campaign to oversee the execution of a convicted killer with an IQ in the 70s.) On the other hand, both before and after the election, Clinton occasionally evinced glimmers of a more sociological analysis of the crime problem. For example, in a speech to the Democratic Leadership Council shortly after the Los Angeles riots, Clinton characterized looters as people whose "lives and bond to the larger community had been shredded by the hard knife of experience." He also criticized the Reagan-Bush administrations for blaming crime problems on "them"—poor, non-White Americans. And he also spoke eloquently of the need to reverse the trend toward racial isolation and of the government's responsibility to reduce social inequalities. A year after the election, Clinton still, at least occasionally, expressed these views:

> We have to rebuild families and communities in this country. We've got to take more responsibility for these little kids before they grow up and start shooting each other. I know the budget is tight, but I'm telling you, we have to deal with family, community and education, and find jobs for members of society's underclass to bring structure to their lives.[80]

Clinton also offered some criticism of the Reagan/Bush war on drugs. In 1992, for example, he argued that "Bush confuses being tough with being smart, especially on drugs. He thinks locking up addicts instead of treating them before they commit crimes . . . is clever politics. That may be, but it certainly isn't sound policy, and the consequences of his cravenness could ruin us."[81] Janet Reno, Attorney General under Clinton, was also known to have derided boasts of drug seizures and arrests as evidence of a misguided "body count mentality."[82] In short, Clinton and his deputies sometimes espoused the notion that crime and drug abuse are related to social conditions, giving some observers hope that the new administration would advocate alternative approaches to these problems.

This potential was not realized. In August 1993, Republicans announced an anticrime legislative package calling for increased federal aid for local law enforcement, enhanced federal support for prison construction for states willing to adopt "truth-in-sentencing" provisions, more mandatory minimum penalties, and new restrictions on the federal appeals process for death row inmates. One week later, Clinton and several key congressional Democrats proposed their own anticrime legislation, calling for federal support for local community policing efforts, enhanced federal support for prison construction, a ban on assault weapons, other gun-control measures, and limits on appeals in capital cases. The most significant differences between the two parties' proposals were their positions on gun control, crime prevention, and the requirement that federal aid to local law enforcement be used to bolster community policing efforts (all of which the Democrats favored and the Republicans opposed).[83] These differences are not insignificant,[84] but the legislation proposed by the mainstream of the two parties was fairly similar: both emphasized the need to spend more on police and prisons. Only the Congressional Black Caucus developed anticrime proposals oriented toward a radically different goal: to "prevent crime [by making social investments, particularly in urban areas] and reform the criminal justice system to make it more fair."[85]

The publicity associated with these legislative proposals appears to have had an impact on public concern about crime. The percentage of those polled who felt that crime was the nation's most important problem increased from 9% in June 1993 to 22% in October and to 32% by January 1994.[86] Attention to the crime issue increased still further when President Clinton used his 1994 State of the Union address to urge more Congressional action, including the adoption of a federal equivalent of California's "three strikes" law (which made life imprisonment mandatory for three-time convicts). Later that year, a national poll found that 72% of the voters endorsed these "three strikes" provisions; 28% opposed them.[87] Most Democrats—pleased with new poll results indicating that Republicans no longer enjoyed an advantage on the crime issue[88]—continued to support the expansion of the criminal justice system while offering only tepid criticism of some mandatory sentencing provisions and mild support for some preventive measures.[89]

The final version of the Violent Crime Control and Law Enforcement Act of 1994 authorized $6.9 billion for crime prevention efforts, $13.8 billion for law enforcement, and $9.8 billion for state prison construction.

The cost of the bill, originally estimated at $5.9 billion, was now estimated to be $30.2 billion over 6 years.[90] This legislation also created dozens of new federal capital crimes, mandated life sentences for some three-time offenders, restricted the scope of court-ordered settlements in lawsuits seeking improved prison conditions, limited inmates' rights to sue over these issues, expanded federal prosecutors' capacity to use illegally obtained evidence, restricted prisoners' ability to file habeas corpus petitions, and strengthened measures to provide for the swift deportation of illegal aliens.[91] The legislation was sent to President Clinton in August 1994 and was hailed as a victory for the Democrats, who "were able to wrest the crime issue from the Republicans and make it their own."[92]

With Republicans demanding still "tougher" solutions to the crime problem, House and Senate campaigns in the fall of 1994 focused more on crime than on any other issue. In Florida, gubernatorial candidate (and son of the former president) Jeb Bush called for corporal punishment of the sort practiced in Singapore. On the television program *Meet the Press*, Texas Senator Phil Graham promised a "real crime bill" that "grabs violent criminals by the throat, puts them in prison, and that stops building prisons like Holiday Inns." In North Carolina, congressional candidate Fredrick Kenneth Heineman urged that provisions of the North American Free Trade Agreement be used to export U.S. criminals to Mexico, "where they can be warehoused more cheaply."

Under the leadership of then House Minority leader Newt Gingrich, the Republican party enthusiastically announced their "Contract With America"—including new anticrime proposals. This legislative package proposed further strengthening truth-in-sentencing, mandatory minimum sentencing, and death penalty provisions and weakening restrictions on the admission of illegally obtained evidence. In addition, despite the fact that less than one fourth of the funds appropriated by the 1994 legislation were earmarked for preventive measures, the Republicans now proposed eliminating all such measures. Privately, Republicans argued not only that they doubted the efficacy of crime prevention programs but that their main beneficiaries were the urban poor—a group famous for its loyalty to the Democratic party.[93]

Despite President Clinton's embrace of virtually all of the components of conservative law and order rhetoric and policy, the election proved to be the ultimate vindication of the GOP's southern strategy. With Gingrich leading the charge, Republicans won congressional victories in state after state, finally achieving the long-sought status of majority party in both the Senate and the House of Representatives. The goals advanced in the Contract with America were subsequently embodied in a series of bills passed easily in the House in February 1995.

Most of the ensuing debate over crime policy centered on House proposals to eradicate federal support for crime prevention programs, allow local law enforcement to use federal funds for purposes other than community policing, and further tie federal prison assistance grants to states' willingness to adopt truth-in-sentencing provisions. Despite rules forbidding changes to existing laws in general appropriations bills, the 1996 Appropriations Act made several key changes to the 1994 crime bill. In particular, 1996 legislation eliminated a large number of prevention programs included in the 1994 act and replaced them with block grants for local law enforcement. The appropriations act also increased federal anticrime monies allocated from $2.3 billion for fiscal 1995 to $4.1 billion for fiscal 1996.

Although President Clinton and the Democrats did manage to retain separate funds for community policing efforts and the ban on assault weapons, the 1996 legislation largely embodied the conservative approach to crime and decimated federal support for crime prevention programs. Asked to explain President Clinton's failure to provide any real alternative to these proposals, one administration official said: "you can't appear soft on crime when crime hysteria is sweeping the country. Maybe the national temper will change, and maybe, if it does, we'll do it right later."[94] Since then, despite evidence of ongoing public support for crime prevention efforts aimed at the "root causes" of crime, neither party has been willing to deviate from the bipartisan consensus in favor of "getting tough."[95]

CONCLUSION

In this chapter, we have argued that contemporary wars on crime and drugs reflect the ascendance of a particular way of framing the crime problem. Over the past three decades, conservatives have promoted the view that a variety of social ills including crime, addiction, and poverty, stem not from blocked opportunities linked to class inequality and racial discrimination but rather from "permissiveness" in the forms of criminal justice leniency, tolerance of drug use, and welfare dependency. Undoubtedly, violence and drug abuse (especially in the age of crack) pose very real and significant problems, and the seriousness of these problems has increased popular receptivity to conservative claims. However, the conservative effort to frame these issues as a consequence of excessive "permissiveness" and "leniency" was not rooted in public opinion, nor is it consistent with the findings of most sociological research.[96]

Instead, these claims-making activities were part of a larger effort to realign the electorate along racial (rather than class) lines and thus forge a new Republican electoral majority. They were simultaneously aimed at shifting the government's role and responsibilities from the provision of social welfare to the protection of personal security.

The fact that liberal politicians largely accepted this reframing of crime, drug use, and other social problems has meant that challenges to the law and order discourse have been few and far between. The liberal about-face on crime-related problems has many causes, including conservatives' ability to disseminate law and order rhetoric through the mass media and its resonance with much of the American public—subjects that will be explored in the following chapters.

5
◆ Crime in
◆ the News

◆ ◆ ◆ Americans have a love-hate relationship with crime. On the one hand, we abhor it, decry its apparent increase, and worry about the safety of our loved ones and ourselves. At the same time, we are fascinated with crime—we can't seem to get enough of it. Indeed, crime-related news stories are among the most widely read, and many of the most popular entertainment shows also focus on crime and violence. Of course, it is difficult to determine whether our enthusiasm for crime stories is a consequence of their ubiquity or whether crime stories are ubiquitous because we so relish them. In either case, crime is one of the most consistent topics covered by the news media, and both news and entertainment programs that focus on crime are highly popular among the public. In fact, the mass media are the main source of the public's information about crime.

In this chapter, our focus is on the news media; in the following chapter, we turn our attention to entertainment media (although we hasten to point out that the line between these genres is often—and increasingly—blurry). Our discussion of the news media begins with a bit of historical background regarding the mass media's coverage of crime. In the sections that follow, we examine the ways in which crime-related topics are framed in the news media and how these representations of crime influence public opinion and criminal justice policy.

Finally, we illustrate some of these issues through a detailed analysis of the mass media's coverage of the "drug crisis" of the 1980s and 1990s.

CRIME AND THE AMERICAN NEWS MEDIA

Printed news about crime is nearly as old as printing itself. In Europe, some newsprint weeklies supplied regular accounts of court cases as early as the 1600s. Over the next two centuries, the print media continued to provide different types of news coverage, including tips on preventing crime, accounts of particularly lurid crimes, descriptions of executions, and details regarding wanted suspects. In the United States, weekly papers proliferated in the 1800s and offered brief summaries of high-profile trials.[1] Not until the emergence of daily newspapers in the 1830s did crime and justice become staples of American journalism.[2]

The *New York Sun* was the first American daily, or "penny" paper, to include a daily column on police and court news. The paper's circulation subsequently increased and, not surprisingly, other papers soon began to pay more attention to crime. These new crime stories were soon subjected to a number of criticisms, including complaints that they encouraged immorality and licentiousness, prejudiced juries, and were simply in bad taste.[3] But the public's appetite for these stories was hearty, and the daily newspapers—as well as weekly news magazines—continued to provide abundant and detailed descriptions of crime and justice matters. In fact, some newspapers (such as the *National Police Gazette*) existed primarily to cover the most significant crimes of the day.

The new crime stories often provided blow-by-blow accounts of crime and courtroom dramas, but they also offered political analysis and commentary regarding the causes of crime. The *National Police Gazette*, for example, focused on the corruption of public officials and those who held excessive economic power.[4] Similarly, the early penny press dailies typically portrayed crime as the result of class inequality and lamented the ways in which the rich and powerful interfered with the process of justice.[5]

By the turn of the century, some newspaper reporters began to specialize in crime. At the same time, the newspapers shifted from being explicitly and openly political—and often critical of the status quo—to being ostensibly "neutral" and "objective" sources of information. As a result, political editorials and commentaries about crime and justice were increasingly eclipsed by news accounts of individual criminal cases—often quite dramatic ones. Crime was rarely discussed as a social issue or problem, and police officials typically served as journalists' primary source of information about the criminal cases covered.[6] These apparently more "objective" accounts of crime were common in both the informational newspapers aimed at professionals and elites and the more entertainment-oriented newspapers aimed at the middle and working classes.

In the 1920s, radio became a primary source of both entertainment and news. The strength of the new medium was its capacity to provide live, on-the-scene reports. Its weakness was its inability to deliver more than one "story" at a time. Unlike print media, which can provide a range of stories from which various readers can choose, radio must find ways to hold the attention of all listeners at once. Dramatic tales of crime and justice thus fit the new medium especially well and quickly became a programming staple. Television soon followed radio, adopting both its format and preference for dramatic stories that grab the attention of viewers. Both radio and television continued to depend largely on police and government officials for their information about crime and justice.[7]

Over the past three decades, the media has further increased its coverage of crime. Between 22% and 28% of all contemporary newspaper stories focus on justice-related topics. Crime is also the subject of 10% to 13% of all national and 20% of all local television news stories.[8] In more recent years, crime has become an even more popular news topic. In the mid-1990s, as the rate of violent crime declined, television and newspaper coverage of crime increased by more than 400% (see Exhibit 5.1).[9] Between 1990 and 1995—a period in which the homicide rate declined by 13%—network news coverage of murder (excluding coverage of the O.J. Simpson trial) increased by 336%.[10] In cities such as Denver (in 1992) and Boston (in 1997), the news media bombarded audiences with saturation coverage of homicide for periods lasting several months.[11] Nationwide, crime was the leading television news topic in the 1990s.[12]

Crimes, Criminals, and Victims in the News

One of the most noteworthy characteristics of contemporary crime news is its tendency to focus on the rarest types of crime, such as murder,

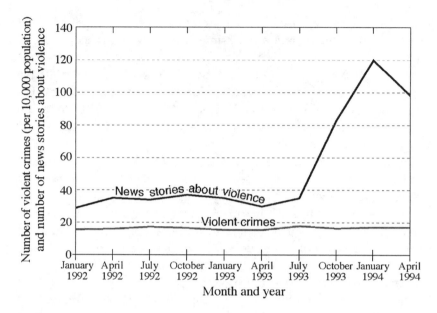

Exhibit 5.1. Television and Newspaper Coverage of Crime

SOURCE: Chiricos et al., "Crime, News and Fear of Crime."

NOTE: Media coverage includes television and newpaper stories about violence. The violent crime rate is measured in terms of the number of violent crimes known to the police per 10,000 households.

rape, and robbery. According to one study, although less than 1% of the crimes known to the police involve murder, over 26% of crime news stories feature a homicide case. Conversely, 47% of the crimes reported to the police are nonviolent, but only 4% of crime news stories depict instances of nonviolent crime.[13] A meta-analysis of 36 content analyses of crime news confirmed these findings, concluding that 8 stories about violent crime appeared for every 2 stories about property crime. By contrast, official statistics show that more than 9 property crimes occur for every 1 violent crime. Other kinds of illegalities, such as corporate and state crime, are also largely ignored in favor of violent "street" crime.[14] This focus on the comparatively rare violent cases is most pronounced in the electronic media (radio and television) and in tabloid rather than "high-brow" newspapers.[15]

The media are also more likely to report instances of violent crime that are committed by strangers than those that are committed by acquaintances or intimates (especially domestic violence).[16] As a result, criminal offenders are typically portrayed as predatory outsiders rather than as friends and family members. Over the last century, these predatory criminals have come to be depicted as ever more barbaric and irrational, while their crimes are presented as more and more violent and unpredictable.[17] Sexual violence, for example, is covered extensively by the news media, but the cases deemed "newsworthy" are almost exclusively ones involving predatory strangers as suspects (especially cases involving multiple victims). These stories reinforce the notion that sex crimes are committed only by "sex fiends"—crazy and irrational individuals—and both reflect and perpetuate the myth that sexual violence is not committed by known and trusted individuals.[18] In fact, the majority of rapes are committed by persons known to victims.[19]

Network news stories in which African Americans are accused of crimes are more likely to involve violence or drugs than news stories featuring White defendants.[20] This fact alone is difficult to interpret: African Americans are also arrested for violent and drug-related crime at a higher rate than Whites. However, Blacks charged with violent offenses are often depicted differently than Whites charged with violent offenses. Studies of local and national news have found that Blacks arrested for violent crimes were more likely to be depicted in the physical custody of police (e.g., spread-eagled against the side of a police cruiser) and to be dressed poorly. Blacks were less likely than Whites to be identified by name in still photographs or to be represented through sound bites from defense attorneys. Together, these differences had the effect of making Blacks accused of violent crimes appear more menacing than Whites accused of violent crimes.[21]

News media depictions of crime victims are also misleading. In the news, when crime victims are depicted, they are typically White, female, and affluent.[22] One content analysis of national and local television newscasts, for example, found that when the race and gender of crime victims could be identified, White females were the most common category of victims (see Exhibit 5.2).[23] In fact, young men of color—especially those living in poor and urban areas—experience the highest rates of victimization, and White females report the lowest. The dynamic is illustrated by a pair of recent New York City homicides. The murder of Marvin Watson, a 22-year-old electrician, elicited no media coverage. The killing a few weeks later of Amy Watkins, a 26-year-old graduate student studying to become a social worker, was covered extensively by local and national media; reporters camped out at the crime scene and

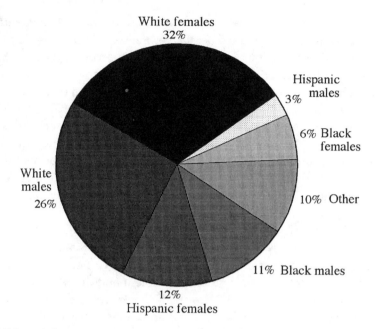

Exhibit 5.2. Crime Victims in the News
SOURCE: Chiricos et al., "Crime, News and Fear of Crime."
NOTE: Figures are based on a 9-week analysis of news in Tallahassee, Florida, in 1995.

tabloids ran the story on their covers. Both Watson and Watkins were new to the City and both were "innocent victims." The only apparent difference between the two is that she was a middle class White woman and he a working class Black man.[24]

Framing Crime

In general, crime-related news stories provide detailed accounts of individual criminal events. Comparatively little attention is paid to broader trends in crime, and few stories attempt to put the crime problem in a larger perspective.[25] As one researcher explained, crime news tends to be framed "episodically" rather than "thematically."[26] Coverage of child sexual abuse, for example, typically ignores issues of gender and power and highlights instead the pathology of individual perpetrators or the failure of social workers in particular cases.[27] Similarly, coverage of urban riots tends to depict such political disorder as instances of criminality and to ignore the larger structural and political forces involved.[28]

Crime stories are somewhat more likely to be framed thematically (in terms of causes and possible remedies) in news weeklies and the commentary sections of newspapers.[29] In these venues, crime is sometimes depicted as a consequence of poverty, family breakdown, or violence in the mass media. The most common frame, however, treats crime as a consequence of the failures of the criminal justice system: Criminals escape punishment because of legal technicalities, liberal judges, and permissive laws. According to this perspective, the best way to lower the rate of crime is to impose more certain and more severe punishment and to incapacitate offenders for longer periods of time.[30]

Understanding Crime News

How do we understand the media's obsession with violent crimes committed by predatory strangers? How do we make sense of the media's tendency to frame crime in terms of failures of the justice system? Three main factors help to account for these tendencies:

◆ *News values.* Journalists define *news* as that which is out of the ordinary.[31] By definition, criminal events involve the violation of norms and thus satisfy this criteria. Crime news also provides the media with the opportunity to perform a vital societal role: identifying and reinforcing moral boundaries by highlighting violations and showcasing punishment.[32] Stories about crime provide society with a fascinating and never-ending series of conflicts between good and evil. This conflict is captured most dramatically in stories about violent, predatory crimes committed against persons believed to be vulnerable and blameless—which helps to explains the overrepresentation of White, female victims in the news.[33]

◆ *Organizational needs.* The regular provision of information from law enforcement and other government officials means that crime stories can be produced quickly and regularly and on the basis of information obtained from sources considered to be legitimate authorities.[34] Moreover, given that the mass media are for-profit enterprises with an interest in increasing market share and advertising revenue, the apparent popularity of crime stories certainly helps to explain why the news media focus on crime.

◆ *Reliance on official sources.* The tendency of journalists to rely on law enforcement agents, politicians, and government officials for information also influences the volume and content of crime news.[35] This practice is by no means unusual: in general, journalists prefer politicians and government bureaucrats as news sources.[36] Officials are often seen as authoritative and thus lend legitimacy to the often ambiguous journalistic enterprise.[37] Officials are also able to supply journalists with a steady diet of appropriately formatted and timely information—a necessity in the deadline-driven world of modern journalism.[38]

Increasingly, criminal justice officials attempt to shape the way in which their performance is depicted in the news.[39] For example, police organizations work hard to ensure that instances of excessive use of force are either discredited or framed within the "one bad apple" theory, which holds that such problems are not institutionally based but are the consequence of a few "rotten" individuals.[40] Not all such efforts are successful. Consider, for example, news coverage of the 1991 beating of motorist Rodney King by officers of the Los Angeles Police Department. News accounts of the Rodney King affair did not represent it as an isolated event but framed the LAPD's excessive use of force as a widespread phenomenon resulting from strained police-community relations. There were two reasons for the reluctance of the media to adopt the LAPD's perspective in their coverage of the King beating. First, the dramatic nature of the videotaped beating made it more difficult for LAPD officials to define the meaning of the event for the public or journalists. Second, the availability of "respectable" independent sources and the presence of conflict between elites on the subject of police brutality in general and the King beating in particular meant that no one source was able to establish a dominant interpretation of these events. [41]

In the routine course of events, however, official sources are often successful in their efforts to shape the news.[42] In the case of drug-related news, for example, stories that relied on official sources in the 1980s were much less likely to offer criticisms of the government's antidrug strategy.[43] Furthermore, although conflict between political elites increases the likelihood that media coverage will present alternative perspectives, the usual reluctance of media personnel to rely on nonofficial sources (such as crime victims, grassroots or public interest organizations, or criminal suspects) means that the range of perspectives depicted in the news typically remains fairly narrow. In short, although nonelite sources are sometimes able to establish themselves as news sources, the media's overall tendency is to reproduce the perspectives of the law enforcement officials and politicians who serve as their main news sources.

CRIME NEWS AND PUBLIC OPINION

The media are a crucial source of information in the modern world and, as a result, play an important role in shaping public perceptions of political and social issues. Historically, much of the research on the impact of the media has been concerned with their capacity to "set the public agenda." This research suggested that although "the press may not be successful in telling people what to think . . . they are stunningly success-ful in telling people what to think about."[44] Indeed, most studies found that those problems receiving prominent attention on national news tended to be identified by the viewing public as relatively important.[45]

Researchers have also examined whether the media shape how we think about social problems. The best-known example of this type of research is the "cultivation analysis" of George Gerbner and his col-leagues. Using primarily survey data, Gerbner found that heavy con-sumers of television are somewhat more likely to see the world as a violent, frightening, and "mean" place.[46] More recent survey research shows that fear of crime among middle-aged White women is related to watching television news and listening to the news on the radio. The authors of this study attributed this media effect to the overrepresenta-tion of White women as crime victims in the news.[47]

Some have challenged these findings, pointing out that correlations between television viewing and either fear of crime or a "mean" world-view may be due to the tendency of people with these kinds of feelings and attitudes to watch more television (rather than vice versa).[48] As will be discussed in Chapter 6, both of these arguments appear to be true: Heavy television consumers are quite probably influenced by what they watch, and those who view the world as a mean and scary place are more drawn to television—especially cop and crime shows—than are those with a rosier perspective. However, experimental studies—which ran-domly assign people into control and experimental groups and can therefore isolate the effects of exposure to media—provide further evi-dence of the media's influence on popular perceptions and attitudes about crime. These studies indicate that those who are exposed to media depictions of violent crimes are subsequently more likely to perceive other crimes as more serious and to support punitive anticrime measures.[49]

Studies have also found that the framing of crime-related news stories affects assessments of the crime problem and support for particular crime control policies.[50] In one particularly innovative study, the television crime story to which people were exposed varied along two dimensions. Some stories framed crime "episodically"—they depicted a single instance of violent crime. In others, violent crime was framed "thematically"—that is, discussed as a social problem and situated in its larger social context. Researchers also varied the racial identity of those visually depicted as "the criminal." Not surprisingly, those who viewed stories that framed violent crime in "episodic" terms were more likely to attribute crime to individual rather than social causes. But the more dramatic finding in this study was the significance of race: Stories that featured violent Black criminals were more than twice as likely as stories depicting violent White criminals to elicit individualistic (rather than social) attributions of responsibility for the problem of crime.[51] In light of the apparently racist tendency of people to hold Blacks but not Whites individually responsible for the crimes they commit, the media's tendency to focus disproportionately on conventional "street crime" (as opposed to corporate, white collar, or organized crime, in which Whites are more likely to be involved) likely reinforces the notion that crime is caused by wicked individuals and the belief that punishment is the best solution to this problem.[52]

Experimental studies, then, confirm that exposure to news stories about crime shapes media consumers' perceptions of the seriousness of the crime problem and beliefs about appropriate responses. However, such media effects vary according to the characteristics of the media consumer, the content of the story, and the medium in which it is presented. People who lack personal experience with crime or have weakly held beliefs about the topic are more likely to be affected by media accounts. Stories about local crimes are more likely to increase fear of crime than stories about crime in faraway places. Finally, television news and tabloid coverage of crime may be more likely to affect attitudes and emotional states (such as fear levels); the print media may have a greater impact on beliefs about the pervasiveness of crime.[53]

In some cases, people may even react to media messages in ways that are directly opposite to what might be expected. Exposure to public service announcements warning youth of the dangers of drugs, for example, may have led to increased drug use, presumably because these announcements created heightened awareness of and interest in drugs.[54] Such exceptions and complications are important to keep in mind. In general, though, research suggests that news stories have an important and relatively direct impact on beliefs and attitudes regarding criminal justice matters. In particular, the media—especially television and the tabloids—tend to increase the fear of crime and the likelihood that people will adopt a "retributive justice perspective."[55]

CRIME NEWS AND CRIMINAL JUSTICE

By shaping public opinion, the media have an indirect impact on criminal justice policy and outcomes. The irony is that because politicians frequently serve as news sources regarding crime, they often end up responding to the very sentiments and views they themselves have cultivated through the media. To further complicate matters, there is evidence that media coverage and media personnel may directly affect the policy-making and legal processes independent of any impact they may have on popular opinion. In the sections that follow, we identify some of the ways in which the media can directly affect criminal justice policies and outcomes without necessarily having any impact on general public opinion.

The Media and Criminal Justice Policy

Politicians often interpret media coverage of an issue as a sign of heightened public concern. In accounting for their legislative initiative on the crime and drug issues, for example, politicians in the 1980s often cited increased media coverage of the drug problem as evidence of the public concern to which they felt compelled to respond.[56] For example, early in the summer of 1986, President Reagan described his renewed interest in the antidrug cause as a response to public opinion, claiming that "the polls show that this [drugs] is, in most people's minds, the number one problem in the country."[57] A reporter attempted to identify the source of this claim at a White House Press briefing with President Reagan's spokesman, Larry Speakes:

Question: The President recently cited a poll in which he said that 71%, I believe, of the American public cited drugs as the number one issue. Do you know what poll that was?

Speakes: I don't know—sure don't. Bill?

Question: Larry, if I could continue—you said that there has been a tremendous outpouring of public feeling since the Len Bias death [death of a professional athlete attributed to drug use]. Do you have any research or evidence of what kind of public feeling there is on this issue?

Speakes: No. I just think it's an obvious feeling about the amount of publicity that was given to the most recent sports drug deaths that have really peaked public interest.[58]

In fact, the national polls administered just prior to this exchange did not indicate that most Americans considered drugs to be the nation's most important problem. According to a New York Times/CBS News Poll taken in April 1986, only 3% of those polled were most concerned about drugs. It was not until after the President announced his national campaign against drugs in early July that concern about the issue increased— and even then, it did not come anywhere near the levels claimed by President Reagan. In this case, Reagan administration officials misintepreted massive media coverage of the death of Len Bias as evidence of high levels of public concern about drugs, and this (mis)interpretation affected the Reagan administration's antidrug agenda.

Under some circumstances, media personnel may also play a direct role in the policy-making process. One of the first studies to suggest that the media may play such a role was Mark Fishman's analysis of an apparent "crime wave" against the elderly in New York City in the 1970s. Fishman showed that journalists, working closely with law enforcement sources, created the impression that crimes against the elderly were increasing dramatically. Journalists thus identified "crimes against the elderly" as a news theme and subsequently focused on those incidents that fit with this theme. Law enforcement agencies responded by drawing reporters' attention to cases that involved older victims. And because media personnel tend to look to other media outlets in defining "what's news," many of the local media reported in ways that gave the perception that crimes against the elderly were increasing dramatically. The consequences of the creation of this "crime wave" included the creation of new law enforcement squads and tactics, the reallocation of public and police resources, and the introduction of legislation aimed at protecting the elderly.[59] Interestingly, police statistics did not indicate any increase in the number of older crime victims during this time.[60]

Similar "crime waves" have since been chronicled in several cities.[61] In most cases, the triggering events included murders of "ideal victims"—individuals deemed by society to be either especially vulnerable or especially blameless. In Boston, for example, the 1997 rape and murder of 10-year-old Jeffrey Curley was linked to a number of other grisly murders and reported intensively by the local press. News coverage of "the killing season" (as one local newspaper dubbed it) was so intense that the state legislature debated and came within one vote of adopting a death penalty statute, despite the fact that the state's overall murder rate had been steadily declining for several years.

The Media and
the Criminal Justice Process

Just as media coverage and personnel may directly affect criminal justice policy, they may also have a direct impact on criminal justice practices and outcomes. In the 20th century, highly publicized trials have emerged as important media events, illustrating the fine line between crime "news" and "entertainment."[62] Historically, the main way the media were thought to influence criminal trials was by prejudicing jury members in cases that received a great deal of media coverage. However, the research findings on the effects of trial coverage are quite mixed: It is not at all clear that jury members are significantly affected by media coverage of the trial itself. However, studies do indicate that exposure to pretrial publicity may have prejudicial and long-lasting effects on jurors and other actors in the criminal justice process.[63] Prosecutors, for example, are less willing to consider plea bargains in homicide cases that receive extensive media coverage.[64]

Most criminal cases are not televised, do not receive much publicity, and do not even make it to trial. Nevertheless, these unpublicized cases may also be affected by media coverage of celebrated cases. In several recent studies, researchers analyzed the impact of highly publicized cases on more ordinary cases involving similar types of offenses and found that media coverage of celebrated cases may have "echo effects." For example, the number of child abuse cases increased markedly and an increased proportion of the accused were found guilty following a highly publicized case that involved allegations of sexual abuse in a day care center.[65] The effects of media coverage of celebrated cases can thus extend well beyond a single case.

In sum, crime-related news stories play an important role in the formation of public beliefs and attitudes and can have both indirect and direct effects on criminal justice policy and processes. Although these media effects are not universal and are not always straightforward, crime-related news stories do have important cultural and political consequences.

In the next section, we examine news coverage of the "drug crisis" in the 1980s and 1990s. This case study draws together and illustrates the various themes addressed in this chapter, including:

◆ The significance of competition for audience share in the selection and framing of crime news
◆ The influence of official sources on news frames
◆ The impact of news coverage on public opinion and government policy

CASE STUDY: CONSTRUCTING THE DRUG CRISIS IN AMERICA

Media coverage of the "drug crisis" in the 1980s played a significant role in justifying and perpetuating the war on drugs. Journalists drew a great deal of attention to the spread of crack cocaine in the inner city and depicted the drug problem primarily as the consequence of insufficient control and punishment.[66] Concern about the drug problem and support for punitive antidrug policies also reached record levels during the late 1980s, and these attitudinal shifts played an important role in legitimating "get-tough" antidrug policies.

In the discussion that follows, we first describe the news media's representation of the drug problem at the height of the drug war. Next, we examine new, more critical themes that began to appear in the 1990s. Finally, we offer an explanation for the somewhat surprising appearance of these critical themes in light of the factors we have identified as most responsible for shaping news about crime.

Constructing the Drug Panic

Researchers analyzing the media's construction of the drug issue in the second half of the 1980s have amassed evidence that

◆ relative to earlier and later periods, the volume of coverage of the drug issue during this period was extraordinary

◆ the framing of the drug issue emphasized the pharmacological (i.e., chemical) properties of crack cocaine as a cause of drug-related violence and implied the need for tough new criminal justice solutions

◆ the media frequently advanced scary but misleading claims about drugs

The following excerpt from a *Newsweek* magazine cover story published in 1986 is a fairly representative example of the kind of drug coverage that proliferated during this period.

It is cheap, plentiful and intensely addictive . . . the crack craze is spreading nationwide. . . . Crack has captured the ghetto and is inching its way into the suburbs. . . . Wherever it appears, it spawns vicious violence among dealers and dopers.

Rock and crack represent a quantum leap in the addictive properties of cocaine and a marketing breakthrough for the pusher. Sold in tiny chips that give the user a 5-20 minute high, crack is often purer than sniffable cocaine. . . . The cycle of ups and downs reinforces the craving and . . . can produce a powerful chemical dependency within two weeks.

There are ominous signs that crack and rock dealers are expanding well beyond the inner city. . . . "In the past six months every city, county and almost every little town has been hit by the crack epidemic," says John J. Barbara of the Florida Department of Law Enforcement.

Crack and rock are spreading because cocaine is so widely available in the United States and because the justice system has been unable to thwart the cocaine trade at any level. Police in every city where crack is now a major problem argue that the courts are too lenient with drug offenders, and they may be right. . . . "We are not thinning out the ranks and making any impact. We are not *deterring*," Cusack says. "As a matter of fact, the opposite is happening. What's the risk? So few are getting caught and the risk of prosecution is so remote that we are encouraging people to traffic."[67]

Although media coverage of the drug issue increased somewhat after President Reagan declared the war on drugs in October 1982, drug coverage increased most dramatically in 1986.[68] The proximate causes of this surge were the cocaine-related deaths of celebrity athletes Len Bias in June and Don Rogers in July. By the middle of the summer, the quantity of drug stories was truly staggering: The three major TV networks aired 74 evening news stories about drugs during July alone.[69] By the November elections, NBC News had aired over 400 stories about drugs (consuming an "unprecedented" 15 hours of air time) and a handful of major newspapers and magazines had produced roughly 1,000 stories about crack.[70] *Time* and *Newsweek* each ran five cover stories on the drug issue in 1986 alone. Attention to the drug issue diminished a bit during 1987 but intensified once again between 1988 and the outbreak of the Persian Gulf War in early 1991.

The changing nature of the coverage of the drug issue during this period is also striking. In the early 1980s, the typical cocaine-related news story focused on White recreational users who snorted the drug in its powder form. These stories frequently relied on news sources associated with the drug treatment industry and emphasized the possibility of "recovery." By late 1985, however, this frame was supplanted by a new one depicting cities in a state of siege. Increasingly, cocaine-related news stories featured poor and non-White users and dealers of crack cocaine. At the same time, law enforcement officials demanding tough responses to the drug problem took the place of the medical and treatment experts previously identified as drug authorities. As the 1980s progressed, journalists increasingly used an overtly "campaigning" voice to demonstrate their clear disapproval of the drug scene and those who populated it. And as a result of their reliance on law enforcement sources, camera crews began using hand-held cameras to cover crack house raids from the vantage point of the police.[71]

In addition to promoting the "siege" frame, the media promulgated misleading information about the drug problem. For example, media accounts during this period claimed that drug use was "epidemic"— sometimes "pandemic"—and thus analogous to a "medieval plague."[72] By contrast, the available evidence suggests that most categories of drug use were declining in the 1980s: National Institute of Drug Abuse data indicate a downward trend in the use of all illicit substances other than cocaine. Even with respect to cocaine use, the data are somewhat ambiguous. Although the proportion of high school seniors and young adults reporting cocaine use in the past year or past month did increase slightly prior to 1986, lifetime use of cocaine by youth and young adults peaked in 1982 and consistently declined after that year.[73] In all other age groups and categories, NIDA's Household Survey indicates that cocaine use was declining. Statistical artifacts and graphic images were nonetheless used to demonstrate and dramatize the claim that cocaine use among the young was a crisis of epidemic proportions.[74]

The nature of crack cocaine was also presented in misleading ways. News stories about crack often claimed that addiction to the drug is "instantaneous" and depicted the violence associated with crack as a consequence of its pharmacological properties.[75] Claims about the addictiveness of crack were clearly exaggerated: In fact, many crack users are not instantly or inevitably "addicted."[76] The media's emphasis on the chemical properties of crack also preempted a more accurate and nuanced understanding of the relationship between crack and violence. Much of this association is a product of the illegal nature of the drug trade and the socioeconomic context in which battles over market share are fought.[77] The media's tendency to overemphasize the chemical causes of crack-related violence led it to exaggerate the "random" nature of drug-related violence, the threat it posed to "innocent bystanders," and the extent to which this violence was "spilling over" into White and middle class neighborhoods.[78] The saturation coverage of the drug issue—largely depicted as a problem of non-White users and dealers laying siege to middle class White America—was thus predicated on misleading claims, most of which reinforced the notion that the best way to deal with the drug problem is through the enforcement of criminal law and the expansion of the criminal justice system.

Explaining the Drug Panic

The media's construction of the drug crisis was not entirely without foundation. Smokeable cocaine did become more available in the 1980s. Furthermore, the harm associated with drug abuse (particularly among the poor) may well have increased with the spread of crack: The number of drug-related emergency room visits increased throughout the late 1980s and early 1990s.[79] Finally, the crack trade did indeed spawn a great deal of violence in the inner city.[80]

Still, the manner in which the drug problem was framed in media accounts during this time is problematic. Most categories of drug use were declining throughout this period, and the data on prevalence hardly support the claim that cocaine use was "epidemic." More important, media promotion of the law and order approach to the drug problem was not a response to the harm associated with the spread of crack (there are clearly other ways of responding to this harm) and may have done more to exacerbate the problem than alleviate it. Finally, as harmful as crack and the drug trade may be, far more destructive social practices and arrangements (including alcohol and tobacco consumption, rising child poverty, and the absence of accessible health care) were not the subject of media hype in the way that crack cocaine was. Thus, although the spread of crack has had tragic consequences for some individuals and communities, the complicity of the media in the war on drugs cannot be explained in these terms alone. Instead, the active participation of journalists in the creation of a moral panic over drugs largely reflects a convergence of political, bureaucratic, and journalistic interests.

As was explained in Chapter 4, conservatives have used crime and related issues to redefine urban social ills as problems related to troublemakers rather than people in trouble. In the early 1980s, President Reagan linked this general ideological framework to the antidrug effort: The drug problem was not related to social conditions but was a consequence of misguided, evil people who must be taught a lesson. In fact, during the first year of the Reagan administration, officials compiled a list of all of the studies funded by NIDA that used the word "social" and from this list determined which ones would no longer receive government funding.[81]

Motivated by the increased availability of antidrug funds and the possibility of enhancing their turf and authority, federal drug enforcement and treatment agencies worked doggedly to promote journalistic attention to drugs. In April 1986, NIDA began its most ambitious outreach program, "Cocaine, the Big Lie." During the spring and summer of 1986, 13 public service announcements affiliated with this campaign aired between 1,500 and 2,500 times per month on 75 local television networks.[82] Meanwhile, the DEA and other government officials issued hundreds of press releases and gave innumerable interviews. Law enforcement agencies invited journalists to ride along and film drug "busts."

These entrepreneurial efforts paid off, if not in reduced drug use, then at least in terms of bureaucratic budgets. Between 1981 and 1993, federal spending on drug enforcement increased from less than $2 billion to more than $12 billion. Law enforcement was a much bigger winner than drug treatment and prevention agencies, which actually saw declining revenues during this period.[83]

Bombarded by the messages of antidrug bureaucrats, journalists readily embraced the official version of the drug problem. To a significant extent, their collusion reflects the fact that covering the "drug crisis" from the point of view of law enforcement agencies (especially when it yielded film footage of drug raids) satisfied the media's interest in dramatic and sensationalistic news. The ride-along footage of drug busts, the touring of enemy territory, the grave assessment of casualties—all of these made for exciting television. And the excitement registered in ratings. The CBS special "48 Hours on Crack Street," for example, was the highest rated of any similar program in 5 years. News agencies' interest in the dramatic and sensational also helps to explain why journalists were loathe to drop their dubious claims concerning the "epidemic" nature of crack use and the "random" violence it spawned.

By 1987-1988, however, stories on the drug crisis were beginning to be more reflective and nuanced. A few reporters began to point out, for example, that the violence associated with the distribution of crack was actually concentrated in a handful of neighborhoods.[84] In 1989, *Newsweek*—initially one of the most vociferous advocates of the view that crack users experience "instantaneous addiction"—now conceded that "crack isn't instantaneously addictive . . . 2.4 million Americans have tried crack, less than half a million now use it once a month or more."[85] Some journalists also began calling attention to the opportunistic uses of the "cocaine crisis" by politicians and the mass media. And in stories like *USA Today*'s 1992 "Drug War Focused on Blacks,"[86] the media even offered some criticisms of the war on drugs. Many reporters who engaged in such "second thoughts" demonstrated no penchant for irony; they uniformly failed to recognize their own complicity in promoting drug hysteria. At the same time, these stories did imply that crack is as much a political issue as a public health or criminal justice problem and provided some sense of the troubling consequences of the war on drugs.

The damage had already been done, however. During the peak of the drug war in 1989, 64% of Americans named drugs as the number one problem facing the nation. Public support for punitive antidrug measures also increased during the second half of the 1980s. And although the public's receptivity to the "tough" rhetoric of the wars on crime and drugs is more ambivalent than is commonly supposed, the news media's cultivation of law and order attitudes reinforced a general shift to the right. This shift in public opinion, superficial as it may have been, had important policy implications. "During a period when people believed that the greatest risk to their well-being came from random violence perpetrated by drug users and traffickers—a notion constructed by the media—attention and resources were diverted from the more intractable social and structural problems"—problems such as homelessness, AIDS, unemployment, and racism.[87] Indeed, the construction of the crime and drug crises as "underclass" problems resulting from insufficient social control laid the ideological foundation for subsequent Republican-led assaults on welfare and affirmative action.

Challenging the Drug War Ideology

In 1995, a new and even more critical discourse on drugs began to emerge. The precipitating cause of this shift was Congress' decision in that year to retain the controversial federal sentencing laws that require far more serious penalties for crack offenders than for any other class of drug law violators. In 1986, the Anti-Drug Abuse Act tied mandatory minimum penalties for drug trafficking directly to the amount of drugs involved, thereby limiting the range of factors that judges may consider in determining the appropriate punishment. Most significantly, this legislation required a mandatory minimum sentence of 5 (and up to 20) years for the simple possession of five or more grams of crack cocaine and 20 years for any offender who engaged in a "continuing drug enterprise." By contrast, the 5-year mandatory minimum sentence for simple possession applies in powder cocaine cases only when the quantity reaches 500 grams—100 times the threshold for crack.[88]

In May 1995, however, the U.S. Sentencing Commission recommended that Congress abandon those provisions of the Anti-Drug Abuse Act that penalize crack offenders so severely. The Commission further suggested that those found with small amounts of crack (or powder) cocaine should be placed on probation as long as they did not also engage in violence or possess an illegal firearm. But in October—shortly after the Million Man March in Washington, DC, in which the Reverend Jesse Jackson and others denounced the crack laws as "unfair," "racist," and "ungodly"—Congress voted to ignore the Sentencing Commission's recommendations and uphold existing sentencing statutes. President Clinton subsequently approved Congress' decision, arguing that punishing crack offenders more harshly is appropriate because crack is more likely to be associated with violence and therefore takes a greater toll on the communities in which it is used and distributed.

That Congress and the president ultimately decided to uphold these sentencing laws is not, at this point, surprising. What was unusual was the intensity and nature of the debate triggered by the Sentencing Commission's recommendations and the decision to ignore them. Although most of the figures participating in these discussions were high-ranking legal and political authorities, some spokespersons from nonprofit organizations (for example, The Sentencing Project, a group that advocates alternatives to incarceration) and grassroots community groups (such as the Atlanta-based prisoner advocacy group Seekers of Justice, Equality and Truth) were also invited to comment. Media coverage of the drug issue suddenly included several new critical themes.[89]

The first of the new themes attributed the distinctively punitive crack sentencing laws and their selective enforcement to racial bias. News stories and editorials reporting this theme typically cited the Sentencing Commission's finding that 88% of crack defendants, but only 30% of powder cocaine defendants, are African American. Most news stories and editorials treated the racially disparate impact of the new drug laws as unforeseen and unintentional, but some raised the possibility that the refusal to modify them is a product of racism. "If these were young white men going to jail," the *New York Times* quoted a defense attorney as saying, "[the sentencing disparity] would not exist. So the war on drugs is essentially being borne by the black community." The same article quoted the Washington, DC, director of the American Civil Liberties Union:

> How can you go to an inner city family and tell them their son is given 20 years [for using crack], while someone in the suburbs who's using powdered cocaine in greater quantities can get off with 90 days' probation? When people understand the truth about the way these laws are imposed, the fact they've had no deterrent [sic], and the race-based nature of these prosecutions, then I think a sleeping giant is going to roar.[90]

News stories also reported the Sentencing Commission's finding that although most users of crack are White, over 90% of all crack defendants charged in federal court—and thus subject to harsh federal penalties— are Black. In a lengthy article, the *Los Angeles Times* reported the results of its own investigation into federal crack prosecutions in L.A. County. In 1993-1994, the newspaper found, there were no federal prosecutions in Los Angeles County of White defendants on charges related to crack cocaine. During the same period, however, 183 Whites were prosecuted in L.A. County courts—where penalties are less severe—for crack-related offenses. The article drives home its point with a quote from a federal district judge: "More blacks are being punished with these crack laws than whites. A red flag has gone up. Now we must work toward a system that is more fair."[91]

The second theme emphasized in news stories and editorials during this period held that racially biased drug laws and their enforcement— rather than an increase in criminal behavior—are largely responsible for the increasing rate of incarceration among African Americans. News stories expressing this theme often quoted Marc Mauer, assistant director of The Sentencing Project, or a report issued by the same organization, to suggest that the rise in the rate of incarceration of African Americans "primarily reflected changes in enforcement policies that have resulted in a greater number of defendants receiving prison sentences, especially for drug offenses, rather than an increase in the number of crimes committed by black men."[92]

The third new theme, appearing somewhat less frequently, suggested that drug abuse and addiction are related to long-term poverty and unemployment. This theme, as well as the others identified above, is illustrated in the following excerpt from a *Boston Globe* column:

> The forces that keep many of his brothers in prison are obvious to Ijalil, one of the young black inmates who make up more than half the population of the Suffolk County House of Correction.
>
> "I don't care what society says, black men do want to take care of their families. . . . But if the doors to higher-paying jobs aren't opened for you, hey, the first order of the day is survival. So you sell a little reefer. And if you get caught, you're in the system from there on out."
>
> [T]he Sentencing Project, a Washington group . . . reported that one in three black men between the ages of 20 and 29 is either in prison, on probation or on parole. . . . Criminal justice professionals agree that the nation's "war on drugs" has focused primarily on low-level drug dealers, a majority of whom are black.
>
> The implications of the high incarceration rate remain deeply troubling for the black community. There are fewer young men for women to marry and start stable families. Doing time has become a fact of life in many city neighborhoods.
>
> Sociologists say there is still another troubling and self-perpetuating trend: the high imprisonment rate leads to the stigmatizing of all Blacks, especially young men, who are viewed by many police and whites as being associated with crime. . . . Imprisonment also fuels under-employment and joblessness.

In lots of communities . . . a 15-year-old can't get a job at the 7-11, but he can get a highly responsible job as a crack dealer.[93]

In short, following the Congressional decision to retain current sentencing laws, discussions in the mass media of the drug issue became less monolithic, more democratic, and more likely to include critical perspectives.

Explaining the Change

Why the sudden change? How can we explain the inclusion of these more critical perspectives on the drug problem? Three main factors help to account for this shift.

◆ The controversy over the racial dimensions of the crack/powder cocaine sentencing disparity occurred during the same period as the O. J. Simpson murder trial. Extensive news coverage of this case frequently highlighted racial differences in assessments of Simpson's guilt and the fairness of the justice system. The discovery of the "Fuhrman tapes," which documented the racist beliefs and actions of the LAPD detective Mark Fuhrman and some of his colleagues, drew further attention to the problem of racial bias in the criminal justice system (as had the videotaped beating of motorist Rodney King by several Los Angeles police officers several years earlier). Thus, in the background of the controversy over the crack/powder sentencing disparity was increased media attention to the problem of racism in the legal system, as well as African Americans' distrust of that system. These developments sensitized journalists to these issues and convinced them of their suitability for more detailed news coverage.

◆ The U.S. Sentencing Commission report on penalties for offenses involving crack cocaine represented a partial breakdown of the elite consensus behind the drug war. High-ranking officials in the government and judiciary—that is, individuals who satisfy conventional journalistic standards as "authoritative"—were now criticizing components of U.S. drug control policy. Conversely, the virtual absence of such "establishment critics" during the drug panic of the 1980s helps to explain the one-sided nature of the news coverage during that period. The significance of the Sentencing Commission report in creating space for dissident voices on the drug issue is demonstrated by its widespread use in the framing of drug-related stories during this period.

◆ The claims-making activities of progressive advocacy organizations also help to account for the changing nature of news stories on drugs. The partial breakdown of elite consensus behind the drug war created the opening for nonelite claims makers critical of U.S. drug policy, and critics seized the opportunity. The Sentencing Project was especially successful in this regard: the organization's 1995 report on African Americans in the criminal justice system (in which it was found that 1 in 3 young Black men is under some sort of criminal justice supervision on any given day) was cited in numerous news stories and editorials. Although elite dissensus created space for progressive perspectives, the fact that the new space was exploited was a product of the independent and skillful initiative of nonelite drug war critics.

The 1996 publication of a series of essays criticizing the drug war in the conservative news magazine *The National Review* suggests that elite consensus in support of the drug war has fragmented still further. The contributors—including the magazine's editor, William F. Buckley, and Baltimore Mayor Kurt Schmoke—declared the drug war a failure, identified drug prohibition (as opposed to drug use) as an important cause of urban crime and violence, warned against the "creeping attrition of civil liberties," and called for one form or another of drug legalization.[94] Financial support from elite philanthropists also appears to have been crucial in the successful campaigns to legalize marjuana for medical use in California and Arizona. The drug warriors persist, but they can no longer do so without prominent opposition from within the circles of power.

CONCLUSION

Over the three decades, crime has consistently been a top item in the news. In this chapter, we have shown that these news stories typically focus on violent assaults by predatory strangers—the rarest types of criminal events. Crime is also typically discussed in terms of isolated events rather than as a broader social problem. When crime is framed thematically, the lenience of the criminal justice system is often identified as the main cause of crime.

These basic features of news coverage of crime, we have argued, result from the news media's definition of newsworthiness, the organizational interests of news organizations, and the reliance of journalists on public officials for information about crime. Our analysis of drug coverage in the 1980s and 1990s illustrates how these values, interests, and practices come into play. In response to the initiatives of conservative politicians and criminal justice officials, the news media provided massive coverage of the drug issue. The willingness of news organizations to fall into line with the official interpretation of the drug problem was conditioned by both their preference for simple morality tales of the neverending conflict between good and evil and their desire for exciting stories that increase audience ratings. It was only when some prominant officials challenged the war on drugs that media coverage became significantly more critical.

This chapter has also shown that news coverage of crime contributed to the punitive turn in criminal justice policy making:

◆ Images of violent crime have encouraged the public to become more punitive.
◆ Coverage of celebrated crimes has encouraged prosecutors to crack down on similar offenses.
◆ Media-generated "crime waves" have pressured politicians to adopt ill-considered anticrime measures.

The media's coverage of the drug issue in the 1980s and 1990s also demonstrates these effects. As the press turned its attention to crack cocaine and adopted the "state of siege" frame, the public became increasingly alarmed, and politicians rushed to pass harsh new antidrug laws—laws that have filled the prisons with low-level, disproportionately African American drug offenders.

The effects of news media representations of crime are likely heightened by complementary images in popular culture and entertainment. In the next chapter, we examine images of crime in police dramas, "reality-based" television programs, and popular movies.

6
❖ Crime as
❖ Entertainment

❖ ❖ ❖ Fictional stories about crime and law enforcement have long been staples of American popular culture—much to the chagrin of social critics and reformers. In the first half of the century, critics worried that popular gangster films glorified criminals and encouraged disrespect for the law. In recent decades, many have argued that media images of murder and mayhem desensitize people to the real-life consequences of violence and may even encourage copycat crime. Today, a new set of concerns has emerged alongside these venerable criticisms: Some observers now worry that the "surplus visibility" of violence and crime in popular entertainment has become a key source of popular fear and anxiety about crime.[1] According to these critics, media depictions of violence are problematic not because they cause crime but because they generate fear and reinforce the popular demand for harsher punishment.

As a result of these various concerns, images of crime and violence in the entertainment media have become one of the most heavily studied topics in the social sciences. Most of these studies compare representations of crime and violence in popular entertainment with crime data. For example, one group of researchers has charted the "crime rate" for the world of prime-time television since the mid-1950s. In the first decade of their study, as shown in Exhibit 6.1, the real-world rate was 2 violent crimes per 1,000 Americans. On prime-time television, however, characters were committing violent crimes at a rate of 40 per thousand

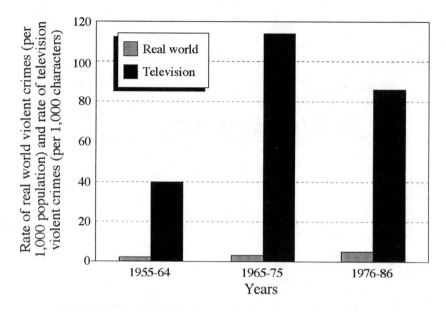

Exhibit 6.1. Real World and Television Crime Rates
SOURCE: Lichter, Lichter, and Rothman, *Prime Time*, p. 276.

characters. In the second decade of the study, the real-world rate of violent crime increased, but on television it shot up even faster. In the third decade of the study, the rate of violent crime decreased somewhat on television while increasing in the real world. Nonetheless, the gap between the two remained huge.[2]

The difference between the televised and the real world is most striking with respect to murder. Over the past four decades, the rate at which Americans have killed one another has varied between seven and 10 murders annually per 100,000 population. On prime-time television, the average homicide rate has varied between seven and 10 for every 100 characters, or about 1,000 times the real-life rate.[3] These figures translate into an average of one dozen televised murders for every prime-time viewing slot, every day of the year.[4]

Depictions of crime and violence are also abundant in film. One recent study found that the share of movies with crime as a dominant theme has remained more or less stable at around 20% since 1945. The volume of violence within these films, however, has increased substantially. Until the mid-1960s, movies rarely depicted crimes other than the ones that animated their central narratives. The murder that sparked the whodunit, in other words, was the only murder in the film. In recent years, films have increasingly depicted a host of ancillary and incidental crimes, to the point where characters like Dirty Harry cannot go for a hamburger without coming across a bank robbery in progress. In the world of feature films, violence is no longer unusual. It is, rather, an pervasive feature of everyday life.[5]

The general picture that emerges from this body of research is that the world of popular entertainment is far more violent than the real world and that it has grown more so in recent history. Does this make-believe violence intensify fear and concern about crime in everyday life? Have fictional representations of crime contributed to Americans' punitive mood and hence their demands for a tougher and more expansive criminal justice system? Comparisons between the fictional and the real are an interesting first step but do not answer these questions. Tallying instances of fictional violence tells us nothing about the meanings these images have for the public. Dramas about crime and law enforcement may foster fear of a chaotic and risky world, but the opposite is also possible: Perhaps such shows reassure people who are already anxious that heroic law enforcers are making the world a safer place. Similarly, whether or not fictional representations of crime encourage popular punitiveness probably depends on the way criminals, law enforcers, and the American justice system are presented and perceived by the audience.

To begin assessing the significance of images of crime and violence in popular entertainment, we ask three sets of questions: First, what stories are told about crime and violence in popular entertainment? What do these stories imply about the nature of lawbreakers, police, and the criminal justice system? Second, how do fictional representations of crime and law enforcement relate to claims-making about these matters in the political sphere? Finally, how do audiences respond to media representations of violence, crime, and law enforcement? What are the "effects" of these representations on the feelings, perceptions, and attitudes of the general public? In the sections that follow, we examine depictions of crime and law enforcement on television police dramas, in films and made-for-TV movies, and in "reality-based" cop shows. In the final part of the chapter, we consider the effects of these popular entertainments on the perceptions and views of the public.

THE POLICE DRAMA

Over the past 40 years, between 20% and 40% of prime-time television programs have focused on law enforcement, making the crime drama the single most popular form of television entertainment.[6] By the late 1980s—the last time anyone counted—more than 500 different television serials had dealt with crime and law enforcement.[7] In a given week of prime-time viewing, the typical audience member will watch 30 police officers, 7 lawyers, and 3 judges but only 1 scientist or engineer and only a small number of blue-collar workers.[8]

The early cop shows of the 1950s and 1960s—*Dragnet, Naked City, The Untouchables,* and *Hawaii Five-0,* to name a few—established the basic parameters for the genre. Like the westerns that they imitated, these shows constructed a two-dimensional moral order. The criminals were unambiguously awful characters. Motivated by either unadulterated greed or mental disturbance, they preyed on innocent citizens: "They threatened helpless widows, accosted women and children, and kicked puppies and kittens."[9] By contrast, the police were exceptionally good, if not quite heroic or larger than life. Epitomized by *Dragnet's* Joe Friday, they were detached professionals simply doing their job.[10] Friday's signature sign-on—"This is the City of Los Angeles. I work here. I carry a badge"—epitomized the law officer's commitment to duty and to the letter of the law. In short, this was "a world where clean cut paragons of decency uphold social mores against deviants and evildoers, where moral and legal standards never diverge, where disorder and ambiguity are dispatched with equal disdain."[11]

Variations on the genre have proliferated over the years:

◆ *Cop as action hero shows.* Shows like *77 Sunset Strip* (1950s), *Starsky and Hutch* (1970s), and *Martial Law* (1990s) featured hip crime-fighting duos: "they make their own rules, they drive a distinctive car, they shoot guns, they save each other's lives, they chase bad guys very fast in their distinctive car, they get hurt, they don't die, they always get their man."[12]

◆ *Cop as social worker shows.* Shows like *The Mod Squad* (1960s) and *The Rookies* (1970s) softened Joe Friday's image for a more socially conscious audience.

◆ *Private eye as cop shows.* Shows like *Charlie's Angels* (1970s), *Cannon* (1970s), and *Magnum P.I.* (1980s) expanded the ranks of crime fighters to include private detectives.

◆ *Civilian-sleuth shows.* These shows opened up the crime-fighting profession to an insurance investigator (*Longstreet*, 1970s), a talented medical examiner (*Quincy*, 1980s), and an author of crime fiction (*Murder She Wrote*, 1990s).

◆ *Cop shows as sitcoms.* Shows like *Barney Miller* (1980s) offered a rare satirical alternative to the regular fare.

◆ *Cop shows as soap operas.* The most recent addition to the mix includes shows like *Hill Street Blues* (1980s), *Cagney and Lacey* (1980s), and *N.Y.P.D. Blue* (1990s), which explore the personal lives and relationships of their characters while tracking multiple story lines across weekly episodes.

The crime shows have, on occasion, reflected changes in the broader political climate. In the early 1970s, for example, network executives tried to capture the rebellious spirit of the times by airing shows about crusading, activist attorneys (*The Young Lawyers, Storefront Lawyers*). Ten years later, they responded to Ronald Reagan's tough-on-crime platform by ordering a new batch of cop shows, including *Hill Street Blues*.[13] A few years after that, television producers dramatized the Reagan Administration's war on drugs in a new *Cop as action hero* show, *Miami Vice*: "The national taste had no problem seeing Colombian drug dealers shot on a weekly basis," commented the show's producer, Dick Wolf.[14] (The networks had already helped set the stage for the drug war by nearly doubling the number of prime-time depictions of drug crimes between 1975 and 1985.[15]) Finally, in the 1990s, network executives rushed to fill the void left by the conclusion of the O.J. Simpson murder trial by airing a prime-time look alike, *Murder One*.

Looking beyond these short-term efforts to tap into the prevailing mood, two developments in the cop show genre are especially striking. The first is a new narrative in which the police take extralegal action to counterbalance what are portrayed as undue constraints on their crime-fighting duties. The second is the introduction of characters—on both sides of law enforcement—who are morally complex, exhibiting both flaws and heroic qualities.

Vigilante Police

Since the 1970s, the theme of bureaucratic and legal constraints on law enforcers—and the concomitant necessity of extralegal police action—has become increasingly prominent. In shows such as *Kojak, Adam-12,* and *Streets of San Francisco*, laws and bureaucratic rules aimed at protecting the civil liberties of suspects were depicted as impediments to police investigations. Faced with the possibility of seeing their honest arrests rejected because of these legal "technicalities," characters such as Telly Savalas's Kojack ("Who loves you, baby?") were obsessed with "the way criminals were 'getting off' because the police were not allowed to do their job properly." A smart legal aid lawyer, this detective would say, wants only to "get criminals back on the street."[16] Dedicated to "getting their man" in the face of these constraints, these law enforcers routinely strong-armed witnesses, conducted illegal searches, coerced confessions, and engaged in other illegal behaviors—all in the pursuit of justice.

Indeed, one analysis of 15 police dramas aired in a single week in the 1970s identified 21 constitutional violations by the police and 15 instances of police brutality.[17] Another analysis from the same period found that "Illegal searches were portrayed as essential, always turning up a vital missing piece of evidence. Witnesses brutalized by police often provided the crucial lead that resulted in the capture of vicious criminals." In over 70% of the cases where the police mentioned the Constitution, the courts, or judges, the reference was negative or critical. These studies concluded that the message on television crime shows is that "The law and the Constitution stand in the way of effective solutions to our crime problem."[18]

This emphasis on legal constraint and the need for extralegal action by law enforcers persisted in the 1980s and 1990s. On *Hill Street Blues*, for example, Captain Furillo has "had it up to here with looters, rapists, con-artists, lawyers, and liberal politicians" and asks sarcastically, "Now, whose civil rights have we violated today, Counselor?"[19] During the show's second season, public defender Joyce Davenport considers quitting her job after the monster who killed her colleague is released on a "technicality." (By the end of the season, Davenport was packing a gun).[20] In the same vein, story lines for the 1990s hit program *Law and Order* typically revolve around "open and shut" cases that get complicated when liberal judges order suppression of key pieces of evidence, effectively sending the prosecutors and detectives back to square one.

Given the apparent difficulty of making arrests stick in court, it is no wonder that television cops do whatever they can to elicit confessions. In *N.Y.P.D. Blue*, for example, Agent Sipowitz, a recovering alcoholic, routinely slaps suspects around during interrogations. On *Homicide: Life on the Streets*, detectives are more apt to resort to deception and emotional manipulation to garner confessions, but in one episode, they drove a frightened teenager to an isolated beach and implied that they would kill him if he didn't provide evidence against guilty friends.

In all of these shows, what makes the suppression of key evidence seem especially outrageous and the frequent police trespasses on suspects' rights apparently tolerable is the fact that in almost every case viewers know for certain who the bad guys really are. The notion that restraints on police conduct exist because the police often do not know who is guilty is difficult to recover from these entertainment narratives.[21]

One reason the theme of legal constraint and police vigilantism has become a key feature of police dramas is that it features the timeless conflict between the individual and the organization and allows for the narration of a kind of rugged American individualism. The maverick who answers to his (and sometimes her) own conscience, works according to his or her own rules, and triumphs where rule-bound organizations have failed is the very stuff of American heroism—and it makes for great television.[22]

But in cop shows and films, this theme has clear political implications. In particular, it resonates with conservative political attacks on Supreme Court decisions that, according to critics, "handcuff" the police. These police dramas, in other words, provide an abundance of images that seem to confirm that "the system is set up to protect the rights of criminals and not victims," "the police are handcuffed by the courts," "prisons have revolving doors," and "criminals get off on technicalities." In reality, few felony arrests are rejected by either prosecutors or judges as a result of procedural errors.[23] Nevertheless, as we will see in Chapter 7, these staple slogans of conservative political rhetoric on crime have become increasingly popular with the general public.

Moral Complexity

The second long-term thematic development in cop shows emerged in the early 1980s. Whereas the police dramas of the 1950s, 1960s, and 1970s depicted a simple struggle of good versus evil, more recent police dramas tend to present characters and situations that are more morally complex. These changes began with *Hill Street Blues* and *Cagney & Lacey* in the 1980s and flowered in the 1990s with *Homicide: Life on the Streets* and *N.Y.P.D. Blue*. Police in these new dramas are depicted more realistically, as complex individuals with personal strengths—which still typically include integrity and commitment to protecting the public—but also with very real personal flaws. In several of the new police dramas, leading characters are portrayed as (surprisingly sympathetic and likable) recovering alcoholics, beneath-the-surface racists, or unregenerate sexists. At the margins of these dramas, moreover, are various "bad cops" enmeshed in criminal conspiracies whose investigation by the "Internal Affairs Division" constitutes an increasingly common subplot.

An episode of *Homicide* illustrates this more complex construction of cops. In the weeks leading up to the episode, Detective Kellerman has been in a downward spiral after covering up the circumstances of his killing of the notorious drug dealer Luther Mahoney. Under investigation by Internal Affairs and taunted by Luther's sister (who threatens that she has a videotape of the killing), he has begun drinking heavily. Then, in the episode in question, after staggering drunk out of a bar, he picks a fight with a couple of men who are simply hanging out on the corner. He beats one of the two mercilessly, stopping only when interrupted by a police cruiser that happens on the scene. Questioned by the uniformed officers, he explains—struggling not to slur his speech—that the man on the ground is a "collar" who should be taken to jail. He then leaves the scene. Eventually, in a later episode, Kellerman is forced to retire.

Kellerman is not, however, simply a "bad cop." When he shot Luther Mahoney and set in motion the events that led to his downfall, his motivations were noble. Mahoney was an especially evil character who had managed time and again to avoid prosecution and threatened to do so again. Moreover, the shooting itself was an ambiguous affair: Kellerman burst onto the scene just as Mahoney was about to kill Kellerman's partner, Detective Lewis. Ordered by Kellerman to drop his gun, Mahoney instead dangled it aimlessly by his index finger. It was only after several attempts to get Mahoney to drop the gun that Kellerman opened fire. In some respects, therefore, even this representation of trigger-happy policing could be interpreted as a familiar tale of justified police vigilantism in the face of a legal system that will not lock up dangerous criminals.

Greater moral complexity sometimes also extends to portrayals of criminals. Most shows still feature odious and evil professional criminals, motivated by greed and rationally calculating their crimes.[24] Increasingly, however, cop shows also situate street crime in the context of the harsh conditions of ghetto life:

In shows like *Cagney & Lacey* and *Hill Street Blues* police officers had to face the fact that not all criminals were bad people, and that all bad people were not necessarily criminals. Driven by passion or desperation, criminals lacked the premeditated, evil nature seen so often in earlier shows. In other cases very abusive or opportunistic people who deserved arrest were beyond the reach of the law.[25]

This more nuanced portrayal of police and criminals reflects, in part, television and film's stylistic turn toward "gritty realism," which has had a variety of implications for police dramas. Since *Hill Street Blues*, for example, shows have been more willing to depict members of minority groups as criminal offenders. Network executives still prefer the politically safe practice of featuring White street criminals, but the new police dramas increasingly reflect the reality that those arrested for drug and violent crimes are disproportionately people of color.[26] These shows are also more realistic in terms of how they represent violence and its consequences, a fact that has earned them the "stamp of approval" from at least one group of researchers monitoring media violence.[27]

But the moral complexity of these new police dramas is about more than mere style; it also reflects political concern about contemporary law enforcement, social inequality, and race relations. In other words, real-world voices of opposition are occasionally given expression in these programs. In general, therefore, we agree with the media scholar John Fiske that these newer police dramas, like most television programs, are "producerly texts": they do not strong-arm their viewers into a single moral conclusion or perspective on reality but are open to multiple interpretations.[28] Although the core of their narratives remains squarely within the cop show genre—valorous law enforcers standing between innocent civilians and the world of violent criminals—the newer cop shows sometimes convey a range of additional images that might be interpreted in a variety of ways.

THE CRIME FILM

In several respects, the evolution of crime films has mirrored the television police drama. Between the end of World War II and the mid-1960s, movies with law enforcement themes uniformly depicted the police as helpful and virtuous and criminals as bad guys responsible for their own troubles. The movies of this period invariably concluded with the villains brought to justice and peace restored.[29] There was nothing accidental about the ubiquity of this simplistic good-versus-evil morality play. To preempt government censorship, the five giant studios that dominated film production during this period promulgated a Production Code that banned more controversial story lines. For example, the Production Code stipulated that "Law, natural or human, shall not be ridiculed, nor shall sympathy be created for its violation. [Crimes] shall never be presented in such a way as to throw sympathy with the crime as against law and justice or to inspire others with a desire for imitation."[30]

In the 1970s, as the big studios' control over the film industry diminished, representations of crime and justice became more ambivalent. Cops were increasingly depicted as either corrupt or as the first to initiate violence. For example, in the film *Serpico* (1974), police officers kill one of their own to cover up widespread corruption. Before 1965, only 1 in 6 celluloid cops committed a crime and 1 in 10 resorted to violence; thereafter, approximately half of all cops were depicted as criminal or violent.[31]

During the same period, criminals were for the first time occasionally represented as victims of circumstances beyond their personal control,[32] even as their violent deeds became more sadistic and gratuitous.[33] Criminals were also scripted as protagonists with greater frequency.[34] These developments did not destroy the conventional crime film model. In the 1990s, most big-screen police officers are depicted as heroic and most criminals as evil. But, like the television police drama, the crime film became more ambivalent after 1970, with cops increasingly depicted as playing by the same rules as criminals.[35]

Images of crime victims have also changed over the past four decades. One content analysis of roughly 150 big box office crime movies released after 1945 found that just 1 in 4 of the earlier movies showed crime victims as traumatized. After 1980, however, roughly three quarters of the films depicted victims as suffering extreme trauma. "By positioning the audience as sympathetic to the victims," the authors of this study speculate, "later films may in fact make the audience more inclined to abhor violence and crime in general."[36]

Like the police drama, the theme of vigilante justice is increasingly central to the crime film. Before the mid-1960s, roughly 1 in 10 celluloid cops resorted to vigilante tactics; thereafter, the number rises to roughly 8 in 10. In the earlier period, movies were as likely as not to conclude with the major villain brought to justice. Nowadays, this is almost never the case. Instead, criminals are typically dispatched in a hail of bullets.[37]

Narratives of the maverick cop have been especially prevalent in *Cop as Action Hero* movies like *Dirty Harry* (1972), *The Enforcer* (1977), and *Death Wish II* (1982), as well as in comedies like *Beverly Hills Cop* (1985). In these movies, conventional police officers are portrayed as too con-strained—either by superiors or by the law—to function as effective crime fighters. Instead, superhuman cops must break department regulations and disregard the civil liberties of virtually everyone to "get the job done." For example, in *Lethal Weapon IV* (1998), the crime-fighting duo of Martin Riggs (Mel Gibson) and Roger Murtaugh (Danny Glover) are promoted to the rank of captain to get them off the streets where their crime-fighting antics are proving too costly for the City of Los Angeles. Nevertheless, in a rapid-fire sequence of car chases, gun battles, and martial arts maneuvers, the maverick L.A.P.D. cops hunt down and kill the movie's Chinese slave-trader villains. Looking back on the last three decades of crime movies, one research team concludes: "Hollywood's representation of police work looks more like organized vigilantism than the measured use of force in bringing criminals to justice."[38]

Now and again, crime films and made-for-TV movies have proven especially effective in drawing public attention to particular crimes and criminal justice issues. For example, the so-called "slasher" films popular in the 1980s and 1990s—including *Scream* (1998), *Silence of the Lambs* (1991), and the *Friday the Thirteenth* series (1980s)—focused attention on the problem of serial murder.[39] Similarly, made-for-TV movies like *The Burning Bed* (1985) drew a great deal of attention to domestic violence.[40] Made-for-TV movies have also helped to disseminate and popularize the core claims of the victim rights movement—claims that will be discussed in Chapter 8.

THE "REALITY-BASED" COP SHOW

As we discussed in Chapter 5, the news media provided intense coverage of the war on drugs in the 1980s, including dramatic footage of border seizures and police raids on crack houses. The news footage for these stories was frequently shot live and from the vantage point of the police, typically by reporters tagging along on police raids. It was in this context that the new "reality-based" police shows were introduced to the American public.[41]

A curious hybrid of news and entertainment, these shows consist of either actual video footage of police pursuing and apprehending suspects or dramatic recreations of crimes and arrests. In those shows that rely on footage of actual events, police officers often serve as program "hosts," providing narrative and commentary. Insofar as they claim to be strictly factual, these shows are distinct from the police dramas discussed in the previous section. But these programs are not exactly "news": The episodes are not dated and are often shown in re-runs. The most popular such show has been Fox TV's Cops, which depicts raw footage from a variety of U.S. cities. Other such programs include Real Stories of the Highway Patrol, Bounty Hunters, L.A.P.D. Life on the Beat, Top Cops, and America's Most Wanted.

One might assume, based on the proliferation of these shows, that they command a large audience. Actually, the evidence suggests otherwise. In one sample week in 1993, the Nielsen Company reported that the reality-based police shows attracted viewers from about 9% of all households with television sets. The comparable figure for the average network prime-time show during that week was 12%; the most popular shows (Seinfeld, Home Improvement, 60 Minutes) drew between 17.5% and 22%. In terms of audience share—a measure of a show's audience size relative to other shows in the same time slot—the reality shows typically drew about 15%, a weak showing compared to the 22% to 39% commanded by the most popular shows. "In short," one observer has noted, "no matter how you measure it, reality crime programs are not wildly popular. They have an audience, but, by industry standards, it is neither large nor particularly lucrative."[42] Although audiences for the reality-based shows may be small by industry standards, they are still quite significant. A rating of 9%, after all, translated in 1993 into nearly nine million households, comparable to the audience for the networks' evening newscasts.[43]

An additional consideration helps to explain why reality-based cop shows have become a staple of prime-time television. Television networks profit by either expanding their audiences or, as in the case of the reality-based police shows, reducing their production costs. Because these shows rely on footage of real-life cops, the producers have no writers, set designers, or make-up artists to pay. Best of all, these shows have no expensive stars. Production of a single episode of the hit comedy

Roseanne typically costs $2-3 million. By contrast, it costs only $250,000 to produce six half-hour segments—a full week's worth of programming—of *Real Stories of the Highway Patrol*. In an era of declining overall audience size for all network television, the cost savings afforded by these shows likely explains why they have proliferated so rapidly.[44]

For viewers who do tune into these cheaply produced pseudodocumentaries, what is the attraction? One keen interpreter of the reality-based shows argues that they offer viewers the twin pleasures of voyeurism and identification with authority:

> Voyeurism is taking pleasure from viewing the private or forbidden. The viewer overrules the wishes of others that the object of viewing remain secreted. Viewing may thus be experienced as an act of domination. The voyeurism of *Cops* is intertwined with its authoritarian pleasures. The seductions or pleasures of one type of power—voyeuristically intruding into the private or forbidden—are meshed with the seductions of another type of power: identifying with the sanctioned authority of the police.[45]

The reality-based programs may also attract viewers by appealing to their sense of civic duty. *America's Most Wanted*, for example, urges audience members to help fight crime by calling a "tips" hotline with information on the whereabouts of criminals depicted in the weekly program. In 1994, this show received three thousand telephone calls per weekly episode.[46]

Reality-based cop shows differ from the new television police dramas in several ways. First, even in the newer dramas, criminals are largely depicted as White and as either professional crooks or corrupt businessmen. By contrast, in the reality-based shows, the objects of police attention are typically poor and members of minority groups.[47] In fact, one content analysis found that the show *Cops* overrepresents Blacks as offenders, especially when it comes to violent crime: "In all, 26 of the 34 violent crimes (76%) and seven of nine property offenses (78%) were allegedly committed by nonwhites." Whereas Blacks tended to be associated with violent crimes, Whites were typically depicted as engaging in less serious crimes, such as prostitution and leaving the scene of an accident.[48]

Second, in the carefully constructed reality-based programs, the moral ambiguity of *N.Y.P.D. Blue* and *Homicide* is nowhere to be found. The cops are portrayed as honest, hard-working, and deeply committed to protecting the public. Whenever the story line permits, they are treated as heroes. The suspects, on the other hand, are frequently "described in terms that connote physical ugliness. They are depicted as dangerous, depraved, unremorseful people."[49] Journalist Debra Seagal, who at one time logged raw footage for the show *American Detective*, explains how the process works:

> By the time our 9 million viewers flip on their tubes, we've reduced fifty or sixty hours of mundane and compromising video into short, action-packed segments of tantalizing, crack filled, dope-dealing, junkie-busting cop culture. How easily we downplay the pathos of the suspect; how cleverly we breeze past the complexities that cast doubt on the very system that has produced the criminal activity in the first place. How effortlessly we smooth out the indiscretions of the lumpen detectives and casually make them appear as pistol-flailing heroes rushing across the screen.[50]

The good-versus-evil story line is constructed from the raw footage by way of exclusion. Images of police brutality, abuse of power, and corruption are edited out. Images of suspects that might elicit sympathy—or of suspects or witnesses responding with hostility to the presence of the television camera—are similarly excised. And in the most straightforward exclusion of all, camera crews are rarely assigned to tag along with police in neighborhoods where middle class deviance might be uncovered.

Seagal describes some of the material that winds up "on the cutting-room floor." In one strip of raw footage, two Hispanic suspects are seen emerging from a car after a high speed chase with their hands in the air. "Get on the ground cocksucker!" a police officer screams. "I'll blow your motherfucking head off." Viewers of *American Detective* will never hear this; nor will they see the violence that ensues as officers kick the suspects in the stomach, face, and head:

> Our main cameraman focuses on the detectives ambling around their fallen prey like hunters after a wild-game safari; a lot of vainglorious, congratulatory back-slapping ensues. Our secondary cameraman holds a long, extreme close-up of a suspect while his mouth bleeds into the dirt. I feel like I'm dying, he wheezes, and turns his head away from the camera. One [*American Detective*] producer shook his head at the violence. "Too bad," he said. "Too bad we can't use that footage." This was clearly a case of too much reality for reality-based TV.[51]

Finally, in the reality-based cop shows, in contradistinction to the best of the police dramas, only one perspective on reality is presented: that of the show's narrating host. Several of the reality-based shows, including *Cops* and *L.A.P.D. Life on the Beat,* have police officers as guest hosts. Others, such as *America's Most Wanted* and *Unsolved Mysteries,* have permanent celebrity hosts. In either case, it is the host's interpretation—and almost never that of witnesses, victims, or suspects—that imbues the images on the screen with meaning. Consider a typical vignette from the show *Cops*: The cameras roll as a Hispanic woman is arrested for selling cocaine to an informant working for the police. When told that she is "going away" for at least 3 years, the woman breaks down sobbing. The host police officer sums up the segment with this observation: "What made her do it? I don't know, the devil made her do it." Audience members are, of course, never made privy to the woman's own explanation for why she "did it."[52]

In these shows, moreover, the host's perspective rarely strays far from the "permissiveness" theme that characterizes conservative political discourse on crime (see Chapter 4). A victim rights activist and host of the show *America's Most Wanted* conveys the central message in these words, broadcast as a teaser for the program:

> You know what I'm sick of? Criminals who serve only a fraction of their sentences. Sexual predators who are released to live next door to you and your children and you don't even know it. Drug dealers who think they run these streets. This is a society where criminals have all the rights and victims don't have any. Well, it's going to change. You're going to make that happen. The new "America's Most Wanted." America fights back. Premieres next Saturday after "Cops" on non-stop Fox.[53]

The moral simplicity and narrative closure of the reality-based shows have led some observers to declare that they are in fact less "real" than the best of their fictional counterparts.[54] Be this as it may, both fictional and reality-based cop shows depict a world that is filled with predatory violence—a world in which well-intentioned police officers are doing their best to protect the public in spite of laws and judges that favor the rights of criminals over the lives of honest citizens. These themes are given the hard sell in the reality-based cop shows and in the more archaic police dramas. In the new "gritty realism" dramas, these themes are soft peddled—and sometimes even contradicted—but are generally present for those who are inclined to seize on them. What is the impact of this narrative on its audience? How have these representations of crime and law enforcement affected the feelings and beliefs of the American public? These are the questions explored in the next section.

AUDIENCE RESPONSE
TO ENTERTAINMENT CRIME

Television and film, like parents and schools, socialize people into ways of thinking, feeling, and being in the world. Whatever effects these socializing agents have on beliefs are likely to accumulate over long stretches of time.[55] This fact makes assessing the effects of media exposure exceedingly difficult. How can we disentangle the impact of television and film from the influences other institutions in society?

In a series of annual content analyses of prime-time television, George Gerbner and his colleagues at the Annenberg School of Communication contrasted the "mean and scary" world of television with the real world as portrayed by official statistics. They simultaneously administered surveys of the general public regarding television viewing habits and perceptions of social reality. To highlight their interest in the cumulative effects of television viewing, they called this methodology cultivation analysis.

In general, Gerbner and his colleagues found that heavy television viewers are more likely to see the world as a mean and scary place than are light television viewers. Heavy viewers, for example, are more likely to overestimate the number of people who commit serious crimes, as well as the percentage of people involved in violence. Similarly, heavy television viewers are more likely to distrust others, fear walking alone at night in their own neighborhood, and report that crime is a "very serious personal problem".[56] In short, as one member of the research team stated, "television's mean and dangerous world tends to cultivate a sense of relative danger, mistrust, insecurity, vulnerability, dependence, and—despite its supposedly 'entertaining' nature—alienation and gloom."[57]

Researchers testing cultivation theory have qualified these findings in a number of ways. One researcher found that the media had a more pronounced impact on people who regard television dramas as "realistic."[58] Other researchers report that heavy viewing contributes to fear of the world "out there" but not of the immediate neighborhood.[59] Gerbner's own research team has suggested that the media's contribution to fear may consist largely of "mainstreaming"—the tendency to heighten fear among heavy television viewers who belong to demographic groups that typically express moderate levels of fear. For example, heavy television viewing tends to increase fear among respondents with medium to high incomes but not among respondents with low incomes.[60]

Most cultivation analysis examines the effects of television as a whole. Some analysts, however, have focused on shows with law enforcement themes. One such researcher found adolescent heavy viewers of fictional crime dramas to be more fearful of victimization and view the police more positively than light viewers. Adolescent heavy viewers were also found to be less supportive of civil liberties.[61] In another study, regular viewers of reality-based crime shows provided higher than average estimates of crime prevalence, and, in contradistinction to heavy viewers of fictional police dramas, higher than average estimates of crime prevalence among African Americans.[62]

Cultivation research has been criticized on a number of grounds. In some studies, the statistical relationship between heavy viewing and fear of crime is either relatively weak or disappears after the introduction of statistical controls for age, education, and income.[63] Cultivation researchers respond that because even "light viewers" watch a substantial amount of television, modest differences between light and heavy viewers may indicate a substantial "cultivation effect" for all television viewers.[64]

Cultivation research has also been criticized for assuming that television viewing causes fear. Perhaps instead, fearful people are drawn to television's depictions of crime and violence.[65] The basic allure of crime dramas, these skeptics contend, is that they promise to reassure the already anxious; their popularity is a measure, not a cause, of popular anxiety about crime. An alternative but similar argument holds that feelings of vindictiveness toward criminals draw certain people to television's images of aggressive law enforcement. The debate continues, but we suspect that both camps are tapping into different dimensions of reality. Although such conclusions are impossible to prove, it makes perfect sense (to us) that televised (and cinematic) crime and violence encourage anxiety and punitiveness and that anxious and punitive people turn to television (and cinema) for either reassurance or vicarious vindication. In short, the prevalence of crime and violence in popular entertainment is probably both the cause and the effect of popular fears, concerns, and sentiments.

CONCLUSION

Looking broadly at entertainment representations of crime and violence, we have noted that the "reel" world of film and television has long been far more violent than the real world. And it has become even more violent in the past 30 years. Moreover, the police are increasingly depicted as stymied in their pursuit of criminals by liberal-minded due-process restrictions. Although the moral categories of the police drama are in some cases less clearly drawn today than in the past, new reality-based television cop shows resemble the crime dramas of the 1950s in their unambiguous "us versus them" depictions. In general, therefore, most contemporary crime narratives still resonate with key elements of the conservative discourse on crime.

In particular, entertainment crime narratives encourage three ideologically loaded notions:

◆ Offenders are professional criminals—clever, clear headed, and motivated by unadulterated greed. (This conception contrasts sharply with the notion that the behavior of many criminals is shaped by the "code of the streets" discussed in Chapter 3).

◆ The interests of public safety and justice are ill served by liberal judges and lawyers who are—sometimes to the point of absurdity—preoccupied with the "rights" of defendants.

◆ Hard-working, dedicated cops are "out there" every day doing their best in the face of these difficult challenges.

Attempts to empirically assess the impact on popular perceptions of mass-mediated depictions of crime, violence, and law enforcement have generated ambiguous results. On the one hand, heavy television viewers tend to be more fearful and mistrusting, to view the police more positively, and to express greater hostility toward civil liberties. On the other hand, these differences may be due, in some measure, to selective exposure: Crime-related programs may in fact attract the already fearful (for reassurance) and the vindictive (for vicarious vindication). We have good reason to believe that both processes are at work.

In the next chapter, we continue our discussion of media effects. This time, however, we approach the subject from the standpoint of popular opinion. Why are people so worried about crime, and why do they seem to favor punitive approaches to the problem?

7

❖ Crime and
❖ Public Opinion

❖ ❖ ❖ One version of the conventional wisdom on the expansion of the penal system goes like this: *Crime rates may be stable, but the American public is growing increasingly fearful of crime and increasingly punitive in its policy preferences. If the imprisonment boom is unnecessary and socially damaging, well, the people are only getting what they asked for. . . .* This view is conveyed in the following excerpt from a 1994 *Time* magazine article entitled "Lock 'Em Up!":

> With outraged Americans saying that crime is their No. 1 concern, politicians are again talking tough. But are they making sense?
> "WHAT ARE WE GOING TO DO ABOUT these kids (monsters) who kill with guns??? Line them up against the wall and get a firing squad and pull, pull, pull. I am volunteering to pull, pull, pull."
> That's not a rap lyric. It's from an anonymous letter to a judge in Dade County, Florida—part of the shared unconscious talking. And suddenly we're all ears. In one of the most startling spikes in the history of polling, large numbers of Americans are abruptly calling crime their greatest concern. Confronted by clear evidence of a big issue, politicians everywhere, including the one in the White House, are reaching for their loudest guns: prisons, boot camps, mandatory sentences. Months before the start of baseball season, the air is full of shouts of "Three strikes and you're out."[1]

In this chapter, we review evidence that casts serious doubt on this "democracy in action" thesis. First, we show that over the past two

119

decades, popular fear of crime has been surprisingly stable and that, with some notable exceptions, it has not been nearly as widespread as media accounts suggest. We also show that over the past three decades the public has seldom mentioned crime as the nation's most serious problem. On the rare occasion when a crime-related issue has risen to the top of the popular agenda, the public appears to be taking its cues from politicians and the news media—not the other way around.

Moreover, when it comes to policy preferences, the public is not uniformly or exclusively punitive. Mounting evidence from surveys and ethnographic research indicates that both tough-on-crime rhetoric and alternatives to it resonate with much of the public. One category of citizens in particular, African Americans, has grown increasingly disillusioned with contemporary crime control policies. We therefore conclude with an analysis of the public's support for alternative responses to crime.

FEAR OF CRIME

In survey research, the standard measure of fear of crime is the question "Is there any area right around here—that is, within a mile—where you would be afraid to walk alone at night?" If rising fear of crime is the basis for the politicization of crime, then we would expect to see the level of reported fear of "walking alone at night" increase over time. As Exhibit 7.1 shows, however, the percentage of Americans reporting fearfulness has remained remarkably stable over time and has even declined in recent years. Slightly over a third of the population consistently reports fearfulness.

But fear is not evenly distributed. As Exhibit 7.2 shows, women, non-Whites, and the elderly are disproportionately among those who fear walking alone at night. Because two of these three groups, women and the elderly, in fact experience below-average rates of officially reported victimization, this finding has often been regarded as paradoxical.[2]

It is not clear, however, how much these survey results really tell us. As several researchers have recently pointed out, the "walking alone at night" question does not tap feelings of fear and dread that respondents experience in the course of their routine activities.[3] Rather, the question asks respondents to imagine how they would feel were they to engage

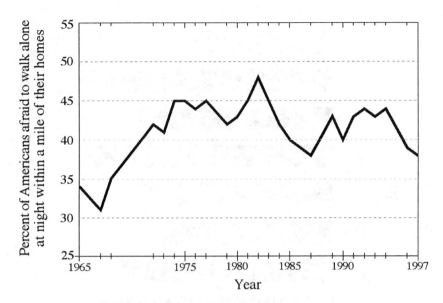

Exhibit 7.1. Fear of Walking Alone at Night
SOURCE: Maguire and Pastore, *Sourcebook of Criminal Justice Statistics 1997*, Table 2.35, and Warr, "Poll Trends."

in the kind of activity that some people—especially women and the elderly—are most likely to avoid.[4] Questions that tap more directly into feelings of fear that people experience in their actual, everyday lives would therefore be more useful and have been incorporated into more recent studies.

In a national 1995 survey, for example, respondents were asked how frequently they worry about various types of crime. Of the survey findings, three are especially noteworthy:

- ◆ In general, respondents appear relatively well informed about the chances of experiencing various kinds of crime. For example, respondents perceive the likelihood of experiencing a burglary or auto theft as much greater than the likelihood of being murdered (see Exhibit 7.3).

- ◆ With a few important exceptions (discussed later), most people do not feel themselves to be personally in great danger of serious victimization. Less than a fifth of Americans, for example, worries "somewhat frequently" or "very frequently" about getting murdered, and less than a third worries about getting mugged (see Exhibit 7.3).

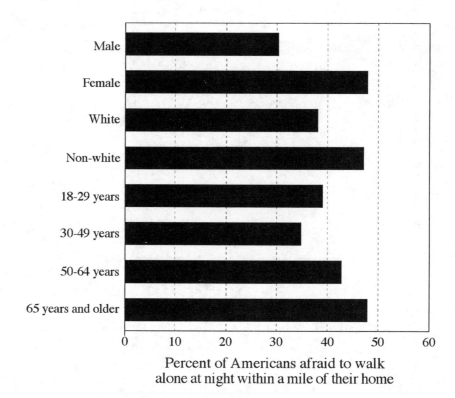

Exhibit 7.2. Fear of Walking Alone at Night by Demographic Characteristics
SOURCE: Maguire and Pastore, *Sourcebook of Criminal Justice Statistics 1997,* Table 2.38.

◆ With the new questions about fear of crime, the paradoxical relationship
between age and fear disappears. For example, younger people report
higher levels of fear of being murdered, which is consistent with the fact
that they experience higher levels of victimization (see Exhibit 7.4).

There are a few important exceptions to the conclusion that levels of
fear are relatively low. Women of all races report relatively high levels of
fear, especially with respect to sexual assault (see Exhibit 7.4). In fact,
women's fear of sexual assault—a crime women worry about more
frequently than murder—is so pronounced as to "cast a shadow" over
their feelings about other personal crimes. As researcher Kenneth Ferraro
explains, "why women fear non-sexual crime appears to be largely due

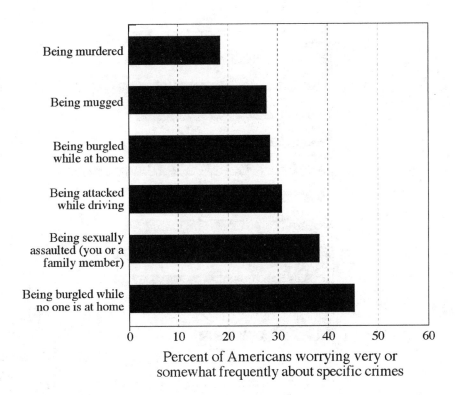

Percent of Americans worrying very or
somewhat frequently about specific crimes

Exhibit 7.3. Worry About Specific Crimes
SOURCE: Flanagan and Longmire, *Americans View Crime and Justice*, p. 25.

to the possibility of sexual crime contingent with any blatantly non-sexual crime."[5] Thus fear of sexual assault appears to be the driving force behind higher levels of female fear of most types of personal victimizations. People of color—both men and women—also report higher levels of fear of violent crime. This tendency is not paradoxical: In the United States, minorities face higher real risks, know it, and are more fearful as a result.[6]

We do not mean to imply that people's feelings about crime are always based on their knowledge of the level and distribution of criminal victimizations.[7] In fact, a number of studies indicate that a variety of environmental stimuli are associated with fear of crime.[8] These triggers include "incivilities" such as aggressive panhandling, signs of urban

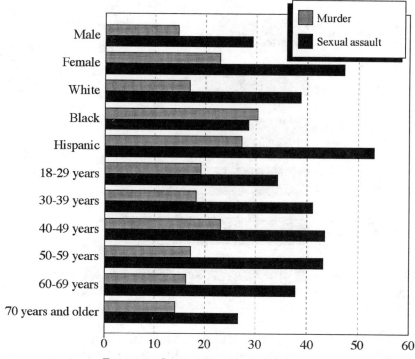

Percent of Americans worrying very or somewhat
frequently about murder or sexual assault

Exhibit 7.4. Worry About Murder and Sexual Assault by Demographic
Characteristics
SOURCE: Flanagan and Longmire, *Americans View Crime and Justice*, p. 25.

decay such as graffiti and vacant lots, and media imagery of the sort
discussed in Chapters 5 and 6. In arriving at assessments of personal risk,
people seem to draw on the various resources available in their immediate environment, including but not limited to information about officially reported crime and personal experiences with crime.

In sum, although fear of crime is not uncommon, attributing the
punitive drift in criminal justice to widespread and increasing fear of
crime seems unwarranted. Whether researchers tap directly into everyday fears of crime or ask the hypothetical "walking alone at night"
question, Americans report a stable level of fear and one that is lower
than media accounts typically imply.

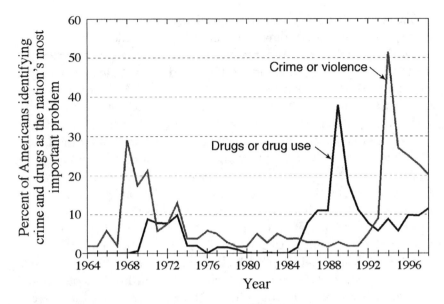

Exhibit 7.5. Concern About Crime and Drug Problems

SOURCE: Maguire and Pastore, *Sourcebook of Criminal Justice Statistics 1997*, Table 2.1, and Gallup, *The Gallup Poll* (Vols. 1 and 2, *Public Opinion from 1938-71* and *Public Opinion from 1972-5*).

NOTE: When more than one Gallup Poll was administered in a given year, we report the results of the last survey taken in that year.

CRIME AS A SOCIAL PROBLEM

Although Americans may not be terribly worried about the potential for personal victimization, they may still be highly concerned about crime as a social problem for the nation as a whole. Information about such concern (as opposed to fear) is generally culled from surveys that ask respondents to name "the most important problem facing the country." As Exhibit 7.5 shows, the percentage of respondents identifying crime as the nation's most important problem is far more volatile than fear of crime. Few Americans named crime or drugs as "the most important issue" until the late 1980s. Prior to this time, issues pertaining to the economy (such as unemployment and government spending) and international relations topped the list of national concerns. In 1988 and 1989, however, "drugs" surged to the top of the list of "America's most serious" problems. In subsequent years, public concern about drugs declined, but it was soon replaced by rising concern about crime.[9]

These data show that Americans consider crime (and drugs) a serious social problem—at least some of the time. But we should not jump to the conclusion that this concern is the driving force behind the politicization of the crime and drug issues in the 1980s and 1990s. Indeed, one study reports that fluctuations in the public's level of concern about crime and drugs correspond to variations in the extent to which politicians and the media highlight the crime and drug issues. This research also found that levels of public concern were directly responsive to levels of political initiative, but that the reverse was not true. In sum, when it comes to concern about crime (and drugs), it appears that the public is following the leadership of politicians and the media, not the other way around.[10]

The surge in popular concern about drug abuse in 1989 provides an especially vivid illustration of this process. "This is the first time since taking the oath of office that I felt an issue was so important, so threatening, that it warranted talking directly with you, the American people," President Bush declared on September 5, 1989, in his first nationally televised address after taking office. "All of us agree that the gravest domestic threat facing our nation today is drugs."[11] The President described a series of new antidrug initiatives, including creation of the office of "drug czar," and stepped up military involvement in drug interdiction. To dramatize the seriousness of the problem, he waved before the cameras a clear plastic bag of cocaine. The groundwork for the President's message had already been established by the national press. Acting on a mid-August announcement by the White House that Bush would deliver a major address on drugs in September, the three major networks increased coverage of the issue. In the 2½ weeks prior to the speech, ABC, NBC, and CBS aired an average of nearly three stories each night on the issue, up from an average of fewer than one story per night in the weeks prior to the announcement of the President's plans. In the week following the address, coverage increased to an average of nearly four stories per night.[12]

The public apparently received the message loud and clear. The share of respondents naming "drugs" as the "most important problem" surged in the aftermath of the President's speech from an already high mark of 27% in May to an astonishing 64% in September. By November, the numbers dropped back to 38%.

Several years later the topic changed from drugs to crime, but the pattern of elite leadership remained more or less the same. In August 1993, the Republicans in Congress—eager to reclaim the crime issue so effectively neutralized by Clinton in the 1992 presidential election—announced a major new package of anticrime legislation. Clinton and the Democrats responded with their own rival package, effectively setting the stage for a contest over which political party is "tougher" on crime. As both houses of Congress debated omnibus crime bills, local Congressional races featured an unprecedented torrent of tough-on-crime posturing.

In December 1993, the Senate passed a version of the crime bill providing for massive federal support to states for hiring police and building prisons. A few weeks later, 37% of Americans, an unprecedented proportion, named crime the most important problem facing the country. In the ensuing months, political and media attention to the issue of crime intensified still further. President Clinton announced his support for a federal "three strikes and you're out" law in his State of the Union address, the House of Representatives adopted its own version of the "crime bill," and the national media covered the issue in a series of magazine cover stories and network news "special reports." In addition, the national press provided saturation coverage of a number of sensational crimes and trials, including the abduction and murder of 12-year-old Polly Klaas, the massacre on the Long Island Commuter Train, and the trial of the Menendez brothers for the murder of their parents.[13] In August, the month President Clinton—amid maximum fanfare—signed the crime bill into law, public concern about crime reached its apex at 52%.

In sum, popular concern about crime and drugs as social problems has historically been lower than concern about such issues as the economy and war and peace. But public concern about crime and drugs has also proven quite volatile, susceptible to mobilization by politicians and the mass media. This should hardly come as surprising news; in general, when people are asked about the country's problems, they reflect not on their relatively narrow range of personal experiences but on what they have seen and heard in the mass media and from their leaders. This is not to say that politicians can mobilize popular concern about any issue or that public concern about crime is not genuine. But on the relatively rare occasions when the public has put crime or drugs at the top of its list of concerns, it has done so in the context of massive political initiative and media coverage. The public worries about crime and drugs, but it is not the driving force behind the massive political and media attention to these issues.

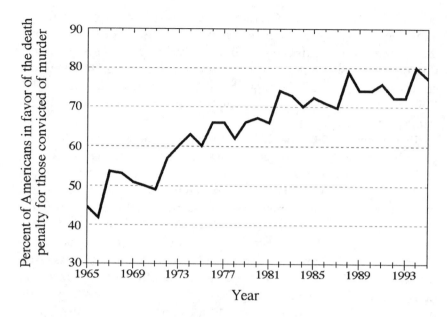

Exhibit 7.6. Support for the Death Penalty

SOURCE: Maguire and Pastore, *Sourcebook of Criminal Justice Statistics 1992*, Table 2.55; 1997, Table 2.55; and Warr, "Poll Trends."

NOTE: When more than one Gallup Poll was administered in a given year, we report the results of the last survey taken in that year.

POPULAR PUNITIVENESS

What about Americans' attitudes regarding crime control policy? Is it true that the public is highly punitive and growing more so over time? There is certainly a kernel of truth to this bit of conventional wisdom. The most reliable trend data on public opinion about crime control consists of questions regarding the death penalty and the harshness of the courts. Between the mid-1960s and early 1970s, fewer than half of respondents in national surveys expressed support for the death penalty for persons convicted of murder. By 1976, the share of the public supporting the death penalty had climbed to 66%; by 1988, it had reached nearly 80%, where it has hovered ever since (see Exhibit 7.6). Regular national surveys similarly indicate a sharp increase, albeit concentrated in the late 1960s and early 1970s, in the percentage of Americans critical of their local courts. In 1965, 48.9% of respondents expressed the view that the courts in their area do "not deal harshly enough" with criminals. Since 1976, however, approximately 80% of respondents have expressed this view.[14]

Because this trend data consists of responses to just two questions, it might be considered a precarious basis for drawing conclusions about the mood of the public regarding criminals. A number of national surveys conducted in the 1990s, however, also found growing and widespread support for most "get tough" policies and initiatives. In particular, large majorities of respondents favor imposing mandatory sentences (including "three strikes" laws),[15] restricting bail and parole for violent offenders,[16] treating juvenile violent offenders as adults,[17] and building new prisons.[18] Moreover, most Americans believe that prison conditions are too comfortable[19] and, according to some surveys, that the government should focus on "punishing," rather than "rehabilitating" violent offenders.[20] Although these harsh attitudes are expressed in all demographic groups, they are more widespread among men, Whites, those who live in the South and West, and self-described conservatives.[21]

Qualitative research also finds widespread support for the notion that the criminal justice system is too lenient with offenders. For example, in focus group discussions conducted in Boston in the early 1990s, a number of participants argued vigorously that the crime problem is in large measure attributable to permissive judges.[22] In the following discussion, for example, participants argue that the hands of the police are "tied" by judges who naively insist that "there's a little bit of good in everybody."

Facilitator: O.K. Next question. "Do you think the crime problem is getting worse or better, and why?"

Edward: I think it's getting worse to some extent, because the hands of the police and the judicial system—not so much the judicial system—the hands of the police and the prison system are somewhat tied, so that the punishment is almost a joke.

Sally: Doesn't fit the crime.

Edward: And if you're a hardcore criminal, you don't really get punished.

Rhoda: When a police officer makes an arrest, before he finishes his paperwork, the damn criminal is back on the street.

Unknown Voice: Right. I know.

Rhoda: The courts have no room for them. There's no follow-up.

Christine: It's easy to be a criminal.

Rhoda: Jails. The courts don't follow through. They're let out in the street, and then the cop doesn't even finish his paperwork and the guy's back out in the street. Ninety percent of the cops don't even want to go to court anymore. It's not worth the effort.

Edward: It's discouraging.

Rhoda: It is. They're discouraged. I mean when we were assaulted, Christine and I, the cop literally said, do you want to push this? Yeah, I want him off the street! Of course I want to push it!

Edward: And the judicial system is very set up to protect the rights—But you're far more protected if you're a criminal than if you're a victim, which is very frustrating.

Unknown Voice: Mmhm.

Martha: You're telling the truth. The police make the arrests, but nothing happens. If you're a policeman and you arrested a hardened criminal, and you're sitting in court and all of a sudden this sweetheart of a judge— "There's a little bit of good in everybody." If he knew how little there was in some of them, he wouldn't sleep nights! So the little so- and-so gets—goes free. And he goes out and he does it again. He says, what do I have to worry about? I can commit this crime many times. And they do. They do. They keep repeating their crime, because they have no fear.[23]

Discussion participants also criticized allegedly cushy prison conditions. In the following extract, they describe prisons as "country clubs" that provide amenities unaffordable to law abiding citizens. Harsher prison conditions, they argue, are both well deserved ("if they're going to act like animals, they should be treated like animals") and more likely to discourage crime:

Deborah: There's no rehabilitation services available, or no deterrent services either. Because we were talking earlier about quadruple bunking them for example. You know, make prison a really—

Lloyd: Not a kiddy club.

Deborah: Yeah. A real terrible place to be—

Karl: Take away the TV.

Lloyd: The gyms, the swimming pools—

Georgia: Let them know that they're there for a reason.

Lloyd: [Take away] the cable TVs.

Deborah: [Over clamor] If they're going to act like animals, they should be treated like animals.

Lloyd: People here in the winter have it so bad that they'd rather go into jail because it's so good there. Three squares. A place to work out. A place to watch TV. A place to go swimming, or whatever. And read and get a little bit of knowledge and stuff, and then it's warm. And then they come out in the summertime.

Georgia: And if they're there long enough, they can come out with a Ph.D.

Unknown voice: Mmhm.

[A few minutes later, in response to a trigger statement:]

Lloyd: I feel strongly on that one. That one is something that has to be addressed. That's why we're trying to make more prisons and stuff like that. But they need to make them less plush, right, and more of them.

Unknown voice: Mmhm.

Chuck: Make it what it is—it's a jail. [Over clamor] It's a prison.

Unknown Voice: Quadruple bunk 'em.

Chuck: It's not a country club. It's not a camp. It's not a summer camp, you know. It's not body-building camp. You know, most of these guys go in the joint, they come out, they look like Arnold Schwarzenegger.

Unknown Voice: Sure you're right. Sure you're right.

Unknown Voice: Pumping iron every day.

Unknown Voice: Eating good.

Chuck: If you don't want to work, you don't have to work.

Karl: You know how much it costs a year to keep one in prison?

Deborah: Something outrageous.

Karl: $46,000.

Deborah: More than they pay me.

Lloyd: Is it?

Karl: To keep *one*. $46,000 for *one*.

Deborah: Wow.[24]

In only 1 of 20 focus group discussions did a participant challenge this characterization of prison conditions. Notably, the dissenter had worked as a top administrator in the Massachusetts prison system.

In sum, both quantitative and qualitative research finds evidence of growing popular punitiveness toward criminals in general. In the next section, we further explore the sources of this "get tough" mood and analyze the coexistence of popular punitiveness with ongoing public support for alternatives approaches to the crime problem.

UNDERSTANDING POPULAR PUNITIVENESS

As discussed in detail in Chapters 2 and 3, the United States endures an unusually high rate of lethal violence. Growing punitiveness toward criminal offenders may be related to this fact. On the other hand, killers make up only a tiny percentage of officially sanctioned criminals. Why then do Americans increasingly express harsh views regarding criminal offenders in general? We begin our analysis with a discussion of certain dimensions of American culture that encourage support for harsher forms of punishment and then consider the more particular contributions of media imagery and race relations to growing public punitiveness.

Individualism and Self-Reliance

Analysts of American political culture have long noted the extraordinary salience of two closely related values:[25]

♦ *Self-reliance* stresses the responsibility of each individual for herself or himself: People should stand on their own two feet! If in the gutter, they should pull themselves up by their own bootstraps! Self-reliance celebrates the self-made person, the one who perseveres in the face of obstacles and through hard work achieves material success.
♦ *Individualism* highlights the importance of individuality, autonomy, and free choice. Each person ought to be regarded first and foremost as a unique individual and only after that as a member of some ethnic group or larger collectivity. Individualism celebrates personal choices—doing your own thing—in matters of politics and lifestyles. Individuality, autonomy, and freedom to choose are valued in their own right and insofar as they permit individuals to discover and develop their "true" selves.

For many Americans, these core values are important wellsprings of optimism. The belief that individual effort alone shapes the quality of one's life means that ordinary people can surmount personal hardships—including handicaps associated with social class, race, and gender—and make something extraordinary of themselves.

The flip side of adherence to the values of self-reliance and individualism is the view that crime, like all forms of action, is strictly a matter of individual choice and motivation. Were crime viewed as a choice made in the context of socially structured beliefs, constraints, and opportunities—as sociological theories tend to posit—then crime-control strategies emphasizing prevention and rehabilitation would seem to be the most logical. But insofar as crime is viewed as a personal choice, pure and simple, crime control strategies oriented toward deterrence and punishment make the most sense. It is in this way that the values of self-reliance and individualism in American political culture provide fertile soil for punitive rhetoric and beliefs.

Media Imagery

If core aspects of American political culture predispose members of the public toward punitiveness, then the crime-related images and messages that saturate the mass media play a vital role in actualizing this tendency. One way the media accomplishes this triggering function is by misleading and misinforming the public about the reality of crime and the criminal justice system. As discussed in Chapters 5 and 6, crime-related news stories and police dramas—especially of the "reality" genre—typically focus on violent crimes committed by strangers. These media images fuel the public's tendency to overestimate the seriousness of the typical criminal offense.[26] Violent crimes committed by strangers are only a minority of those that result in arrest and prosecution, but for most people they are far and away the most disturbing types of crime. The media thus encourages "categorical contagion," a social-psychological process whereby "citizens come to fear many forms of criminal behavior because they imagine them all committed by extremely violent protagonists."[27] People who regard typical criminals as dangerous, malevolent outsiders are likely to support harsher crime control measures.[28]

The mass media similarly misleads the public with regard to the reality of criminal justice practice. Routine news stories about criminal trials, for example, rarely provide adequate information to allow members of the public to grasp the reasons for an apparently lenient sentence.[29] Thematic news stories about the criminal justice system, as discussed in Chapter 5, typically highlight only the institution's most egregious failures such as the early release of offenders who go on to commit new violent crimes.[30] Entertainment crime programs return time and again to narratives of police vigilantism necessitated by judges and criminal justice bureaucrats more concerned with protecting the rights of criminals than with ensuring the public's safety. In these various ways, the mass media depict the criminal justice system as inefficient, ineffectual, and toothless. Not surprising, then, in survey after survey, roughly 8 in 10 respondents express the opinion that their local courts are "not harsh enough" on criminals.[31]

In fact, research suggests that most people significantly underestimate the severity of punishments actually meted out by the justice system.[32] Moreover, mounting evidence indicates that the public's sentencing preferences are actually less punitive than those administered by the criminal justice system. In one study, researchers compared sentences prescribed by the Federal Sentencing Guidelines to sentences preferred by members of the public for selected crime vignettes. (Each crime vignette described a criminal event and provided brief background information on the defendant to be sentenced.) In most cases, the public's sentencing preferences closely matched those prescribed by the Federal Guidelines. However, in almost every case in which there was a disparity between survey respondents and the Federal Guidelines, the Federal Guidelines were far harsher. For example, the Federal Guidelines sentence for the 'trafficking in crack cocaine' vignette (22 years in prison) was more than twice as long as the median respondent sentence for the same crime vignette (10 years). Federal Guidelines sentences were about twice as severe as those preferred by the public for kidnapping in which a victim is unhurt (11.3 years versus 6 years), carjacking in which the victim is unhurt (11.3 versus 5 years), and bank robbery in which a weapon is fired at the ceiling (11.3 versus 5 years). In sum, when it comes to the concrete task of sentencing criminal defendants, the public does not in fact appear to be harsher than the courts.[33]

Evidence of the mass media's influence on popular conceptions of the criminal justice system can also be found in the everyday discourse of regular people. Consider, for example, the extracts from focus group discussions quoted earlier. In the first extract, participants claim that "the hands of the police are . . . tied," the punishment "doesn't fit the crime," and "you're far more protected if you're a criminal than if you're a victim." These slogans were not conceived from scratch by the discussion participants but were borrowed from the larger public discourse presented in the mass media. Similarly, these discussion participants routinely advanced claims about the criminal justice system that originate in the broader public discourse—for example, claiming in the second extract that prisoners enjoy cable television, swimming pools, and the opportunity to work toward a Ph.D. They also refer to the cost to taxpayers of keeping an offender behind bars for a year. These slogans and "facts" about the justice system are part of a larger public discourse whose principal venue is the mass media.[34]

Modern Racism

There is evidence that growing punitiveness is also, at least among some, a manifestation of hostility toward African Americans. Survey research shows that people who report higher levels of racial prejudice also tend to have more punitive attitudes on the topic of crime control. In one national survey, for example, both antipathy toward Blacks and racial stereotyping were found to be statistically significant predictors of support for the death penalty, even after controlling for a battery of alternative predictors.[35] Similarly, in the study comparing popular sentencing preferences to the Federal Guidelines, respondents' attitudes toward civil rights were found to be a key predictor of punitiveness. Specifically, respondents who believed minorities have "too few" civil rights (about a quarter of the sample expressed this view) assigned an average sentence of 2 years. By contrast, the average sentence assigned by respondents who believed minorities have "too many" civil rights (also about a quarter of the total sample) was 3.8 years. The difference was even more stark with respect to the specific crime of drug trafficking: The average sentence assigned for this crime by civil rights supporters was 3.4 years; by opponents, 8.8 years.[36]

It is important to note that survey respondents who express racial prejudice through criminal justice punitiveness have had a great deal of encouragement. Conservative law and order discourse—with its rhetorical origins in the struggle waged by southern politicians against civil rights—has frequently been mobilized to make veiled (and hence deniable) references to threats posed by minorities.[37] In more recent years, this discourse has been joined by race-coded claims about the burdens imposed on taxpayers by welfare cheats, freeloaders, drug users, and so on, especially in the context of the debate over "welfare reform." Finally, television crime news and the new reality crime programs associate Blackness and crime and do so in emotionally charged ways that encourage punitiveness among the viewing public.

The picture of an angry and vengeful public tainted by racism and clamoring for more prisons and more executions is, however, partial at best. As we shall see, mounting evidence suggests that Americans, although growing weary of crime and eager for something to be done about it, continue to support alternatives to the get-tough policies emanating from the state and federal governments.

ALTERNATIVES TO PUNITIVENESS

Despite the growth of punitiveness, most Americans still prefer that money be spent on crime prevention—especially initiatives targeted at young people—rather than on law enforcement and prison construction. In the 1995 National Opinion Survey on Criminal Justice, respondents were asked whether government, in its attempt to lower the crime rate, should spend money on "social and economic problems" or on "police, prisons and judges." As indicated in Exhibit 7.7, more than half of the sample indicated that money should be spent on solving "social and economic problems," significantly more than those indicating support for strengthening the criminal justice system.[38] In another recent national survey, respondents were asked to choose one of four possible areas—crime prevention, law enforcement, punishment, or rehabilitation—on which the government should spend money to reduce crime. Forty-one percent chose crime prevention (including community, education, and youth programs); only 19% chose law enforcement, 25% punishment, and 12% rehabilitation.[39] These findings are not a recent anomaly: In a 1989 Gallup survey, two thirds of respondents endorsed spending more money on education and job training rather than on more prisons, police, and judges.[40]

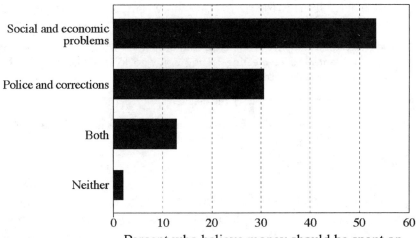

Percent who believe money should be spent on
social and economic problems or police and
corrections to lower the crime rate

Exhibit 7.7. Support for Various Anticrime Strategies
SOURCE: Flanagan and Longmire, *Americans View Crime and Justice*, p. 25.

Popular support for crime prevention is rooted in the widespread notion that crime is a result not only of criminal justice leniency but also of environmental factors, such as family and community breakdown, poverty, drugs, and guns. In fact, in survey research, respondents are sometimes more inclined to identify these environmental factors than criminal justice leniency as a cause of crime.[41] Ethnographic research also finds that many people attribute crime to a breakdown in the moral order, especially in the traditional authority structures of family and community.[42] "Basically the reason [we have so much crime]," explained one participant in the Boston focus group discussions, "is because society's whole moral structure and moral fiber has broken down, where people don't feel like they have to live by the rules." These discussions focused heavily on the failures of parents to supervise, discipline, and accept responsibility for their children. For example:

Gloria: I feel as though [crime is] happening because of the homes that some of these young people may come out of. Lack of supervision, lack of parents—parents being parents.

Ben: No guidance. ["Right!"—a voice interjects.] A few years back on TV, you remember, "It's 11:00 o'clock, do you know where your children are?" And the answer to that today is "Yeah, they're outside on the street somewhere."

Gloria: No commitment in the home, no commitment in schools. Parents do not go to parent/teacher meetings. They don't go to the schools until the student has a real serious problem.

Ben: And then they get angry with the teacher.

Gloria: Yes. Or angry with the principal, or angry with the guidance counselor, or angry with the bus drivers. It's everybody else's fault.

Ben: There is no respect.[43]

Discussion participants also attributed crime to the disintegration of the close-knit communities of their childhoods. These communities, they suggested, provided both mutual support as well as discipline. As one discussion participant vividly recalled:

> I'll chime in. I grew up in a neighborhood—what I'll call a real neighborhood. And I grew up very poor. But one thing about growing up as poor as I did is that we had a sense of community. And we really had to work as a community, because individually the people of the community could not have survived by themselves. The only way that we could survive is that we had to pull together as a community. An example of that is that we were constantly without food. I did not eat every day. What we do sometimes is we would go around to the various neighbors, I need a cup of flour, I need a cup of milk. Go tell Ms. Sue to send me some baking powder and salt. And we would borrow amongst ourselves in order to make that bread. Children just got together and played. This is one thing that—children today, I come in the neighborhood and say "where are the children?" [In my] day you see like tons of children. We just played together as big groups of children when I was growing up. And there was spanking rights throughout the neighborhood and this type of thing. And I long for that.[44]

This "social breakdown" perspective is often the basis for the public's abiding support for crime prevention initiatives. To the extent people believe that faltering families and communities are the wellsprings of crime, they support efforts to shore up these institutions and provide alternative means of encouraging young people to stay on the straight and narrow. The relationship between this emphasis on social breakdown as a cause of crime and support for crime prevention initiatives was sometimes made quite explicit in the discussions:

> When you talk about education and family values and all that sort of thing, it's giving people options—it's—there are some very [good] programs in terms of when you challenge the kids and when you get them involved in art programs and sports programs and you basically get them using their time in more of a constructive fashion, [then] they don't have as much time to basically sit around and feel bored and look for trouble to get into. I think we've all been there as kids ourselves. . . . I think that would help, definitely, in terms of reducing the crime. And also, it's not only going to do it because you're keeping the kids busy, but it's also because you're teaching them good value systems at the same time.[45]

The social breakdown perspective, of course, is also potentially compatible with key elements in conservative political discourse. In particular, widespread popular concern about family breakdown and the decline of traditional authority structures resonates with conservative attacks on the welfare state and attempts to impose order through "get tough" criminal justice initiatives.

In addition to crime prevention, most Americans continue to support rehabilitation, so long as programs are administered in the context of prison sentences.[46] In fact, in one national survey, a plurality of respondents indicated that the most important goal of prison, for those already behind bars, is "rehabilitation" rather than "punishment" or "crime prevention/deterrence."[47] In a separate study on public attitudes toward rehabilitation, criminologist Frances Cullen and his associates conclude:

> [C]itizens do not feel that time in prison should be wasted; prisons should not be warehouses or places that inflict pain without clear purpose. Instead, most citizens take a more pragmatic stance: Inmates should be given the education, training, employment experiences, and, perhaps, counseling that will enable them to become productive citizens.[48]

Finally, a growing body of evidence indicates that most Americans respond favorably when asked about specific alternatives to both incarceration and capital punishment. In focus group interviews, for example, researchers found that most participants support intermediate sanctions—such as community service, boot camp, and restitution to crime victims—as alternatives to incarceration, especially for nonviolent offenders. "As long as the crime did not involve violence," one group of researchers reports, "only small numbers favored incarceration after learning about alternatives, even with offenders who had multiple convictions."[49] Support for alternatives even extends to the death penalty.

In one national survey—as well as statewide surveys in Florida, California, Georgia, and New York—a majority of respondents preferred a sentence of life in prison without the possibility of parole to the death penalty for first-degree murderers when restitution to the victims' family is ordered as part of the package.[50]

These findings suggest a need to qualify the image of a highly punitive public. Americans continue to believe that the best crime-fighting measure is prevention, not punishment. The widespread perception that the criminal justice system is too lenient seems to be based on the impression that the punishments handed out are much less severe than they actually are. What most people seem to be demanding of the criminal justice system is protection from violent offenders and punishments that effectively communicate societal disapproval of crime.[51] Most Americans express support for alternatives to incarceration and execution that are consistent with these goals.

MINORITY DISSENT

African Americans experience disproportionately high rates of serious criminal victimization and express higher than average levels of fear. It is therefore hardly surprising that attitudes among African Americans toward individuals charged with criminal offenses, although still less severe than those of Whites,[52] have hardened somewhat in recent decades. The share of African Americans expressing support for the death penalty for persons convicted of murder, for example, increased from 44% in 1976 to 54% in 1996.[53]

At the same time, African Americans, especially young men, have been the targets of aggressive law enforcement initiatives and, as a consequence, have been disproportionately affected by the expansion of incarceration.[54] This fact, along with highly publicized cases of police brutality and harassment of African American suspects, explains African Americans' growing alienation from the institutions of criminal justice. This alienation was widely recognized for the first time during the 1995 murder trial of Black football superstar O. J. Simpson. Although most White Americans believed Simpson to be guilty, most African Americans believed it was plausible that he was framed by racist cops.[55] Undoubtedly, African Americans' views on the case were influenced by the

"Fuhrman tapes"—audiotapes in which the lead police investigator in the Simpson case is quoted saying "anything out of a nigger's mouth . . . is a f—ing lie" and that "if you did the things that they teach you in the academy, you'd never get a f—ing thing done" (text omitted in original). In the words of one journalist writing at the time of the trial, "Those tapes confirmed what many African-Americans had always known or suspected—that many White cops hate Black people, and see nothing wrong with violating civil rights or tampering with evidence to put away anyone they're convinced deserves it."[56]

When asked in a national survey whether the police treat people fairly, 68% of White Americans answered in the affirmative compared to 38% of African Americans. Similarly, when asked "Who do you think is treated more harshly in this country's criminal justice system?" 74% of African Americans (compared to 35% of Whites) indicated that Blacks are treated more harshly. Notably, African American perceptions of injustice are not limited to the issue of race. In the 1995 National Criminal Justice Opinion Survey, African Americans were substantially more likely than Whites to perceive judicial bias in the "treatment of rich and poor" as well as in the "treatment of minorities."[57]

Ethnographic researchers have reported that conspiracy theories about crime and drugs are widespread in African American communities.[58] Typically communicated by word of mouth—"through the grapevine"— these theories allege that crime, drug dealing, and other crime-related problems endured disproportionately by Black communities are the result of a White effort to destroy those communities. In the discussion that follows, participants in one of the Boston focus groups charge police with intentionally "tunneling" drugs and guns into Black neighborhoods as part of a genocidal plot:

Facilitator: Who's doing these crimes [that concern us most]?

Lynette: We are. Society.

Ertha: But most of these crimes, a lot of these crimes, are provoked by—

Sandra: Them—

David: The White Man.

Ertha: A lot of times it is those that wear the uniforms.

Sandra: Yes! Them!

Ertha: Not only—and not blaming the police themselves. But they are getting really careless [Ertha is referring to an incident in the news at the time of the interview in which a Black man was killed by a White police officer].

Sandra: They're not being careless. It's *acceptable* to shoot us. Do you see what I'm saying? So it's not really carelessness—it's a *plan*. It's genocide.

David: That's the way they get rid of you. . . .

Sandra: Where do [the drugs] come from? Where do the guns come from?

Lynette: Because the kids can get a gun since they were like day one.

Sandra: Who's tunneling all this into our community?

Elaine: The White man. The White man is tunneling and we've been the foolish ones buying.

Sandra: That's the point. They tunnel in the drugs. They tunnel in the guns. They're all coming our way.[59]

Such accounts are not always believed literally, even by those who tell them.[60] Their popularity, however, is a good indicator of the alienation many African Americans feel from the criminal justice system. This alienation is one among many of the harmful consequences of the get-tough policies on crime and drugs.

CONCLUSION

In this chapter, we have argued that most Americans are not typically worried about being struck by crime in the course of day-to-day life, although from time to time Americans have become quite concerned about crime and drugs as social problems afflicting the country as a whole. However, public concern about crime-related issues cannot be taken as support for a "democracy in action" thesis, which explains the get-tough policies of the 1980s and 1990s as a political response to public opinion. Instead, Americans have become most alarmed about crime and drugs on those occasions when national political leaders and, by extension, the mass media, have spotlighted these issues.

Although mobilized by political elites, public concern about crime and drugs is genuine and should be taken seriously. (Were Americans indifferent to the issue, elite efforts to mobilize popular concern would surely have fallen flat.) In this spirit, we have argued that although journalistic depictions of a bloodthirsty public are overdrawn, popular attitudes toward crime and criminal offenders have hardened over the past three decades. But growing punitiveness has not come at the expense of reason: Most Americans regard crime as a consequence of environmental factors, including family and community breakdown, and support a range of crime prevention initiatives. Most Americans also support rehabilitation efforts for offenders already serving time behind bars, as well as alternatives to incarceration and the death penalty. Politicians who believe that the public will respond only to "get tough" appeals are underestimating the complexity of popular thinking on crime.

8

◆ Activism and
◆ the Politics of Crime

◆ ◆ ◆ In the previous chapter, we argued that although members of the public have become more punitive, popular beliefs about crime and punishment remain complex and ambivalent. In this analysis, we treated the public as a largely reactive rather than proactive player in the war on crime. However, many members of the public have not merely responded to politicians, but have actively attempted to shape crime policy. In this chapter, we describe a number of social movements and organizations that have mobilized to influence crime policy—including community anticrime organizations, the victim rights movement, and movements against police brutality, the death penalty, and the drug war—and analyze the conditions that shape the capacity of each to achieve its goals.

One of the most important conditions for the success of a social movement is its ability to capitalize on opportunities created by the larger political environment. When powerful elites with strong views on particular issues ascend to office, new opportunities for political activists with complementary views rapidly materialize. For example, the election of Ronald Reagan in 1980 gave a dramatic boost to the anti-abortion movement.[1] Social movements whose goals and objectives are compatible with those of powerful elites are therefore more likely than adversarial movements to achieve their goals (although their goals may be altered or redefined as a result of their interaction with elites).

This dynamic helps to explain the growth and direction of anticrime activism and the victim rights movement. Both have genuine "grass roots" support, but their development cannot be understood in these terms alone. Rather, because anticrime and victim rights activists pursue goals that are largely compatible with those of political leaders and criminal justice agencies, they have received a great deal of encouragement, guidance, and material support.

By contrast, human rights groups that oppose the death penalty, police brutality, and the drug war have been unable—for obvious reasons—to form alliances with either criminal justice instituions or leading politicians. Although this fact helps to explain why adversarial groups attain a high degree of independence, it also helps explain their comparative lack of succes. Nevertheless, human rights activism may eventually serve as an important catalyst for change.

COMMUNITY-BASED
CRIME PREVENTION EFFORTS

In the United States, community-based programs and organizations received a tremendous boost from the Kennedy Administration, which increased federal financial aid for a variety of local endeavors in the early 1960s. As a result, the number of community organizations in the United States increased rapidly, and many of these included crime on their list of concerns.[2] Surveys administered in the 1970s suggest that 11% to 20% of the public participated in local organizations that included crime prevention as one of their issues.[3]

Interestingly, though, most of these organizations did not treat crime as separate from other neighborhood issues. Instead, they sought to address the social causes of crime, such as insufficient job opportunities, poor educational facilities, and inadequate recreational activities for youth. The widespread nature of this "social problems approach" to crime prevention was related to the then-prevalent belief that crime is a product of social conditions and is often perpetrated by individuals who belong to the community. These beliefs stand in sharp contrast to the now-common assumptions that crime is a problem caused by dangerous outsiders and can be addressed independently of other community issues and problems.[4]

Government support for community anticrime efforts increased significantly in the years following the Kennedy Administration. In 1965, President Johnson created the President's Commission on Law Enforcement and Administration of Justice to make recommendations for enhancing the efficiency of the criminal justice system. In its report, the Commission identified criminal victimization and the fear it engendered as important national problems and suggested that local communities should receive greater support to organize effective responses.[5] Over the next decade, several other national commissions also recommended expanding the citizen's role in the war on crime, and law enforcement agencies increased their "crime prevention" educational efforts. As a result, financial support for community-based crime prevention increased throughout the 1970s.[6] These funds were further augmented with the passage of the Community Anti-Crime Program of 1977 and the Urban Crime Prevention Program of 1980, which provided funds directly to community organizations (rather than to law enforcement agencies) engaged in crime prevention activities.[7]

In recent years, government funds have been allocated to both law enforcement agencies and community organizations, and the emphasis has been on the need for "partnerships" between the two.[8] Although some community organizations remain committed to addressing the social conditions that cause crime, an increasing number have come to focus on enhancing the effectiveness of social control mechanisms in their communities. Some community-based anticrime groups remain independent of government authorities, but many have taken advantage of the opportunity to form partnerships with the police and local officials. Before exploring these developments in greater detail, however, we first address a prior question: What accounts for the growing popularity of community-based crime prevention programs over the past 30 years? Why has the government made involving the community in crime-prevention efforts such a priority?

The Appeal of Community Crime Prevention

The term "community" has become something of a buzzword in policy circles. We hear, for example, of the need for "community policing," "community health care," and "care in the community." In this context, both local governments and the national government have embraced the concept of community crime prevention.[9] The reasons for this policy development appear to be both practical and political. At the practical level, many of these programs are touted as cheaper alternatives to the criminal justice system (although many such programs would—if successful—funnel more people into the system).[10] In addition, the focus on community may help to mobilize individuals to take direct action against crime and to identify particularly high-risk areas for more intensive police intervention.[11]

Political considerations may also have helped catapult community-based crime prevention efforts to the top of the policy agenda. Several analysts have suggested that by declaring a war on crime, government officials increased the public's expectations regarding the state's responsibility and capacity to fight crime.[12] Unfortunately, neither local governments nor the national government have been successful in this war. By emphasizing the need for community involvement, officials may be attempting to reduce public expectations and shift responsibility for dealing with crime back to the community.[13] The rhetoric surrounding community-based programs does indeed imply at least some crime-fighting responsibility for civilians: In the past, the public was told that policing "must be left to the professionals"; now it is informed that "policing cannot be left to the police alone."[14] To the extent that this rhetoric becomes part of the political culture, the government reduces its responsibility for crime control.[15]

Community-based crime prevention programs rest on two main, often competing visions of community:

◆ *Attitudinal:* In this conception, community is defined primarily as a set of collective sentiments: "Community, in brief, is in people's heads . . . if you wish to improve community conditions you are in essence in the business of changing attitudes, or altering the symbols of community, in the hope that improved personal relations will follow."[16]

◆ *Structural:* In this conception, community is defined in institutional terms, "not just as a set of attitudes we can implant or mobilize, but as an interlocking set of long-standing institutions which in turn are deeply affected by larger social and economic forces."[17] As Chapter 3 explained, these larger socioeconomic forces are crucial to our understanding of the nature and distribution of serious crime in the United States.

In what follows, we discuss three main types of community anticrime programs: efforts to maintain (or create) order, efforts to reduce opportunities for crime, and efforts to address the social problems that give rise to crime. Anticrime programs of the order maintenance and opportunity reduction varieties rest on the attitudinal conception of community, which, we believe, helps to explain the limited success of these programs. Community anticrime programs based on the social problems approach address the root causes of crime. Although the structural conception of community around which these movements are organized is more analytically sound, their capacity to alter the fundamental structural forces that shape community life is, unfortunately, quite limited.

Order Maintenance

Many community-based crime prevention programs are primarily attempts to restore or maintain order. Disorderliness can take both physical and behavioral forms. Its physical manifestations include broken windows, graffiti, and other architectural symbols of neighborhood decline.[18] Its behavioral manifestations include panhandling and sidewalk soliciting by individuals, which make many residents feel unsafe. By increasing fear, these manifestations of disorder are presumed to weaken the informal community controls that prevent crime (see Chapter 3). According to this theory, reducing disorder will reduce fear and enable residents to take more pride in and responsibility for their communities—all of which will eventually result in a long-term reduction in crime.[19]

Order maintenance programs often seek to organize community members to "take back their communities" by painting over graffiti, maintaining and cleaning public spaces such as parks, and ensuring that structures that invite "trouble," such as abandoned buildings, are removed or made impenetrable. The object of these activities is ultimately to restore a "sense of community," thereby strengthening both informal and formal social control mechanisms. Insofar as these programs emphasize the need to strengthen community morale and solidarity, they rest primarily on the attitudinal conception of community. Sponsors of these programs typically lack an analysis of why manifestations of disorder—

such as homelessness, panhandling, abandoned buildings, and so forth—might increase in particular areas at particular times. A structural conception of community would suggest that these problems are manifestations of neighborhood decline, which are in turn related to much larger socioeconomic forces such as deindustrialization and residential segregation. In the absence of such an analysis, those who are victims of structural developments (such as the homeless and prostitutes) tend to be identified as the cause rather than the symptom of neighborhood decline.[20]

Some of the more controversial aspects of order maintenance programs are now on display in New York City, which has adopted what is sometimes called "quality-of-life" policing. Under this approach, discussed in greater detail in Chapter 10, the authorities deal aggressively with those who supposedly cause fear in the citizenry—panhandlers, subway turnstile jumpers, the homeless—to help restore order and to empower "law-abiding citizens" to "take back their communities." Defenders of this strategy argue that urban disorder intensified in the 1970s after deinstitutionalization of the mentally ill and the decriminalization of their obnoxious behavior.[21] To counter this development, advocates of quality-of-life policing tout an aggressive and interventionist police strategy and criminalization of the behavior and lifestyles of "undesirables."

By contrast, critics of quality-of-life policing point out that far from being decriminalized, public order and drug offenses are being dealt with in an increasingly draconian fashion, a development that has helped to produce in the United States one of the highest rates of incarceration in the world. Furthermore, critics blame the growth of urban disorder not on the mentally ill, but on an individualistic economic philosophy that has helped to justify a massive redistribution of wealth from the poor to the rich. Thus, according to this argument, social structural conditions (such as the grossly inequitable distribution of wealth) are causing the problems of disorder and crime in the first place, a fact that advocates of order maintenance policing ignore.[22] Finally, critics note that rude or hostile treatment of citizens by the police provokes anger and resentment—reactions that increase the likelihood of future offending. For this reason, "flooding high crime communities with aggressive police could backfire terribly, causing more crime than it prevents, as it has in repeated race riots over the past quarter century."[23]

Opportunity Reduction

"Opportunity reduction," another popular approach to community crime prevention, seeks to reduce the number of situations that invite or encourage crime by intensifying community members' surveillance activities. Surveillance—that is, watching out for and over one's community—may be promoted by social and community organizations or through the modification of the physical environment in ways that are thought to facilitate more "natural" surveillance. In either case, the idea is that residents can be an effective self-policing force by observing one another's property, looking out for suspicious persons and activities, and so forth. Like order maintenance programs, these programs focus on enhancing social control mechanisms and removing or reducing opportunities for crime rather than changing offenders' motivation to commit crime or addressing the social conditions that give rise to crime.

Neighborhood Watch is the clearest example of a program seeking to reduce criminal opportunities by enhancing informal social control and community surveillance. Although there is a significant degree of variation in the implementation of Neighborhood Watch, most groups are organized at the block or neighborhood level and are sponsored by a criminal justice agency, usually a police or sheriff's department. In fact, most local law enforcement agencies now have on staff "crime prevention specialists" who promote and organize Neighborhood Watch-type groups. Although these law enforcement organizers stress that community residents must take greater responsibility for crime through their daily activities, they also instruct members of the public not to intervene in potentially dangerous situations but rather to "observe and report." For this reason, some Neighborhood Watch groups function largely as the "eyes and ears" of the police.[24] These groups are also encouraged to take household security measures, such as property engraving, form crime-tip hotlines, improve street lighting, and engage in "block parenting."

Neighborhood Watch and other block-watch programs are more popular in mostly White, middle class neighborhoods than in high-crime ghetto neighborhoods.[25] This fact is perplexing: One might reasonably expect that people living in the most dangerous areas would be drawn to these crime prevention programs. There are several reasons why this is not the case. First, White residents of middle class communities are likely to believe that crime is caused by "outsiders" rather than by members of their own community.[26] As a result, they appear to be more confident in their ability to identify "suspicious" persons and to be more comfortable doing so.[27] Second, in high-crime areas, residents report higher levels of fear and suspicion of their immediate neighbors, which makes it more difficult for them to organize collectively. Middle class communities, in contrast, have higher proportions of homeowners and married persons, are more homogeneous, and are therefore easier to organize.[28]

Race and class influence not only levels of participation but also the meaning and hopes that participants bring to such programs as Neighborhood Watch. In an analysis of participants' motivations for joining Neighborhood Watch, researchers found both similarities and differences between the African American and White members. Participants of all races hoped to enhance their personal security and improve the quality of neighborhood life. However, African American (but not White) participants also saw crime-watch groups as a way to restore the authority of older residents, whose ability to supervise youth is perceived to have diminished.[29] By contrast, White participants hark back to an era not when neighboring was more intensive but when mothers were more vigilant and involved in their children's lives. These racially based differences reflect the fact that kin networks have historically been more extensive and responsibility for children more diffuse in African American communities.[30] This study reminds us that although the basic content and philosophy of crime-watch programs has largely been determined by law enforcement and government agencies,[31] participants clearly bring to these programs their own meanings and intentions.

Rates of participation in Neighborhood Watch programs remain quite low in most cities, and efforts to raise them have proved discouraging.[32] Research also suggests that crime-watch programs have not been terribly effective. Contrary to what supporters of the programs claim, the most methodologically rigorous studies show that neighborhoods with crime-watch programs experience rates of crime comparable to neighborhoods without programs. Similarly, fear of crime is either unchanged or increases after implementation. Nor do these programs have the desired effect on social cohesion; they also do not activate social behaviors that are presumed to reduce crime.[33]

Civilian or citizen patrols represent an alternative for those inclined to be more actively involved in neighborhood surveillance. Civilian patrols first emerged in the 1960s, mostly in minority communities hoping to reduce police brutality by "policing the police." Not surprising, these patrols tended to have quite adversarial relationships with law enforcement.[34] Others, such as the Guardian Angels, focused more on preventing conventional street crime. The Angels' tactics have sometimes been of dubious legal propriety, and some argue that the organization is best understood as part of the American vigilante tradition. Nonetheless, these patrols have typically been on much more favorable terms with the police than those aimed specifically at monitoring police behavior. Still other neighborhood patrol groups have been founded by Whites hoping to "defend" their communities from "invading" minorities. In Brooklyn, for example, White residents created the Civilian Observation Patrol to keep watch over the neighborhood—and to deny information about housing availability to Hispanics.[35]

Although neighborhood patrols report some crime incidents to the police, they do not have any clear effect on the overall crime rate. These patrols have also been credited with reducing levels of fear among some while making other residents nervous about the nature of their activities.[36]

The Social Problems Approach

The social problems approach to community crime prevention rests on the theory that crime is caused by and related to a number of different social ills, especially conditions that encourage youth to engage in delinquent activities.[37] Groups adopting this approach therefore endeavor to create positive opportunities for young people, including athletic activities, employment services, drug prevention programs, social and academic clubs, and literacy programs. Other common activities include efforts to improve the social, economic, and physical environment in which community members live.[38]

Interestingly, just as crime-watch programs are most popular in mostly White, middle class neighborhoods—where residents believe that crime is perpetrated by outsiders—the social problems approach is most popular in racially heterogeneous and working class communities.[39] In such communities, those who get into trouble with the law could well be friends or family members of residents.[40] As a result, community members are less interested in merely detecting and reporting crime than in preventing it from occurring in the first place. Insofar as community groups adopting the social problems approach recognize the ways in which larger social forces influence the crime problem, they draw much more heavily on a structural conception of community.

The fate of community organizations adopting a social problems approach to community crime prevention is quite different from the fate of those focused on order maintenance and opportunity reduction. On the one hand, groups with multi-issue agendas are much more likely to sustain high levels of participation than are groups that focus exclusively on crime (such as Neighborhood Watch).[41] However, multi-issue groups are often considered to be "insurgent" and are less likely to receive government support.[42] Indeed, federal aid to urban areas has declined sharply since 1980, and most of the funds that are available to such communities are attached to programs that do not attempt to redistribute urban resources in any significant way.

Despite anecdotal accounts of communities that have successfully reduced crime by adopting the social problems approach, little hard evidence of such success can be found. Some analysts suggest that this lack of evidence is not due to ineffectiveness but rather to the lack of "strong evaluations" of such programs.[43] Others argue that try as they might, community activists simply do not have control over the larger social forces (such as the labor and housing markets) that so profoundly influence local crime problems:

> The scientific literature shows that the policies and market forces causing criminogenic community structures and cultures are beyond the control of neighborhood residents, and that "empowerment" does not include the power to change those policies. . . . While programs aimed at linking labor markets more closely to high crime risk neighborhoods and individuals could have substantial crime prevention benefits . . . no program has yet shown success in tackling the unemployment rates of high crime neighborhoods. Yet of all the dimensions of neighborhood life, this one may have the most pervasive influence on crime.[44]

Assessment of Community Efforts

Studies evaluating community crime prevention programs are aimed primarily at determining whether or not these programs "work"—that is, whether they reduce crime and fear.[45] As we have mentioned, such studies indicate that community-based crime prevention efforts have not been particularly successful and have been least successful in communities that need them the most. But ineffectiveness is not the only reason to worry about community crime prevention efforts, particularly the order maintenance and opportunity reduction varieties now favored by government agencies. Another concern centers on their ideological effects: To the extent that these programs draw on an "attitudinal" conception of community, their rhetoric helps to obscure the ways in which structural forces shape community life. This tendency is exacerbated by government funding programs that encourage communities to define and treat such issues as homelessness, AIDS, and drug abuse as criminal rather than social problems.[46] In short, the rhetoric and philosophy of order maintenance and opportunity reduction programs encourage people to identify those affected by these conditions as "people who make trouble" rather than "people in trouble."[47]

A related concern has to do with the ways in which at least some community crime prevention programs may actually encourage social divisiveness. Although the goal of many of these programs is to promote a "sense of community" and hence promote informal social control, many also encourage communities to unite in opposition to "strangers" and "people who do not belong." This understanding of the source of crime is more pronounced in mostly White, middle class communities, and the fact that programs like Neighborhood Watch focus almost exclusively on the kinds of crimes that are more likely to be committed by "outsiders" exacerbates this tendency. Some researchers have argued that these programs are less popular in African American and working class communities precisely because they require that people adopt a sort of oppositional stance against "criminals," a stance that troubles those worried that their own children might one day get into trouble.

The focus on the threat posed by "outsiders" and the need to "defend our neighborhoods" against them is highly controversial. Social critic Mike Davis, for example, argues that this mentality has led to a dramatic transformation of the urban built environment. Gated communities, restrictions on access to public spaces, and ubiquitous signs warning of a potential "armed response" indicate, he argues, a new "fortress mentality"; they are the architectural embodiment of intensified racial and class warfare. Indeed, Davis suggests that " 'security' has less to do with personal safety than with the degree of personal insulation . . . from 'unsavory' groups and individuals."[48] The fact that some community crime prevention programs actually increase residents' fear of crime (presumably because their constant focus on the local crime problem

undermines participants' sense of security)[49] suggests that crime prevention programs may indeed contribute to this fortress mentality. Other
critics worry about the extent to which the rhetoric of "community
empowerment" and "self-help" may encourage vigilantism and other zeal-
ous efforts to establish "community control" over local crime problems.

In sum, although many of the stated goals of the movement for
community-based crime prevention are laudable, these efforts—particularly those types now favored by government agencies—may be ineffective, and they raise many complex moral and political questions. Similar
questions have been raised in response to the growth and transformation
of the victim rights movement.

THE VICTIM RIGHTS MOVEMENT

What is now called the "victim rights movement" first emerged in
the United States in the 1960s. Although its origins are complex, the birth
of this movement was clearly facilitated by President Johnson's declara-
tion of war on crime. Indeed, using the term "movement"—which
implies both cohesiveness and a grassroots foundation—may not be the
most accurate way of naming the complex of social forces and actors that
have worked to put victims at the center of criminal justice policy. Many
grassroots organizations have been involved in this campaign, but the
goals and ideals that now characterize the victim rights movement have
been profoundly shaped by government policies and funding opportunities. In this section, we describe the emergence of the victim movement
in the United States and analyze the process by which the mainstream
of this movement came to accept and promote policies associated with
the government's war on crime.

The Origins of the
Victim Rights Movement

In the United States, the idea of providing greater support to crime
victims was a response to the growing perception that criminals were
being "coddled" by the courts. In the 1960s and 1970s, conservatives
argued that Supreme Court decisions protecting defendants' rights had
unfairly tipped the balance in favor of criminals. The courts had become

so concerned with procedure and "technicalities," conservatives argued, that they were regularly letting violent criminals off the hook. These critics also suggested that measures designed to protect the rights of the accused were a direct attack on crime victims. Defenders of the Warren Court counterargued that the Constitution and the Bill of Rights offer protection to all individuals from a potentially overzealous and intrusive state, and pointed out that someone who at one time is a victim of crime may very well at another be accused of a crime. This debate over the "rights revolution" of the 1960s was an important impetus for the victim rights movement and shaped the nature of the demands it eventually made.[50]

Not all of the actors involved in setting the stage for the victim rights movement had the same motivations. President Johnson and other liberals hoped to undercut the Republican "ownership" of the crime issue, and one of their tactics was to create, in 1965, the President's Commission on Law Enforcement and Administration of Justice. In its final report, the Commission raised concerns about the reluctance of many crime victims to cooperate with prosecutors and testify in the courts. This report attributed what it saw as a low conviction rate—a sign of inefficiency—largely to this reluctance.[51]

The Commission's concern was echoed in the first National Crime Surveys (administered in the late 1960s by the Law Enforcement Assistance Administration [LEAA]). These surveys revealed that because many victims did not even bother to report their victimization to the police, the true prevalence of criminal victimization had been greatly underestimated.[52]

These concerns led the LEAA to create a number of "victim-witness assistance" programs (operated mainly out of prosecutors' offices) in the early 1970s. The main goal of these programs was to increase the conviction rate by encouraging crime victims to cooperate with the police and prosecutors. By 1980, over 400 such programs were operating in the United States.[53] Although a few states had already created victim compensation programs,[54] the LEAA's victim-witness assistance program was the first nationally coordinated effort to provide material support to victims of crime. In addition to providing this financial aid, the LEAA employed a group of specialists whose primary responsibility was to address the social and emotional needs of crime victims. The primary motivation for offering such counseling was to increase victims' cooperation with the state in criminal proceedings.[55]

Another important source of activity on behalf of victims came from feminists concerned about the plight of victims of rape and domestic violence. Feminist activists set up the first rape crisis centers in the early 1970s, which provided support and assistance to rape survivors. Initially, many of these centers were quite distrustful of the police and prosecutors and criticized the ways in which the criminal justice system "re-victimized" rape victims: by treating them with disrespect, by assuming that they were lying or "hysterical," and by putting their sexual histories on trial. Feminist organizers also established emergency shelters for battered women and their children in the 1970s. As with rape crisis centers, these shelters initially were independent of the state.[56]

In the late 1970s and into the 1980s, a variety of other voluntary organizations were created to fight on behalf of crime victims, usually victims of a particular type of crime. Many of these were initiated by family members of crime victims to draw particular attention to the emotional pain the families endure. Some of the best-known examples of such organizations are Mothers Against Drunk Driving (MADD), Parents of Murdered Children, and the National Center for Missing and Exploited Children. Most of these organizations emphasize the need for grassroots efforts, but they have also been quite successful in attracting government support. These groups also tend to combine a service orientation with a more political approach aimed at increasing public awareness and reforming criminal law and penal practices.[57] Increasingly, these organizations have come to identify enhanced victim rights—as opposed to victim services—as the best way to meet victims' needs.[58]

The Shift From Victim Needs to Victim Rights

The idea that crime victims should have legal rights is both very old and very new. In the early Middle Ages, crime victims primarily achieved "justice" by avenging their crimes through blood feuds. In those cases that did involve authorities, victims were sometimes awarded restitution—compensation for their pain and losses. Gradually, the notion that crimes are committed "against society" rather than against an individual led authorities to frown on private means of resolving disputes (feuds, duels, and so forth) and to replace the "private" legal system with a more "public" one. Increasingly, authorities (rather than the victim) took responsibility for initiating legal proceedings. Gradually, the state was empowered to levy fines (which went into the Crown's purse) and to punish offenders who were found guilty of committing crimes against society.[59] Despite this shift, the victim was still the primary initiator of criminal proceedings under colonial law, and restitution—compensation for victims—was still the main rationale for doing so. Victims continued to play an important role throughout the 19th century (in Europe and the United States) in determining whether or not a prosecution would take place (although they could be overruled by authorities).

Only with massive industrialization and urbanization did a fully public system of criminal law emerge in the United States. Under this system, involving the victim in the legal process was thought to promote vigilantism and vengeance. Furthermore, the state began to play a more important role in protecting the rights of the accused. Simultaneously, the goal of punishing the offender rather than producing justice for the offended began to take precedence in the criminal system. By contrast, the civil courts have retained more of the characteristics of earlier "private" legal systems: Cases are initiated by one or both of the parties involved, and the goal is compensation rather than punishment.[60]

Nowadays, many progressives complain that victims have been unfairly pushed out of the criminal justice process. According to this argument, state organizations have "stolen" conflicts from those actually involved, leaving both victims and offenders alienated from the dispute resolution process.[61] In most cases, they argue, justice is better served by restitution than by punishing offenders.[62]

Conservatives also criticize the exclusion of victims from the criminal process, but they attribute this development to an unwarranted expansion of the rights of defendants. For example, the President's Task Force on Victims of Crime, created by President Reagan in 1982, suggested that the victim's role in the legal process should be "restored," that defendants' rights had been extended at the expense of victims, and that victims would be best served by enhancing the state's capacity to punish wrongdoers.[63]

Many of those involved in the victim rights movement have accepted the conservative argument that victims should be more central to the criminal justice process, that the courts have gone too far in protecting the rights of the accused, that this protection comes at the expense of victims, and that punishment of the offender is a victim's right. As a result, some victim rights measures promote a return to a more private and, critics would argue, vindictive legal system. For example, some victim rights groups propose that suspects remain in custody after arrest (before conviction and despite the presumption of innocence); that delays be minimized between arrest and the preliminary hearing and between hearing and trial (despite the fact that defendants may need time to raise money for and organize a defense); that plea bargaining be eliminated or be victim determined; that exclusionary rules regulating the way evidence is collected and presented in court be abandoned or weakened; that the *Miranda* rule protecting the rights of the accused be overturned; and that victims' testimony regarding their emotional experience be considered at the time of sentencing, especially in capital cases.[64] Thus, although victims groups continue to press for services and restitution for crime victims, the emphasis for many has shifted to victims' legal rights.

Both political forces and pragmatic considerations appear to be fueling this trend. Over the last three decades, conservative political rhetoric has charged that excessive leniency on the part of the courts is responsible for much of the U.S. crime problem. Criticism of the Supreme Court's "rights revolution" during Chief Justice Earl Warren's tenure has been a centerpiece of this rhetoric. As we saw in earlier chapters, the mass media has also emphasized criminal justice leniency. In this context, it is not surprising that victim rights activists increasingly interpret the "right not to be a victim" to mean that punishment is a "victim's right."[65]

A more practical reason for emphasis on victims' rights over restitution and conflict resolution is that much of the available funding for victims groups comes from the government—with strings attached. One of the main goals of the LEAA—the primary source of funding for victims groups in the 1970s—was to increase the willingness of victims to cooperate with the police and prosecutors, thereby increasing rates of conviction. The LEAA (like other granting agencies) not only selected which organizations it would fund but could stipulate which organizational activities its funds would support. In general, the LEAA (and the state governments that administered the block grants provided by the LEAA) opted to fund organizations that prioritized services for victims rather than those that engaged in suspect political activities or that criticized police, prosecutors, or judges.[66]

Since the disbanding of the LEAA in 1980, the Crime Victim's Fund (created under the auspices of the Crime Victims Act) and state block grants (provided by the Justice Assistance Act of 1984) have been the main sources of federal support for crime victims. These funds are not derived from tax revenues but are generated from fines levied against those convicted of federal crimes.[67] This funding arrangement may seem fair, but it has had important consequences for the political orientation of the victims movement. If, for example, drugs were decriminalized, the federal prison population—and the funds available for victims organizations—would shrink dramatically (over 60% of all federal prisoners are drug offenders). Many state governments also fund victim services at least in part through criminal fines, forfeited assets, and prisoner wages, and these funds would shrink if the war on crime were scaled back.[68]

Furthermore, because current compensation arrangements segregate crime victims from other recipients of social services, crime victims are less likely to see their cause as linked to efforts to improve schools, enhance employment opportunities, or reduce social inequality.[69] Many states also earmark specific surcharges (on divorce proceedings, for example) for crime victim groups, a practice that also isolates victims organizations from other social service and welfare agencies.[70]

In sum, both the political climate and funding arrangements have contributed to the tendency of many victims organizations to identify punishment as their primary "right." Mainstream victim rights organizations, however, do not represent the views or desires of all crime victims. According to one study, those involved in the victims organizations are overwhelmingly White, female, and middle aged—a group demographic that is hardly representative of crime victims in general (see Chapter 5). These activist victims tend to be more supportive of the death penalty and significantly more likely to believe that the sentences given their offenders are "much too lenient" than are victims of crime who are not involved in the movement. Somewhat more surprisingly, activist victims are also more supportive of the police, prosecutors, and judges than their nonactivist counterparts.[71]

Moreover, not all victims groups are punitive. Indeed, some organizations—such as Murder Victims' Families for Reconciliation—explicitly reject the "politics of vengeance." Similarly, advocates of "restorative justice" challenge the idea that victims are best served by a punitive orientation and seek instead to enhance the capacity of victims and offenders to reach mutually acceptable ways of resolving disputes and compensating victims for the pain they suffer.

Legal Reforms

The victims movement has been quite successful in persuading legislatures to modify laws to promote victims' interests. Some critics of the movement point out that this very success belies the movement's claim that the criminal justice system favors criminals. Indeed, it is difficult to imagine associations of prisoners or criminal defendants exercising comparable influence over the law. State statutes designed to protect and serve victims are now on the books in all 50 states, and as of 1996, 21 states had amended their state constitution to achieve these goals. Most recently, victim rights activists have begun lobbying for an amendment to the U.S. Constitution aimed at "balancing" the protections offered to criminal defendants with provisions for victims' rights.[72]

As a result of this activism (and the government's desire to increase victims' cooperation), funding for victim services has increased sharply. These services come in a variety of forms, including financial aid, psychological support, and assistance in managing the criminal justice process. All but six states have also adopted statutes that enhance the courts' capacity to order restitution (although because criminal offenders are overwhelmingly poor and are paid very low wages for prison work, only about four cents on the dollar for every fine and restitution order is actually collected).[73] Funding for victim services is more generous in the United States than in most other countries.[74] Nonetheless, the availability of these services varies significantly from state to state, and overall, only a small percentage of victims of violent crime actually receive them.[75]

Other largely noncontroversial reforms include the victim's right to be notified of court dates and other relevant judicial proceedings, the right to be present at these hearings, the right to be treated with dignity and respect, and the right to be free of intimidation and harassment by the defendant. As with orders of restitution, these rights are often difficult to ensure.

Reforms aimed at enhancing the role of the victim in judicial decision making have been more controversial. About half the states now require that victims be consulted before any plea bargaining takes place, and many grant the victim veto power in these proceedings.[76] By the mid-1980s, 43 states had passed legislation allowing victims to make personal statements (Victim Impact Statements [VIS]) describing their experience of the crime in question. Inclusion of these statements in courtroom proceedings apparently leads to more punitive sentences,[77] and parole boards appear to be less likely to grant parole when a VIS is presented to the board.[78] Research also suggests, however, that victims are not usually informed of their right to submit a VIS, and of those who are informed, only a small percentage actually file a VIS with the court.[79] Nonetheless, the idea that victims' feelings and experiences should be taken into account at the time of sentencing represents a significant challenge to the principle that crimes are committed against society rather than individuals. It also introduces a more personal—some would say vindictive—quality to the judicial process. The question of the appropriateness of taking victims' feelings into account is even more relevant in states that also allow victims to provide a "victim statement of opinion" regarding the appropriate sentence, especially in capital cases.

Also controversial are those victim rights reforms that undermine the rights of the accused. Some "victim rights" measures, for example, have lowered evidentiary requirements, eliminated the insanity defense, and weakened exclusionary rules designed to block the introduction of illegally obtained evidence.[80] These goals reflect the beliefs that the protection of defendants' rights comes at the expense of victims and that more punishment would serve the victims' interests. They also reflect the belief that victims and accused offenders constitute distinctive and nonoverlapping groups.

The Politics of Vengeance

To the extent that the victim rights movement defines its interests in terms of "getting tough"—demanding faster executions, longer sentences, and restrictions on defendants' rights—it has become part of the very powerful conservative effort to expand the penal system. In fact, the mainstream of the movement seems to have allied itself with other forces promoting the war on crime. In California, for example, the Doris Tate Crime Victim's Bureau obtains 78% of its funding from the California Correctional Peace Officers Association (the prison guard's union) and was the driving force behind California's "three strikes" law. This union also provides over 80% of the funding for a new political action committee called "Crime Victims United," an ally of former Governor Pete Wilson, one of the state's strongest and most influential advocates of penal expansion.[81]

Ironically, victims will pay a significant price if the victim rights movement succeeds in equating victims' interests with the war on crime:

◆ The policies associated with the war on crime actually undermine (rather than protect) the most fundamental right: the right not to be a victim. The war on crime does nothing to address the causes of serious crime discussed in Chapter 3. In fact, we will argue that its main affect is to exacerbate these conditions by creating a large pool of "unemployable" ex-cons and contributing to family and neighborhood disruption.

◆ Vengeance does not clearly serve the interests of victims, even at a psychological level. Many victims do not seek revenge to alleviate their pain, and those who believe that revenge will bring them relief often discover that it does not.[82]

Furthermore, as the victim rights movement has become a partner in the war on crime, it has come to define both "crime" and "victimization" very narrowly. The fact that the organized victim rights movement is largely White and middle class has meant that many victims are not represented by the mainstream of this movement. Among those left out are the many victims of corporate and state crime. In many urban areas, victims of "environmental racism" are organizing to demand that corporations run manufacturing facilities and dispose of hazardous waste in a safer and more responsible fashion—but thus far they have not been included in the victims movement. An even broader conception of victimization would include victims of human rights abuses and those (such as the homeless) denied what the United Nations terms basic human rights—including the right to food, shelter, and clothing. In short, the victim rights movement's growing tendency to equate victims' rights with greater punishment and its almost exclusive focus on "street crime" represents a very narrow interpretation of what it means to be a victim— and a similarly narrow sense of who is doing the victimizing. The same cannot be said of those protesting the aggressive policies and practices associated with the war on crime.

HUMAN RIGHTS ACTIVISM

Unlike many community crime prevention and victim rights organizations, human rights groups confronting the criminal justice system seek to restrict the authority and power of state and criminal justice agencies. They are thus much less likely to receive government aid. Although this fact works to their detriment in many ways, it also allows such groups to define their goals and objectives independent of political fashion and pressures. In this section, we discuss three main areas in which human rights organizations are most active in relation to criminal justice: police brutality, capital punishment, and the war on drugs.

Fighting Police Brutality

The excessive use of force by police officers has long been a topic of concern, particularly in minority communities. Indeed, most of the major urban riots of the post-World War II period have been triggered by allegations of police brutality. Current estimates are that between 1% and 5% of police encounters with criminal suspects involve the excessive use of force, some of which is deadly.[83]

With recent legal reforms, however, fewer people are dying at the hands of the police. Until the 1970s, most police departments allowed officers to shoot anyone suspected of committing a felony (such as larceny) who attempted to flee. During this period, seven Blacks were killed by the police for every White killed. In 1985, however, the Supreme Court ruled this "fleeing felon rule" unconstitutional, and police departments were required to place greater restrictions on the circumstances under which officers are allowed to shoot. As a result, the number of people killed by police officers dropped significantly (from 559 in 1975 to 300 in 1987), and the ratio of African American to White suspects killed by police officers fell from 7 to 1 to 3 to 1.

Nevertheless, in high-crime communities, minorities continue to be subject to police brutality. Indeed, many large cities pay out millions of dollars each year to settle lawsuits over the excessive use of force by police officers. Minorities are also more likely to report being harassed, questioned, and frisked by the police than are Whites.[84] Each of these problems is aggravated by the new "quality-of-life" policing.[85]

Some community groups have organized specifically around the issue of police brutality. These groups tend to have an "adversarial" stance: They see the government and police as the cause of the problem and hence do not seek further government involvement.[86] Instead, these groups typically seek to enhance the ability of community residents to oversee and regulate the police. In Los Angeles, for example, activists recently attempted to create an independent civilian police review board to review complaints of police brutality and harassment, on the assumption that citizen-run review boards will provide more independent and meaningful oversight than police-run boards. This is not always the case, however: One study found that police officers were primarily responsible for investigating complaints in two thirds of all "civilian" review programs.[87]

Well-publicized cases of police brutality—such as the LAPD beating of motorist Rodney King—often trigger widespread protest against police brutality. In the aftermath of the 1998 assault by New York police officers on Haitian immigrant Abner Louima, for example, activists from a number of different organizations (including Haitian, immigrant, and antiracist groups) joined together with anti-police brutality groups. Pointing out that in a recent 20-month period over 100 people had died while in the custody of the NYPD, these groups organized the Coalition Against Police Brutality and sponsored the National Day of Protest to Stop Police Brutality in which thousands of people demonstrated.[88] Historically, the challenge for such groups has been to sustain this level of activism in the absence of well-publicized instances of police brutality and in the face of opposition from law enforcement and local officials.

Opposing Capital Punishment

In 1972, in *Georgia v. Furman*,[89] the Supreme Court accepted the arguments of the National Association for the Advancement of Colored People and the American Civil Liberties Union and found capital punishment to be unconstitutional. This ruling was highly controversial and ignited an energetic campaign to reinstate the death penalty. In 1976, the Court overturned its 1972 decision, declaring capital punishment to be constitutional after all.

Since the Court's reversal, capital punishment has been debated largely as a political rather than a legal issue. The death penalty has many quite vocal supporters, and public enthusiasm for it has grown considerably (although much of this support disappears when people are presented with the option of a sentence of life without parole as an alternative to death [see Chapter 7]).[90] But capital punishment also has many opponents, including a growing number of religious bodies (such as the World Council of Churches, the American Friends Service Committee, the American Jewish Committee, and the U.S. Catholic Conference), and these opponents have been quite active in their opposition.

The anti-death penalty movement subsided somewhat in the 1980s and early 1990s[91] but seems to have revived a bit in recent years. Several factors appear to have facilitated this revival, including the release of the well-known film *Dead Man Walking* and publicity surrounding the film's protagonist, anti-death penalty activist Sister Helen Prejean. In addition, in 1997 the American Bar Association took the unprecedented step of calling for a moratorium on the death penalty, arguing that issues of racial inequality in capital sentencing, inadequate legal representation for capital defendants, and evidence of wrongly convicted persons necessitated a rethinking of the issue.[92]

Credit for sustaining the movement against the death penalty is also due to grassroots groups such as Murder Victims' Families For Reconciliation (MVFFR), a Virginia-based organization of relatives of murder victims with over 4,000 members. MVFFR activists have been quite outspoken in opposing the argument that retribution serves victims' interests.[93] Activist SueZann Bosler, for example, spent much of the 10 years following her father's murder working to prevent the execution of his murderer. She told the press that she cannot understand "why we kill people to show that killing people is wrong."[94] The fact that this opposition comes from those who have lost a loved one makes it especially powerful. Thus far, however, the louder and more publicized voices of the mainstream victim rights movement have dominated in the media, and it remains to be seen whether groups such as MVFFR can make their voices heard.

Seeking Truce in the War on Drugs

Although the war on drugs apparently enjoys support from much of the public, it has become increasingly controversial. Pockets of resistance are cropping up in a variety of places—even among criminal justice officials. A poll taken in 1996 found that over 60% of police chiefs believe that antidrug strategies have been ineffective,[95] and over 50 federal judges (many of whom are Reagan and Bush administration appointees) have refused to hear any more drug cases. As one retired judge explained, "I can't continue to give out sentences I feel . . . are unconscionable."[96]

Grassroots opposition to the war on drugs takes a variety of forms. One arena of debate and resistance has been around the issue of access to clean needles. An increasing number of public health and community activists argue that needle exchange programs are necessary because over one third of all current AIDS cases are linked to drug injection.[97] But these activists are stymied by drug war policies that ban the sale or possession of hypodermic needles. In 1998, the Department of Health and Human Services under President Clinton refused to lift a ban on federal funding for needle exchange programs.[98] In this context, activists around the country have been arrested for implementing their own needle exchange programs. In many areas, however, activists have forged alliances that have successfully overcome political opposition and have therefore been able to legally implement such programs and reduce the transmission of the virus that causes AIDs and other infectious diseases.[99]

Opposition to other antidrug laws—particularly mandatory minimum sentencing statutes—is also growing. These sentencing laws require that judges impose specified minimum penalties for drug offenders. Although ostensibly aimed at "drug kingpins," they predominantly affect low-level drug couriers ("mules").[100] Most politicians are opposed to scaling back the mandatory minimum drug laws. However, proposals to do just that are increasingly backed by police, judges, and attorneys, many of whom point out that the cost of incarcerating low-level, nonviolent drug offenders is quite high. Another catalyst for the campaign to repeal mandatory sentencing laws comes from grassroots organizations, especially Families Against Mandatory Minimums (FAMM). The membership of FAMM has grown from a few dozen in 1991 to over 33,000 in 1997. One of the main strategies of this group has been to publicize the nonviolent nature of the crimes committed by many individuals sentenced under these laws and to draw attention to the effects of harsh punishment on families and children.[101]

Other groups have targeted not just the laws, but the drug war's overarching goal—a "drug-free America." These activists argue that some drug use is inevitable, and that the goal of drug policy should be to reduce the harm associated with drug abuse rather than eradicating all drug use through criminalization. This "harm reduction" philosophy has attracted many supporters and may serve to unify academics, local officials, community activists, and others opposed to the war on drugs. In Oakland, California, for example, the first national conference of the Harm Reduction Coalition in 1996 drew over 1,000 participants.[102]

Harm reduction also appears to have some appeal among the electorate. In California and Arizona, for example, voters recently passed measures allowing for the medical use of marijuana; the Arizona legislation also mandated that first- and second-time drug offenders receive treatment rather than prison sentences.[103] The impact of these measures is currently unclear. The U.S. Justice Department continues to threaten doctors who recommend or prescribe marijuana to their patients with criminal prosecution, and politicians in both Arizona and California struggle to reverse the results of the election. Still, the fact that these measures were written, advocated, and eventually approved by the voters represents a major victory for opponents of the drug war.

CONCLUSION

Far from being passive players in the wars on crime and drugs, some members of the public have quite actively attempted to shape crime policy. Most of this activism has been aimed at reducing crime through community-based crime prevention efforts or at providing for the needs and rights of crime victims. The fact that these forms of activism are largely consistent with the goals and philosophy of current anticrime policies has meant that they have received a great deal of government support. In fact, these movements have been profoundly shaped by their interaction with government and criminal justice officials.

By contrast, those elements of these movements that are less compatible with the philosophy of the war on crime—such as community groups that adopt a "social problems" approach to crime prevention and victims associations that do not advocate more punitive sentencing laws—have received significantly less government support and have remained much more independent of the government. Similarly, groups that actively oppose aspects of the government's war on crime typically have an adversarial relationship to the government and receive very little support from it. The fact that these opponents of the war on crime have a more difficult time making their voices heard has contributed to the punitive climate in which new tough-on-crime laws have been adopted. In the chapter that follows, we examine these laws and their implications for American society.

9
◆ Crime and
◆ Public Policy

◆ ◆ ◆ Throughout this book, we have argued that the dramatic expansion of the U.S. penal system is a consequence of the politicization of crime-related issues. Over the past three decades, politicians have kept the issues of crime and drug abuse at the top of the national agenda and have framed these issues in ways that suggest a need for a harsher and more expansive system of criminal justice. This interpretation of crime and related issues has been amplified through the mass media and, from time to time, has resonated with large segments of the American public.

The political obsession with crime and the spread of support for "getting tough" has precipitated a series of policy developments:

- massive increases in drug arrests
- new, more punitive sentencing schemes
- revival of capital punishment
- retreat from juvenile justice
- hardening of prison regimes
- intensification of community surveillance

In this chapter, we take a closer look at these policies and practices, paying particular attention to their significance for criminal punishment. In the last section, we examine the implications of these changes for the control of crime and for the quality of social life more generally.

171

DRUG POLICING

Most of the public discussion of policing in the 1980s and 1990s focused on the kinds of collaborative, "order maintenance" and "quality-of-life" initiatives discussed in Chapter 8. The image conveyed in these discussions has been that of the congenial "beat cop" of an earlier, gentler era. In reality, however, the most significant practical development in policing over the past two decades has been the crackdown on drugs.

Since the Reagan Administration's Omnibus Crime Bill of 1984, police departments around the country have been encouraged to pursue drug offenders by the promise that they can confiscate any assets believed to be acquired with drug money—including cars, boats, houses, and bank accounts. Moreover, law enforcement agencies were allowed to keep a portion of seized assets, whether or not their owners were ever convicted of—or even formally charged with—a drug offense.[1] As a result of the new law, asset forfeiture receipts increased from $27.2 million in 1985 to $874 million in 1992; the assets and goods seized between 1985 and 1990 alone were estimated to be worth between $4 and $5 billion. By 1990, over 90% of police and sheriff's departments serving populations of at least 50,000 had received money or goods from a drug asset forfeiture program.[2] Indeed, as critics of these statutes point out, the lucrative nature of drug law enforcement means that law enforcement agencies may prioritize the prosecution of drug offenders over those who commit violent offenses.[3]

It is not surprising, therefore, that the annual number of drug arrests has increased in recent years (see Exhibit 9.1). In 1996, more than 1.5 million Americans were arrested on drug charges, roughly three times the number of annual arrests for aggravated assault and ten times the number for robbery. Indeed, someone is arrested for a drug violation every 20 seconds.[4] Since the early 1980s, in any given year the vast majority of drug arrests—between two thirds and four fifths of the total—have been for the crime of simple possession.[5]

A popular interpretation of these numbers is that the drug problem in the United States worsened during the mid-1980s and mid-1990s. Indeed, in a special report on the explosion of drug arrests, researchers at the Federal Bureau of Investigation contend that "The Nation experienced its highest level of illicit drug activity in 1995 when measured by the total number of reported drug arrests since 1980."[6] The problem with this claim is that the number of annual drug arrests is a poor index of

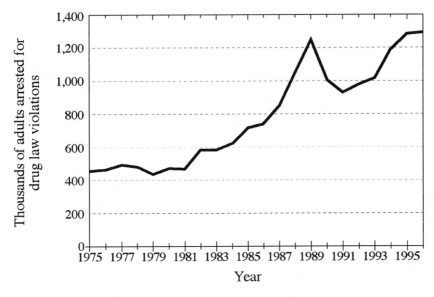

Exhibit 9.1. Drug Arrests.
SOURCE: Federal Bureau of Investigation, *Uniform Crime Reports, 1996.*

underlying drug activity. According to the National Institute of Drug Abuse's (NIDA) most recent National Household Survey, more than 10% of Americans used a prohibited drug during the past year—mainly marijuana, cocaine, or a hallucinogen such as LSD—and more than 6% used one in the last month.[7] The pool of potential "drug offenders" is thus huge. Moreover, if we examine the results of the NIDA surveys since 1980, the image that develops is not one of rising drug use but the opposite. Among adults, the rate of illegal drug taking declined between 1980 and 1993 and has remained stable ever since (see Exhibit 9.2). Among high school seniors, the rate of drug use declined through 1993 but has since increased modestly due to rising use of marijuana (see Exhibit 9.3).[8] The surge in drug arrests does not reflect changes in drug taking so much as the policy choice made by politicians and the police to fill the prisons with drug offenders.[9]

The crackdown on drug dealers and users has focused disproportionately on inner city minority neighborhoods. According to the annual NIDA survey, African Americans make up about 13% of monthly users of illegal drugs, a number roughly proportionate to their share of the U.S.

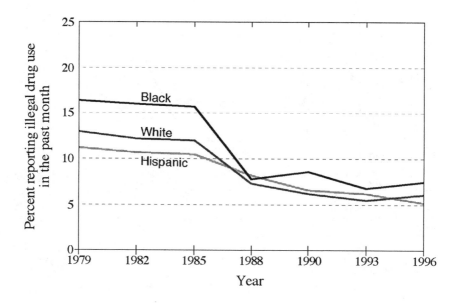

Exhibit 9.2. Illegal Drug Use Among Adults

SOURCE: National Institute on Drug Abuse, *Household Survey on Drug Abuse,* 1979, 1982, 1985, 1988, 1990, 1993; National Institute of Drug Abuse, *Preliminary Results.*

population.[10] Between 1980 and 1989, however, the proportion of drug arrests involving African Americans increased from about 1 in 4 to about 4 in 10.[11] Some portion of this disparity may be due to the fact that some disproportionately poor and minority addicts slip through the cracks of national surveys. But as one research team concluded, "the degree of disparity between drug use and drug possession arrests is of such magnitude that it clearly points to disproportionate arrest practices."[12]

The police have focused their efforts in minority communities for several reasons:

◆ Drug dealing in predominantly minority inner city neighborhoods, in contrast to middle class areas, is more likely to occur in public places. "Open air" drug markets are more likely to generate citizen complaints and are more susceptible to police intervention through "buy and bust" undercover operations.[13]

◆ The residents of inner city neighborhoods tend to be politically powerless. Unlike their counterparts in upscale suburbs and on college campuses, they are unlikely to cause headaches for police and local politicians when arrested.[14]

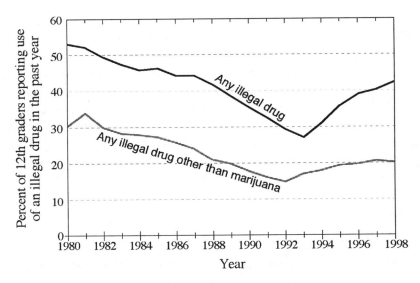

Exhibit 9.3. Illegal Drug Use Among High School Seniors
SOURCE: University of Michigan, *Monitoring the Future Study,* Table 3.

◆ Inner city drug dealers fit the image of drug traffickers constructed in political discourse and in the news and entertainment media.

In and of itself, the astronomical growth in the number of annual drug arrests would have contributed to growth of both prison populations and racial disparities among the incarcerated. But the impact of surging drug arrests has been compounded by harsh new mandatory sentencing laws. These are among several new punitive sentencing practices, a topic to which we now turn.

PUNITIVE SENTENCING

Many politicians, neoconservative intellectuals, and members of the public are convinced that the sentences handed down by the courts are far too lenient. Their concerns have precipitated major changes in sentencing. For most of the century, a guilty verdict was followed by the proclamation of an open-ended, "indeterminate" sentence—5 to 20 years, in a typical case—with the precise release date to be determined by a parole board. This system honored, at least in principle, the notion that prisons ought to treat individual offenders on the basis of their particular situations and to release them once they have been "rehabilitated."

Since the early 1980s, a new system of "determinate" punishment, founded upon a repudiation of rehabilitation, has been taking shape.[15] In the new regime, sentences are calibrated to punish offenders, deter would-be offenders, and incapacitate offenders who might pose a danger if free in society. The shift to determinate sentencing is taking shape primarily through three sentencing innovations: mandatory minimum sentencing laws, "three strikes" legislation, and "truth-in-sentencing" requirements.

Mandatory Minimum Drug Sentences

Over the past two decades, mandatory minimum sentencing laws have become one of the most popular sentencing innovations. They have been adopted by state legislatures and the U.S. Congress as a way of "sending a message" that particular offenses will be punished severely while simultaneously limiting the discretion of judges to do otherwise. Between 1985 and 1991, the U.S. Congress enacted at least 20 new mandatory sentencing laws, bringing to more than 100 the number of federal offenses governed by such laws.[16] Mandatory sentencing laws also proliferated at the state level. Massachusetts, for example, enacted mandatory penalties for unregistered firearms, drug law violations, drunk driving, and murder. By 1994, every U.S. state had adopted at least one new mandatory penalty, and most had adopted several.[17] These laws typically apply to the most serious crimes, such as murder, rape, and felonies committed with a firearm. But they also apply to drunk driving and drug offenses.

In fact, the mandatory penalty laws that have had the greatest impact on the nature and scope of criminal punishment have been those aimed at drugs. As with all laws of their type, mandatory minimum drug laws oblige judges to ignore information about an offender's job status, family obligations, history of victimization, and potential for rehabilitation. Moreover, because these laws punish according to the volume of the drug seized, they oblige judges to overlook even the particular details of the offense. It thus matters not at all whether the offender is a 17-year-old transporting drugs from one location to another (a "mule"), the battered girlfriend of a small-time distributor, or a genuine "drug kingpin." In Federal Court, 1 gram of LSD, 5 grams of crack cocaine, and 100 grams of heroin each gets you 5 years.[18] In Massachusetts, 200 grams of cocaine or heroin gets you 15 years, and 10,000 pounds of marijuana gets you 10 years.[19]

The results are sometimes surreal. Consider the following vignettes, culled from a *Boston Globe* "Spotlight" study of mandatory drug sentencing in Massachusetts:

> Rachel Acevedo, a poor mother of three, was caught with her former boyfriend selling four ounces of cocaine to an undercover police officer. Arrested in 1993, 22 years old, she is serving 10 years without any possibility of parole. She is a first-time offender with no criminal history.

> Victor B. Ramos, a 17-year-old high school student, was caught selling $40 worth of marijuana to a "pretty student" who turned out to be an undercover cop. "I was just trying to pick the girl up," Ramos explained to the *Boston Globe* reporter. He is serving a 2-year mandatory sentence without the possibility of parole for selling drugs within a "school zone."

> Undercover agents ran Stanley Forrester, a "novice" with "no prior criminal record," through five separate cocaine "buys" without arresting him. Their aim was to induce the 19-year-old father—a high school dropout employed in a "dead end" job—to sell more than 100 grams of the drug and therefore trigger the 10-year mandatory minimum sentence. "I should do some time for what I've done. But show some mercy. Give me a chance to change. . . . There is much better treatment for those who do violent things to society. They come and go. I deserve punishment—just not 10 years."[20]

"Massachusetts has overdosed itself on the drug war—filling the state's prisons with hundreds of nonviolent, low-level offenders," conclude the *Boston Globe* reporters.

Globe reporters also discovered that high-level offenders, with "assets to forfeit and information to trade," have managed to evade the mandatory sentences. In such cases, prosecutors have used their discretion to either charge high rollers with lesser offenses or drop charges altogether. "An average payment of $50,000 in drug profits," the *Globe* calculated, "won a 6.3-year reduction in a sentence for dealers."[21]

The case of Massachusetts drives home one difficulty associated with mandatory minimum sentences. Such sentencing schemes turn judges into machines (input type of drug plus volume of drug, output sentence). Real sentencing power is shifted to prosecutors, who determine the original charge. It is not surprising, therefore, that in a 1993 survey of judges belonging to the American Bar Association, 82% of state judges and 94% of federal judges (many of whom are conservative appointees of the Reagan and Bush administrations) expressed opposition to mandatory minimum sentences.[22]

There is no evidence that the proliferation of mandatory drug sentences has deterred would-be users and dealers.[23] Instead, the real impact of these laws has been to fill the prisons with drug addicts and small-time user-dealers. Between 1980 and 1992, largely because of the new mandatory drug laws, the share of arrested drug offenders sentenced to prison terms increased by 400%.[24] As a result, the proportion of new court commitments to state prisons for drug crimes (as opposed to violent, property, and public order crimes) increased from 13.2% to 30.9% between 1985 and 1995.[25]

Because the rate of incarceration for drug offenses has increased more rapidly than for any other category of crime, the composition of the nation's prison population has shifted. Between 1985 and 1996, the proportion of state prison inmates serving sentences for violent crimes fell from 54% to 47%, while the proportion serving sentences for drug crimes rose from 9% to 23%. The shift was still more dramatic in the smaller federal system: The proportion of violent offenders declined from 28.1% to 13.1%, while the proportion of drug offenders increased from 33.3% to 59.9%.[26]

Mandatory minimum drug sentences also contribute to minority over-representation among the imprisoned. First, these laws magnify the effects of the already disproportionate arrest of minorities for drug crimes. Second, some mandatory sentences have been written in ways that exacerbate racial disparities in incarceration. One example is the distinction made in the Federal Sentencing Guidelines and in most states between powder cocaine and crack cocaine. The two substances are pharmacologically similar, but the user populations of the two forms of cocaine are noticeably different. In the mid-1980s, when the federal government established its first mandatory penalty laws for drugs, powder cocaine was typically viewed as a recreational drug of upscale Whites, and crack cocaine was depicted as the scourge of the ghetto poor.[27] Around the time of the new federal law, about 9 out of 10 arrests

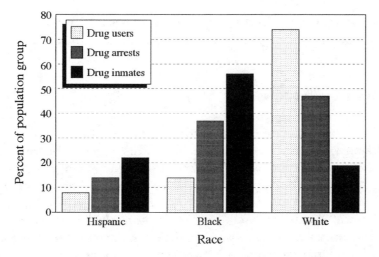

Exhibit 9.4. Race of Drug Users and Drug Offenders in the Criminal Justice System
SOURCE: National Institute of Drug Abuse, *Preliminary Results*; Maguire and Pastore, *Sourcebook of Criminal Justice Statistics 1996*, Table 4.10; *National Corrections Reporting Program 1992*, Table 1-13.

for crack but only 3 of 10 powder cocaine arrests involved an African American.[28] The decision by the U.S. Congress to impose a 5-year mandatory prison term (with a statutory maximum of 20 years) for five grams of crack but for 500 grams of cocaine therefore had a racially discriminatory impact.[29]

"School zone" laws are another example of mandatory sentences with discriminatory impact. These laws impose a mandatory penalty for drug sales within a specified distance—usually 100 yards—of a school. Schools, it turns out, are much more densely concentrated in inner city neighborhoods than in suburbs and exurbs. Thus the likelihood that an "ordinary" drug transaction (one not involving students or teachers) will be within the proximity of a school is much greater in largely minority neighborhoods.

Nearly three quarters of those admitted to state or federal prison for drug crimes in recent years were African American.[30] Between 1985 and 1995, the number of Whites behind bars for drug crimes increased by 306% while the number of Blacks increased by 707%.[31] In 1996, among state prison inmates serving time for drugs, 56% were Black, 22% were Hispanic, and 19% were White.[32] This large and growing disparity between Blacks and Whites in the incarcerated population (see Exhibit 9.4) is to a large extent a product of the surge in drug arrests in combination with the introduction of mandatory minimum penalties for drug offenders.

Three Strikes Laws

The baseball metaphor "three strikes and you're out" refers to new laws aimed, at least in official pronouncements, at incapacitating dangerous repeat offenders. Since 1993, 23 states and the federal government have passed laws bearing the "three strikes" slogan.[33] These laws typically oblige judges to increase penalties for second felony offenses and to sentence "three-time losers" to life in prison. Neither the particular circumstances, nor the seriousness of the crimes charged, nor the duration of time that has elapsed between crimes is given consideration. Moreover, like other mandatory penalties, three strikes laws oblige judges to ignore mitigating factors in the background of offenders, as well as their ties to community, employment status, potential for rehabilitation, and obligations to children.

Under Washington State's new three strikes law, 35-year-old Larry Fisher was sentenced to life in prison without the possibility of parole for robbing a sandwich shop of $151. At the time of the robbery, he was carrying a knife. Rather than display the knife, however, he jammed a finger in his coat pocket and pretended to have a gun. His previous two felony convictions were for stealing $360 from his grandfather and $100 from a pizza parlor. Fisher's lawyer argued that his client, who was raised in state custody after being pronounced "incorrigible" at age 12, is a product of the prison system: "We trained him that when he needs help to go out and commit a petty crime."[34]

Fisher's case is by no means extraordinary. California's three strikes law requires that the penalty for a second felony be doubled and that a third felony result in 25 years to life. To be convicted under the law, only the first two felony convictions must be for "strikeable" (serious but not necessarily violent) offenses; the third can be any offense, no matter how minor.[35] Among the more notorious three strikes cases in California have been individuals sentenced to serve 25 years to life for theft of a pizza slice,[36] theft of meat from a grocery store,[37] and theft of chocolate chip cookies from a restaurant.[38]

The extent to which these laws are being used in the states where they have been adopted varies significantly. In some states, such as New Mexico, virtually no offenders have been sentenced under the new "three strikes" laws. However, in a few states—especially Georgia and California—these laws have made a significant contribution to the expansion of the prison population.[39]

Although three strikes laws are typically represented as efforts to stem the tide of violent crime, in California, nonviolent property and drug offenders are the ones who have been most affected. One systematic review of the impact of the California law 2 years after its implementation found that 75% of third strike and 85% of second strike cases did not involve violence against persons. Indeed, more than half of all third strike cases involved the crimes of burglary, theft, and drug possession; less than 2% involved murder, rape, or kidnapping. The majority of both second and third strike offenders were classified as either "minimum" or "low medium" security risks for purposes of incarceration—a further indication of their nonthreatening nature.[40]

The long-term impact of three strikes laws on prison populations and costs may be devastating in states where they are widely used. Imagine what prison populations would be like if we were still incarcerating octogenarians whose crimes consisted of bar fights and auto thefts they had committed in the 1930s. One RAND Corporation research team has estimated that California's law will cause its prison population, already the largest in the nation at over 150,000, to more than triple within 20 years after implementation. The RAND team further estimated the cost of implementing California's three strikes law at about $5.5 billion per year over the next 25 years.[41] A 1996 study conducted by the same organization concludes that a million dollars invested in prisons would prevent 60 crimes a year, but the same amount invested in graduation incentive programs would prevent 258 crimes per year.[42]

The actual impact of the three strikes law in California may prove less daunting. In 1996, the California Court of Appeals ruled the law unconstitutional on the grounds that it shifted discretion over sentencing from judges to prosecutors.[43] (Under the original statute, prosecutors are permitted to ignore one or more strikes but judges are not). The state's revised three strikes law will allow judges the same discretion as prosecutors. The number of cases charged under the law will thus likely prove fewer than originally projected. In other states, however, judicial discretion remains tightly circumscribed. And two states, Georgia and South Carolina, recently passed two strikes laws.

Truth-in-Sentencing

Like the other sentencing innovations discussed in this section, truth-in-sentencing reflects the underlying shift from indeterminate, rehabilitation-oriented sentences to determinate sentences aimed at administering punishment. The new truth in sentencing rules require that felony offenders serve most of their court-ordered sentence prior to parole eligibility. By 1993, several states and the federal government had adopted one or another version of truth-in-sentencing. In the 1994 Crime Bill, however, the U.S. Congress mandated that states applying for $10.5 billion in federal assistance for new prison construction have laws on their books requiring that felony offenders serve at least 85% of their sentences.

"Truth" has a neutral ring to it, but its probable impact on prison populations is anything but neutral. In principle, the shift to "truth" would not necessarily entail longer sentences because judges would be free to order shorter terms. However, in the prevailing punitive environment, few judges are likely to be willing to pronounce prison terms that are substantially shorter than has been their habit in the past. It is probable, therefore, that these new laws will prove a major new source of prison overcrowding, as average time served per offense continues to increase.

In summary, as a net result of mandatory sentences, three strikes laws, and truth-in-sentencing requirements, as well as the generally punitive climate, offenders who once might have drawn probation are now going to prison, and prison-bound offenders are staying behind bars for longer stretches of time. Between 1980 and 1996, the number of new court commitments to state prison per 1,000 arrests grew by 29% for aggravated assault, 46% for burglary, 85% for larceny and motor vehicle theft, and 400% for drug offenses.[44] Also, according to estimates compiled by the National Corrections Reporting Program, persons committed to state prison in 1995 were expected to serve an average of 43 months behind bars, up from 38 months in 1990 and 31 months in 1985.[45]

RETURN OF
CAPITAL PUNISHMENT

The drive for tougher punishment has also prompted reinstatement of the death penalty. Since the 1976 United States Supreme Court decision in *Gregg v. Georgia* ended the decade-long moratorium on executions, nearly 5,000 offenders have been sent to death row. Between 1995 and 1998, the United States executed prisoners at an average rate of one per week. In 1997, 74 were executed, more than in any year since 1955. By the year 2000, more than 500 prisoners will have been executed in the United States since the return of the death penalty. Most will have been electrocuted or poisoned. A smaller number will have been gassed, shot with bullets, or hung by the neck. The condemned include numerous mentally retarded prisoners and prisoners who committed their crimes as juveniles aged 16 or 17.[46] The United States is the only Western democracy that still executes convicted criminals.

Death penalty opponents have made a number of arguments against the reinstatement and recent acceleration of judicial executions:

◆ Mistakes have been made in conviction and sentencing and inevitably will be made again in the future. Between 1973 and 1998, 75 people were released from death row after evidence of their innocence emerged.[47] In many cases, this evidence did not surface through the normal appeals process but as a result of new DNA tests and the investigations of journalists, students, and devoted attorneys. These prisoners were not simply removed from death row due to procedural errors related to conviction; rather, they were fully exonerated of the crimes for which they were condemned to die. Because most death row inmates are not fortunate enough to have such individuals scrutinizing their cases, it seems quite likely that innocent people have been put to death in recent years.

◆ The death penalty has never been shown to deter crime.[48] In fact, there is some evidence that the opposite is true—that executions *encourage* violence among those already "ready to kill."[49] Furthermore, states that execute in the largest numbers, such as Texas and Florida, also have the highest rates of homicide.[50]

◆ The death penalty is administered in a racially discriminatory fashion. Studies consistently show that prosecutors are far more likely to seek death and juries are more likely to vote for death in cases involving Black defendants and White victims.[51] In 13 death penalty states, significant race-of-offender bias has also been documented.[52]

◆ The death penalty is not cost effective: It costs more to litigate capital cases and execute people than it would to incarcerate them for life.[53] This is the case because of the necessary safeguards that must be in place to diminish the likelihood that an error will be made.

◆ Finally, although a majority of Americans now report that they support capital punishment, fewer than half favor the death penalty when they are given the option of a life sentence without the possibility of parole for convicted murderers.[54]

RETREAT FROM JUVENILE JUSTICE

In the late 1980s and early 1990s, the mass media provided saturation coverage of a putative wave of juvenile violence. In Denver, Colorado, for example, the city's leading newspaper printed 44 front page stories and 48 editorials on the topic of juvenile crime in the summer of 1993. During the previous summer, the paper had printed just two front page stories and three editorials on the topic.[55] Several prominent criminologists provided fodder for the unfolding media spectacle by dubbing juvenile offenders "superpredators" and warning of an unprecedented wave of youth violence as the proportion of young people in the population increases in the next decade.[56]

A quick review of the actual data on crime patterns in the 1980s and 1990s reveals a more complicated picture. In fact, juvenile arrests have accounted for the same proportion of all violent crime arrests—about 20%—for the past 20 years. To the extent that a juvenile crime wave occurred, it consisted largely of a spike, from about 10% to 17%, in the juvenile share of all homicide arrests (see Exhibit 9.5).[57] As we argued in Chapter 3, this jump in juvenile murder was largely a consequence of the arms race set in motion by the trade in crack cocaine.

Nevertheless, rising public concern about youth violence and declining faith in the capacity of the juvenile justice system to rehabilitate its charges has fueled major changes. Most significantly, states have expanded the range of offenses for which juveniles can be tried in adult court and sentenced to prison. Many states have also lowered the age at which juveniles become eligible for waiver into adult court. For example, in 1996, without holding hearings and after only brief debate, Massachusetts adopted a juvenile justice law that automatically transfers juveniles 14 years old and older who are charged with murder to adult court. The law also features the equivalent of a juvenile "second strike": prosecutors are empowered to charge any juvenile in adult court if he or she has

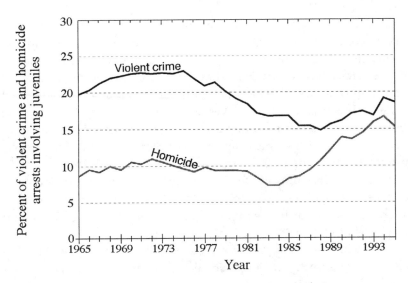

Exhibit 9.5. Juvenile Violent Crime and Homicide Arrests
SOURCE: Cook and Laub, "The Unprecedented Epidemic of Youth Violence," Figure 3.2.

already served time in juvenile detention on a previous charge. Similarly, in 1998, New York expanded its juvenile code to allow trial in adult court and possible detention for up to 7 years for youngsters 14 and older who carry loaded guns to school.[58] Meanwhile, in response to the school massacres in Arkansas and Colorado, the U.S. Senate debated legislation to expand federal jurisdiction over youth gun crimes and give prosecutors unreviewable power to charge and punish children as adults.

Here's how *Time* magazine recently summed up the trend:

> In the past five years, most states have made it easier to charge and punish children as adults. Thirteen-year-olds are therefore getting mandatory life-without-parole sentences, and there's nothing appellate courts can do to help them. We have effectively discarded these lives. Should we make 11-year-olds eligible for life behind bars? Nine-year-olds? Seven-year-olds? We are inching closer and closer to a moral line.[59]

PRISONER WAREHOUSING

Over the past two decades, about 1,000 new prisons and jails have been built in the United States. Despite this fact, at least 45 state prison systems are operating at or above capacity, and 22 states are under court order to contain the size of their inmate populations.[60] Double bunking inmates in cells and cubicles designed for one has become the norm in prisons across the country. So too has the practice of housing inmates in prison gymnasiums and dayrooms or in county jails. In some states, such as Massachusetts, Hawaii, and Vermont, overcrowding has prompted prison authorities to ship inmates out of state to the small number of prison systems with surplus capacity. The State of Texas, for example, incarcerates more than 5,000 inmates from 14 other states.[61]

Prison overcrowding causes massive loss of privacy for inmates and has become a significant source of prison violence. Moreover, in combination with the voguish views that in rehabilitation "nothing works" and that prisons are "country clubs," overcrowding has precipitated a wholesale retrenchment in programs for inmates. Education, vocational, rehabilitation, drug treatment, and recreation programs have been dramatically cut back in many prison systems.[62] Growing numbers of inmates are confined to their cells for 23 hours a day in "lockdown." One journalist described the consequences, based on an encounter with inmates at the New Folsom maximum security prison in California:

> Behind the need to blame others for their predicament and the refusal to accept responsibility, behind all the denial, lay an enormous anger, one that seemed far more intense than the typical inmate complaints about the food or the behavior of certain officers. Shirtless, sweating, unshaven, covered in tattoos, one inmate after another described the rage that was growing inside New Folsom. The weights had been taken away; no more conjugal visits for inmates who lacked a parole date; not enough help for the inmates who were crazy, really crazy; not enough drug treatment, when the place was full of junkies; not enough to do—a list of grievances magnified by the overcrowding into something that felt volatile, ready to go off with the slightest spark.[63]

In the words of two notable scholars, contemporary prisons represent a "new penology" that seeks not to deter or rehabilitate individual offenders but merely to warehouse the riskiest segment of the so-called urban underclass.[64]

Indeed, prison design increasingly expresses an overriding concern with the facilities' strictly custodial function. The new "supermax" prisons for hard-to-handle inmates are designed to minimize all human contact among prisoners and between prisoners and their guards. Prisoners are held for long stretches of time in states of virtual sensory deprivation. During their one daily hour of exercise, supermax inmates are released into narrow chain-linked cages resembling dog runs. In 1997, there were 57 supermax prisons spread across 36 states, housing more than 13,000 prisoners.[65]

At the less serious end of the spectrum are the new mass-produced, prefabricated ("cookie-cutter"), medium security prisons popping up in rural communities across the country. These new facilities are designed around huge dormitories that house 80 or more inmates in tiny cubicles, often double bunked. In the words of two industry insiders, these prisons reflect "the most critical factor in contemporary correctional facility design: low cost."[66]

The cutback in prison programs and the emergence of a more frankly custodial approach has occurred as general inmate populations have become increasingly diverse. Between 1980 and 1996, the proportion of women, Blacks, and Hispanics in the state inmate population increased, and the proportion of White males declined.[67] Over the same period, the annual share of new prison commitments for nonviolent (including drug) offenses increased from about half of all new prison commitments to nearly three quarters.[68] The share of inmates addicted to drugs and the share suffering from serious mental illness also increased markedly.[69] In short, although prisons continue to house many serious, dangerous offenders, they have increasingly become "dumping grounds" for nonviolent petty offenders, drug addicts, and the mentally ill.

And as they have always been, United States prisons continue to be violent and degrading places. In the words of the international human rights organization Amnesty International:

> Every day in prisons and jails across the USA, the human rights of prisoners are violated. In many facilities, violence is endemic. In some cases, guards fail to stop inmates assaulting each other. In others, the guards are themselves the abusers, subjecting their victims to beatings and sexual abuse. Prisons and jails use mechanical, chemical and electroshock methods of restraint that are cruel, degrading and sometimes life-threatening. The victims of abuse include pregnant women and the mentally ill.[70]

The routine violence and degradation of prison life is nothing new. The dramatic expansion of incarceration in the United States, however, means that the number of Americans subjected to these experiences is without precedent.

THE SURVEILLANCE SOCIETY

Concern about crime, together with the technologies and interests that have grown around it, has fueled and legitimated new strategies for keeping tabs on people. Surveillance practices long associated with prison have thus spilled into communities, as law enforcers and security guards increasingly monitor public places—a trend captured in the phrase "the prisonization of society." Nowadays, everyone is watched by security cameras and frisked electronically when entering and exiting stores and public facilities. Increasingly we are subjected to drug testing, background checks, metal detectors, and security gates.[71]

Schools are also increasingly deploying technologies once reserved for prisons:

> The sprawling new brick building next to the Dallas County Probation De-partment has 37 surveillance cameras, six metal detectors, five full-time police officers, and a security-conscious configuration based on the principles of crime prevention through environmental design. It is not the Big House. It is a schoolhouse: Dallas's $41 million state-of-the-art Townview Magnet Center, which has been touted as a model for high-tech school security since it opened for the new school year.[72]

The recent spate of school shootings will surely catalyze the trend toward "maximum security" schools:

> Going to class will be a little more like boarding an airliner for many U.S. pupils this year as educators try to prevent another year of bloodshed in America's schools. They'll walk through metal detectors and past police or other guards. . . . [They'll] be wearing photo ID badges and toting book bags made of see-through materials, if they're allowed to carry book bags at all. They're being given hot-line numbers to report, anonymously, signs that a schoolmate could turn violent, and some will face punishment if they don't. . . . Principals in places like Evansville, Ind., are getting handheld metal detectors for frisking students suspected of being armed. Each Evansville high school is getting a breath machine to test if students have been drinking.[73]

All Americans are experiencing stepped-up surveillance. Suspect populations, however, are kept under far tighter scrutiny. Black men, regardless of their involvement with the justice system, are routinely subjected to motor vehicle stops for the crime of DWB—Driving While Black.[74] Members of minority groups are often stopped in airports, bus terminals, and other public places and questioned about drugs, a practice legitimated by typically ambiguous "drug courier profiles," which open the door for unlimited police discretion.[75]

For individuals of all races who have been sentenced by a court, forms of surveillance range from regular probation, which might entail nothing more than a notification requirement concerning change of address, to electronic monitoring, day reporting, halfway house residency, and house arrest. Probationers and parolees suspected of substance abuse problems must submit to regular drug and alcohol testing. Sex offenders must register with local police, who in turn, in many jurisdictions, notify area residents and prospective employers.

In the United States, on any given day, nearly 1 in 3 young Black men is under one form or another of criminal justice supervision. In many U.S. cities, the proportion is even more dramatic. As noted in Chapter 1, in 1997, 50% of Black males in Washington, DC, between 18 and 35 years old were either in jail or prison, on probation or parole, out on bond, or wanted on an arrest warrant. In neighboring Baltimore, Maryland, in 1991, the comparable statistic was 56%.[76] In high-poverty "ghetto" neighborhoods, the percentage is still higher.

One unsurprising consequence of the expansion and intensification of community surveillance (e.g., probation and parole) is the burgeoning number of persons sent to prison for violating the conditions of community release. In 1980, new court commitments were responsible for 82% of prison admissions; parole and probation violations were responsible for 17%. By 1995, the share of prison admissions from the courts had declined to 64%, while the share stemming from conditional release violations surged to 34%. Although probation and parole were conceived, at least in part, as mechanisms for reintegrating offenders into community life, they have recently become major reasons United States prisons are bursting at their seams.

CRIMINAL JUSTICE AND DEMOCRACY

In the previous section, we discussed the most important developments in criminal justice policies and practices over the past two decades. These innovations have dramatically expanded the scale and scope of institutions of criminal justice in the United States. Many are rightly asking whether such costly policies have been effective in reducing crime. Some are even more concerned about the effect of these policies on the health and vitality of American democracy.

Crime Control

Defenders of the get-tough approach point to dropping crime rates as evidence that this approach is effective. Indeed, the violent crime rate has dropped considerably in the last several years, especially among older Americans. But a closer look reveals a more complicated picture. If filling the prisons reduces crime, then it ought to have begun to do so in the 1980s. Although the average prison sentence per violent crime tripled between 1975 and 1989, there was no discernable impact on the overall rate of criminal violence during this period.[77] The historical evidence also shows no correlation between patterns in incarceration and patterns in crime.[78]

In addition to the problematic historical evidence, the get-tough faction's argument is inconsistent with the current cross-sectional evidence. Between 1992 and 1997, for example, New York experienced one of the sharpest drops in serious crime in the country but one of the smallest increases in prison population (just 13.4%) and no increase in jail population.[79] Similarly, Canada's rate of violent crime has been dropping since 1991, but its rate of incarceration has increased only slightly.[80] In sum, the correlation between dropping overall crime rates and U.S. penal expansion in the 1990s appears to be a largely spurious one.

Filling prisons to the rafters fails to markedly reduce the rate of crime for many reasons:

◆ By the time offenders have accumulated enough charges to justify a long prison sentence, by and large they are on the verge of "maturing out" of crime.[81] Efforts to devise schemes to identify and incarcerate high-rate offenders before they have done much damage inevitably run the risk of "false positives." In the United States, we still do not imprison people on the basis of what they might do in the future.

◆ Incarcerating offenders for participation in the underground economy— for example, for drug dealing, gambling, or prostitution—often generates a "replacement effect": Persons who are otherwise law abiding are recruited to fill what amount to job vacancies in illegal trades.[82]

◆ Many people fail to make risk-benefit calculations before engaging in criminal behavior—or, having done so, they determine the risks to be acceptable. As criminologist Alfred Blumstein puts it, "There are some people who simply do not respond when a threat is presented to them. . . . For people who see no attractive options in the legitimate economy, and who are doubtful that they will live another ten years in any event, the threat of an extended prison stay is likely to be far less threatening than it would be to a well-employed person with a family."[83]

◆ As we argue in the next section, the experience of incarceration typically has contradictory effects on prisoners: It may motivate them to "go straight" to avoid another stint behind bars, but it also socializes offenders in the "code of the street," diminishes their chances of finding decent work, severs their ties to families and straight friends, and opens up new opportunities and contacts for criminal activities.

If the dramatic growth in correctional and prison populations does not explain the recent drop in serious crime, what does? Epidemiological research sponsored by the National Institutes of Health finds that drops in homicide by city are correlated with changes in the drug market, especially the crack market. These changes, in turn, are a consequence of the natural course of the drug epidemic and not law enforcement interventions.[84] This research supports the argument presented in Chapter 3 concerning the role of illicit drug markets in the etiology of homicide. Researchers seeking to explain the recent drop in serious crime have also cited declining opportunities in the illicit labor market, demographic changes, and declining levels of unemployment.[85]

Unintended Consequences

In his book *Search and Destroy: African American Males in the Criminal Justice System*, crime policy analyst Jerome Miller uses the term "social iatrogenesis" to describe the impact of the new "get tough" policies on drug dealing and crime. The term *iatrogenesis* refers to a "cure" that is actually responsible for the underlying illness. Miller uses the term in relation to crime policy to describe "a 'treatment' that maims those it touches and exacerbates the very pathologies which lie at the root of crime. It suggests that the criminal justice system itself has been a major contributor to breakdown in the inner cities."[86]

For example, consider the war on drugs. Like alcohol prohibition in the 1930s, the contemporary prohibition on marijuana, cocaine, and other drugs is directly responsible for the black market and for the violence it has spawned. Crackdowns on drug dealers, moreover, tend to drive up prices and profits and hence make the risk taking associated with the trade more rational. Similarly, massive drug arrests in effect create new "job openings" for dealers while setting the stage for battles over ever-shifting turf. Finally, prohibition has facilitated the formation of violent drug cartels, especially in Colombia, Peru, and Mexico, which have seriously destabilized those states. In a word, drug prohibition has proved a boon for daring criminals but has done little to stem the tide of drug use and abuse.[87]

More generally, the get-tough approach to crime and drug dealing fuels the material, social, and cultural ills that are the root causes of crime and drug dependency:

◆ These crackdowns divert resources from education and social welfare initiatives. In individual states, the trade offs are sometimes quite stark. In California, for example, between 1980 and 1995, the proportion of state spending devoted to prisons increased from 2% to 9.9% while the proportion devoted to higher education dropped from 12.6% to 9.5%.[88] Nationwide, more Black men are behind bars than enrolled in colleges and universities.[89] Spending on social welfare for the poor has also declined over the past two decades. In 1993, more money was spent nationwide at the federal, state, and local levels on the war on drugs alone ($31 billion) than on the nation's premier "welfare" program, Aid to Families with Dependent Children ($25 billion).

◆ Massive criminal justice interventions foster joblessness and family disruption. Most prisoners have unimpressive work histories. Having served time and earned the label *ex-con*, former prisoners typically find it more difficult than ever to secure stable employment.[90] Jobs and stable, two-parent families are among society's most important bulwarks against both poverty and crime.[91] Jobless men and men currently behind bars are among the least likely to get married and support children. Predictably, therefore, in high-poverty, inner city neighborhoods, both the rate of out-of-wedlock births and the share of unmarried women have risen in tandem with the incarceration rate of minority men.[92] Female-headed households are also disrupted by incarceration. For example, three fourths of the 54,000 women incarcerated for drug crimes have children.[93] Overall, nearly 2 million children have a parent in prison.[94] Thus criminal justice interventions increasingly represent a major cause of, rather than cure for, contemporary urban social ills.

◆ Massive criminal justice intervention in the lives of poor people and minorities increases their political and social isolation and reinforces the "code of the streets." In 14 states, exfelons are denied the right to vote, a fact that now translates into the disenfranchisement of 13% of African American men.[95] In the State of Florida, 31% of Black men are barred from voting because of criminal records.[96] In big cities, meanwhile, imprisonment has become virtually a formal "rite of passage" for young minority men, signaling their transition into a new way of life. Sadly, what prison best prepares its visitors for is survival in a violent, predatory world—that is, for survival on the inside. Beyond the prison walls, the skills and beliefs cultivated within prisons frequently lead ex-cons back into lives of crime, addiction, and trouble.

In summary, "get tough" policies are not merely ineffective strategies for crime reduction. To the extent that these practices contribute to social inequality, family and community breakdown, and a predatory street culture, they are increasingly significant causes of the very problems they purport to correct.

The Penal-Industrial Complex

As if the picture were not sufficiently grim, many analysts are now warning of the emergence of a "prison-industrial complex." These critics argue that the dramatic escalation of criminal justice spending has generated constituencies with vested interests in existing practices and perspectives. Police departments, for example, are political sacred cows, immune to budget cuts, and strong supporters of the war on drugs—an increasingly important source of revenue. The private prison industry is also rapidly expanding, profitable for investors, and politically well connected. More than 90,000 prisoners are currently held in private facilities, up from about 5,000 a decade ago.[97] In several states, unions of prison guards are well organized and politically influential. In California, for example, the guards' union played an instrumental role in funding the state's three strikes law and donated $1 million to the 1992 re-election campaign of Governor Pete Wilson.[98] Depressed rural communities in places like upstate New York have become an important constituency for new prison construction.[99] Finally, as any casual glance at one of the many new glossy magazines or web sites dedicated to the prison industry reveals, businesses that provide prisons with goods and services are flourishing. These include the telephone companies AT&T and MCI, which compete for lucrative prison contracts, and firms that build prisons, supply medical services, and market electronic surveillance and security devices.[100]

In short, concomitant with the growth of spending on criminal justice has been growth in the number of players with financial or professional interests in get-tough approaches to crime and drugs. This new "prison-industrial complex" poses a potential challenge to those who would scale back the criminal justice system.

CONCLUSION

In this chapter, we have examined the policies that have grown out of the politicization of crime. These policies have dramatically increased prison populations and the scope of the criminal justice system. They have not, however, contributed much to public safety. Indeed, the criminal justice system is increasingly a major source of the problems it is supposed to contain.

When we consider the criminal justice trends discussed in this chapter in connection with the simultaneous reduction in welfare programs, the contours of our general predicament become more clear. In the United States, we are increasingly substituting for the welfare state, based on the principles of mutual responsibility and common destiny, a neoliberal security state. In this emerging social formation, race and class inequalities harden, and social peace is accomplished not through the promise of full citizenship and a decent life but rather with the stick of punishment. In the next and final chapter, we discuss the choices still potentially within our grasp if only we find the political will to act.

10

❖ Alternatives

❖ ❖ ❖ In the previous chapter, we described and critiqued many of the anticrime policies adopted in the rush to "get tough" on crime. These policies are predicated on the view that crime and drug use are primarily the consequence of immoral individuals and a permissive criminal justice apparatus that fails to punish their immoral acts. As we have seen, this way of framing crime was initially promoted by conservative opponents of civil rights and welfare reform. For these political actors, the emotionally and racially charged crime issue—especially in the context of urban riots—provided a means of legitimating individualistic explanations of a range of social problems. Over the years, liberal politicians have largely accepted the premise that the best way to deal with social problems such as crime, delinquency, drug abuse, and even poverty is to "get tough." In short, the expansion of the criminal justice system has been the consequence of political activism. Political elites highlighted and framed crime-related issues in particular ways to realign the electorate and mobilize support for their political agenda. As a result of their initiative, the "get tough" approach to crime and drugs enjoys strong, bipartisan support, and virtually all politicians now accept the basic reorientation of domestic policy from social welfare to social control.

As we have made clear, we believe that this policy shift is based on unsound evidence and is an ineffective response to crime. Furthermore, many of the new "get tough" policies are inhumane and reflect a disturb-ing tendency to scapegoat, exclude, and stigmatize those now seen as members of an "underclass." The logical consequence of the war on crime—the incarceration of huge and growing numbers of people, espe-cially young minorities—is at least in political and moral terms a crime of the state, the significance of which is far greater than the petty crimes committed by many of today's offenders.

It was political activism that led us down this path, and it is through political activism that the current crime and social policies will be trans-formed. There is evidence that people are mobilizing for such change. As we discussed in Chapter 8, a variety of religious, social, and political organizations are challenging practices and policies associated with the war on crime, such as capital punishment, bans on needle exchange programs, and harsh mandatory minimum sentencing laws for drug offenders. There is also evidence of more general opposition to the prioritization of social control over social welfare. In Concord, Califor-nia, for example, over 2,000 high school students recently marched to protest declining educational funds, calling for "Education, Not Incar-ceration!"[1]

This type of activism is needed to raise awareness of the costs of the war on crime and to pressure politicians to adopt more sensible and just anticrime policies. In what follows, we identify some alternative policies and programs that, if implemented, would not only address crime and drug abuse in a more effective and humane fashion but would reduce the enormous human, social, and fiscal costs of incarcerating over 1.8 million people. Our discussion of these policies is informed by an awareness that lethal violence is the primary U.S. crime problem, that current policies do not address the causes of serious violence, and that massive incarceration is an ineffective and inhumane solution to the problems associated with social marginality.

SOCIAL INVESTMENT

One of the most effective ways we can reduce crime—especially the very serious problem of lethal violence—is to reduce poverty and in-equality. As we saw in Chapter 3, serious interpersonal violence is concentrated in very poor, racially segregated communities. Studies consistently report that these areas are characterized by "resource deprivation," including high levels of poverty, joblessness, and single-headed households.[2] It is not surprising that cities with more generous welfare programs have less poverty (especially among children) and lower levels of crime, including homicide.[3] Comparative studies provide further evidence of the association between poverty, inequality, and crime: Countries with higher levels of poverty and inequality are also characterized by greater levels of serious violence.[4] Thus, there is ample evidence that it is not welfare dependency but inequality and poverty that give rise to high levels of interpersonal violence.

Despite this, our politicians have systematically adopted policies that have exacerbated inequality and increased poverty, reversing the gains won earlier by welfare and civil rights activists. The welfare state retrenchment of the 1980s and 1990s has been particularly devastating for poor people in this country. Efforts to reduce social spending and remove families from the welfare roles resulted in a 33% decline in per-child welfare spending between 1979 and 1993.[5] The most recent revisions to the welfare system (contained in the 1996 Personal Responsibility and Work Opportunity Act) further tightened eligibility requirements. As a result, the number of families receiving Aid to Families with Dependent Children (AFDC) in the United States declined by another 42% between 1993 and 1998.[6] Declining wages for workers at the lower end of the occupational ladder and regressive tax policies have also contributed to heightened poverty and inequality. As a result of these developments, child poverty rates in the 1980s and 1990s have been about one third higher than in the 1970s.[7] The severity of poverty has also increased: The average payment required to lift the poor above the poverty line was more than 20% higher in the 1980s and early 1990s than in the 1970s.[8]

In sum, recent economic and policy developments mean that more children and their families in this country are poor and living in communities characterized by extreme and concentrated poverty.[9] As we have seen, this kind of poverty encourages serious violence. To begin to address these problems, we need to adopt policies that invest in communities and families and that reduce high levels of inequality. Examples of such policies include "living wage" legislation (laws that require employers to pay their workers enough to support a family above the poverty line); increased social support and services—especially for those raising children; universalization of child and health care; increased support for high-quality public housing; investment in mental health care;[10] and job creation programs that provide work for the unemployed and increase the provision of needed services.[11] These and other policies aimed at reducing poverty, inequality, and unemployment would not only ameliorate criminogenic social conditions but would be a first step in the creation of a more just and inclusive society.

HARM REDUCTION

Current drug control laws are aimed at eradicating all illegal drug use through punishment. This "zero tolerance" approach treats the official distinction between legal and illegal drugs as entirely rational and refuses to acknowledge any difference between recreational, experimental, or occasional drug use and chronic, uncontrolled, personally harmful, or socially disruptive drug abuse. The zero-tolerance approach also depicts drug use as an immoral individual choice that is unrelated to larger social conditions.[12] The costs of this approach to drug use are alarmingly high: These policies have made a significant contribution to the expansion of prisons and jails and, by contributing to family and community disruption and siphoning resources away from social services and programs, have aggravated the social conditions that give rise to the worst forms of drug abuse.

We should reorient our drug policies toward the goal of *harm reduction*. The harm reduction approach begins from the premise that consciousness-altering substances have been used in all known societies in which they are available, and that some drug use is inevitable. Furthermore, this approach suggests that not all drug use is personally or socially harmful. To the extent that it is, it may be the social context in which drugs are used or the policies that prohibit drugs that are responsible for at least some of this harm. The goal of drug policy should be to minimize the harm associated with drug abuse, not to punish those who use them.[13] This perspective has a number of important policy implications.

First, reorienting drug policy toward harm reduction would encourage policy makers to differentiate between drug use and drug abuse, to recognize, for example, that recreational use of some drugs does not constitute a major social problem. It would also imply the need to distinguish between drugs that pose a higher risk of serious harm and drugs that are relatively safe. Toward that end, we recommend that marijuana be legalized. Of the approximately 60 million Americans who have used marijuana in their lifetime, not one has died of an overdose.[14] And although smoking marijuana does pose certain health risks, so do many legal practices such as eating saturated fat and smoking tobacco. In fact, even among regular marijuana smokers, the amount of smoke and carcinogens inhaled is less than that inhaled by tobacco smokers. There is no evidence that marijuana is conducive to dependence or necessarily leads to the use of harder drugs.[15] Furthermore, legalization of marijuana would lead to the separation of the cannabis and hard drug markets so that in the course of buying pot, people would not also gain access to harder drugs. Finally, legalizing marijuana would reduce the prison, jail, and probation populations and decrease law enforcement costs considerably.[16] Indeed, a record number of marijuana arrests were made in 1997, nearly 90% of which were for simple possession.[17]

Orienting drug policy toward harm reduction would also require that we think critically about the origins of the harm that is associated with drug abuse. Advocates of the harm reduction approach distinguish between "primary" and "secondary" drug problems. Primary drug problems are those that result from the use of the substance itself, such as liver damage caused by alcohol use and lung damage that results from smoking tobacco and marijuana. By contrast, secondary drug problems are the consequence of the social context in which drugs are used or of drug prohibition itself. Turf wars, for example, are a consequence of the criminalization of drugs that increases their profitability and of the poverty-induced desperation that leads many to turn to the illegal drug market. Other examples of secondary drug problems include the spread of infectious diseases through the use of dirty needles (a consequence of a ban on needle exchange programs and other policies that restrict access to clean needles) and drug users' unwillingness to seek medical help for fear of detection.[18]

One of the most effective ways of minimizing both the primary and secondary harm associated with drugs is by addressing the social conditions that underpin our most serious drug problems. A substantial body of sociological research demonstrates that the distribution, seriousness, and consequences of drug abuse are shaped by social conditions. It is clear, for example, that those who have a "stake in conventional life" are much better able to establish control over their drug use[19] and are more likely to benefit from treatment programs.[20] There is also evidence that the impact of drug use by pregnant women on fetal health is mediated by diet, prenatal care, and other factors associated with social class.[21]

Dramatically reducing our reliance upon the criminal justice system in dealing with drug abuse would also reduce both primary and secondary drug problems. Making drug treatment more available and getting drug users out of the criminal justice system would not only reduce the size and expense of the system but would encourage people with drug problems to seek help rather than go underground. According to one recent study, investment in drug treatment is 15 times more "cost effective" than spending on federal mandatory minimum drug sentences.[22] Nevertheless, fewer than 1 in 6 individuals in need of drug treatment are admitted to programs each year.[23]

The most common argument against the harm reduction approach is that the threat of punishment is a significant deterrent and that removing it would result in dramatically higher rates of drug use. In fact, it is difficult to predict whether drug use would increase or decrease if drug penalties were reduced and the state took a "hands off" approach to drug law enforcement.[24] We think it is likely that experimental and recreational drug use would increase, perhaps temporarily, under such a decriminalization scheme.[25] But it is drug abuse—the uncontrolled use of "hard drugs"—that worries us, and we are not persuaded that punishing drug abusers while creating the very social conditions that encourage drug abuse is more effective or more humane than decriminalization. In fact, there is evidence that making the kinds of social investments discussed earlier—including health care, clean needles, and drug treatment services—instead of punishing drug abusers significantly reduces the harm that is associated with drug abuse, and may reduce the incidence of drug abuse as well.

The Dutch experience provides support for this argument. In the Netherlands, the use of cannabis is ignored and the use of "hard drugs" is treated as a social and health problem. Under this decriminalization model, the government ensures that the appropriate services are available to those with serious drug problems. Furthermore, through their more developed welfare state, the Dutch provide basic housing, nutritional, and medical services to all, thereby addressing the social conditions that exacerbate drug problems and reducing the incentive to get involved in the drug trade.

Decriminalization has not given rise to high rates of drug use or abuse in the Netherlands. In fact, the consumption of cannabis products declined following their decriminalization in the 1970s. Although the incidence of pot smoking has increased some in recent years, the percentage of people ever having used marijuana is still lower in the Netherlands than it is in the United States.[26] More important, the incidence of heroin use remains quite low, and crack is nearly absent in that country.[27] Finally, the Dutch government's efforts to ensure that those who inject drugs use clean needles means that rates of infectious disease remain quite low.[28]

Opponents of decriminalization argue that the Dutch experience is unique and does not apply to the United States.[29] The historical evidence from our own experience is contradictory. On the one hand, alcohol use did increase after the repeal of Prohibition, suggesting that the ban on alcohol consumption had some effect. On the other hand, the incidence of marijuana use did not increase in states that decriminalized marijuana in the 1970s.[30]

Although there are clearly important differences between the United States and the Netherlands, and the precise impact of decriminalization cannot be predicted, there is evidence that such a policy would reduce the harm associated with drug abuse without leading to unacceptable levels of drug use. The alternative is not an attractive one: The zero-tolerance approach has not reduced serious drug abuse, has led to the incarceration of many whose main problem is their addiction to drugs, and leaves many of these individuals without access to treatment and services that might enable them to establish control over their drug habit—and their lives. The harm reduction model, including the decriminalization of drugs, offers a more humane and potentially more effective way of addressing the problem of drug abuse and reducing our nation's overcrowded prisons and jails. This approach would also provide a useful framework for rethinking the criminalization of prostitution, gambling, and other victimless crimes.

ALTERNATIVE SENTENCING

The enormous and ever-increasing cost of incarcerating 1.8 million people—the majority of whom have committed nonviolent offenses—has led some to advocate the use of "intermediate sanctions," such as boot camps, house arrest, intensive supervision, and electronic monitoring. Advocates of such programs point out that they are significantly cheaper than incarceration and offer judges a wider range of options when making sentencing decisions.[31] Unfortunately, most of these programs only provide new ways of supervising and controlling offenders, and it is not surprising that they do not lower rates of recidivism.[32] Nor do these programs challenge the notion that by depriving offenders of their liberty, the wrongs they committed have been redressed and justice has been done.

More promising, from our perspective, are programs aimed at "restoring justice." Restorative justice programs derive their theoretical inspiration from early European and indigenous procedures for resolving disputes. In these systems, crimes are treated as wrongs against individuals rather than against the state. Restorative justice programs therefore stress "making amends" to victims rather than retribution for offenders. In the words of one proponent, restorative justice emphasizes "the importance of elevating crime victims and community members, holding offenders directly accountable to the people they violate, restoring emotional and material losses of victims, and providing a range of opportunities for dialogue, negotiation, and problem solving."[33] Toward these ends, restorative justice "conferences" allow victims a meaningful role in the dispute resolution process and are aimed at allowing offenders to make amends to those they harmed and, also, at identifying offenders' needs.[34]

Interest in restorative justice has grown tremendously in recent years. Programs based on its ideals have spread throughout Europe and are especially popular in Australia and New Zealand. In the United States, victim-offender mediation (a component of restorative justice programs) is being practiced in more than 290 communities. As of 1998, 15 states had drafted or proposed legislation promoting restorative justice programs within their juvenile justice systems. In 1994, the Vermont Department of Corrections went even further, identifying 50% of their probation caseload that they believed should be dealt with by Reparative Probation Community Boards made up of citizen volunteers.[35]

Although most of these programs are quite new, some early results of the first evaluation studies are trickling in. Preliminary results from the Reintegrative Shaming Experiments in Australia, for example, suggest that restorative justice conferences were more satisfying to victims, more emotionally intense for offenders, and perceived as more fair by both victims and offenders than traditional court procedures.[36] Analyses of outcomes in other locales are also positive, reporting victim and offender satisfaction, reduced victim fear and anxiety, more successful completion of restitution agreements, and reduced offender recidivism.[37]

Thus, there is evidence to suggest that restorative justice programs offer an attractive alternative to traditional criminal justice solutions to a variety of crimes and, if adopted, would help to reduce our nation's overcrowded prisons and jails. Despite this, it is important to keep in mind that in and of themselves, restorative justice programs do not reduce the scope of criminal law (only decriminalization of victimless crimes can do this). Nor do these programs do anything to alter the social conditions (especially concentrated poverty in racially segregated communities) that underlie our most serious crime problems. Still, with these caveats in mind, restorative justice programs appear to provide a promising means of settling disputes while reducing our reliance on institutions that incarcerate.

REHABILITATING REINTEGRATION

Not all offenders can or should be dealt with in alternative venues such as restorative justice programs. For those who serve terms in prison, we need to place greater emphasis on reintegration into society after release. Despite the fact that most of those in prison will eventually leave, very little emphasis is now placed on the need to facilitate their reintegration into society. The current tendency to ignore the (re)integration process marks a significant shift in penal policy.

For much of the 20th century, a philosophy called "penal-welfarism" served as the foundation of our penal system.[38] According to this philosophy, deviant behavior is at least partially caused by factors beyond the control of individual actors, but the nature of these factors varies from case to case. Criminal justice practitioners therefore identified rehabilitation—defined as the use of "individualized, corrective measures adapted to the specific case or the particular problem"—as the most appropriate response to deviant behavior.[39] The rehabilitative paradigm certainly did not preclude the use of incarceration, but juvenile justice, probation, and parole institutions were aimed at keeping those deemed "reformed" or "reformable" out of prison. And although efforts to "treat" or "correct" inmates were often underfunded and misguided, the possibility that offenders might be rehabilitated served as the primary ideological justification for incarceration.

The situation is quite different today. Rehabilitation is no longer the primary rationale for incarceration, probation, or parole, and this is why relatively little emphasis is now placed on reintegrating prison inmates back into society.[40] The rehabilitative approach was flawed in many ways, but it is also clear that the new approach does not work well. Despite increased efforts to supervise and control offenders in the community, rates of recidivism remain quite high for probationers and even higher for those released from prison, whether directly into society or onto parole.[41] In addition, the new emphasis on supervision and surveillance has meant that more and more parolees are being readmitted to prison for violating the "technical" conditions of their parole programs. These high rates of revocation for technical violations have made an important contribution to the expansion of the prison population.[42]

So many exprisoners, parolees, and probationers are rearrested primarily because the social circumstances that led them to stray from the straight and narrow in the first place have not improved—and, in fact, in most cases have worsened. In addition, incarceration makes it even more unlikely that exoffenders will obtain legal work and therefore more likely that they will reoffend.[43] High rates of recidivism may also reflect the propensity of the police to "round up the usual suspects," that is, people known to have a criminal record.[44] Addressing the social conditions into which offenders are released and reducing our reliance on the criminal justice system as a way of dealing with minor offenders might therefore lower rates of recidivism.

There is also reason to suspect that programs aimed at improving the reintegration of former prisoners would lower rates of recidivism. Exconvicts face what has been called the "reentry problem": the task of surmounting the psychological, social, and financial consequences of incarceration and reintegrating into mainstream society.[45] Providing needed social services (including drug treatment, counseling, education, and vocational training) to inmates, parolees, and some probationers would facilitate the reentry process.[46] A study of persons sentenced to intensive probation, for example, found that offenders who received drug treatment and other social services had lower rates of recidivism than those who were subjected to intensive supervision but did not receive such services.[47] Because the ability to find stable, legal work is a crucial component of the reintegration process, services aimed at helping exoffenders find decent jobs might also reduce rates of recidivism. An experimental program aimed at reintegrating violent young offenders by strengthening their ties to family and work (the Violent Juvenile Offender program, or VGO), for example, was quite successful in reducing recidivism.[48]

In sum, the current emphasis on surveillance and rule enforcement in probation and parole offices increases the likelihood that offenders will be reincarcerated but fails to address the causes of their offending. Significant declines in spending on education,[49] vocational training, and drug treatment[50] within prisons also leaves many exconvicts without the resources and capacities to deal effectively with the challenge of reentering society. Providing job training for prisoners, creating and locating jobs for probationers and exconvicts, subsidizing low wages, and providing incentives for employers to hire probationers and exconvicts would all increase the ability of former prisoners to sustain themselves through legal employment.[51]

TOWARD DISARMAMENT

As was discussed in Chapter 2, the extraordinary availability of guns has made a significant contribution to high rates of homicide in the United States. Americans fight, rob, and attack each other about as often as people living in other industrialized countries. But when we do, we often use guns, especially handguns.[52] And although we do not necessarily intend to kill, the ubiquity of guns means that, often, we do.[53]

The National Rifle Association (NRA) spends millions of dollars every year representing the interests of gun owners (and some would argue, the gun industry).[54] These advertising, public relations, and lobbying efforts result in the dissemination of a great deal of anti-gun control propaganda. Much educational and political work is needed to heighten the public's awareness of the role of guns in producing distinctively high rates of lethal violence in the United States. People need to be informed, for example, that over 75% of all murders in the United States involve guns and that many of these are the unintended consequence of fights and assaults—often between acquaintances and family members. Heightening popular awareness of these basic facts about gun violence would be a first step in changing cultural attitudes and public policy about guns.

In the long term, getting as many guns out of circulation as possible is one of the best ways we can reduce lethal violence.[55] The question is how to do this. Scholars in the field distinguish between laws that regulate the sale, possession, and use of guns and laws that ban the possession of handguns altogether. Laws regulating guns by restricting their sale, purchase, and ownership are common but vary tremendously across the United States. Most of these laws are designed to keep guns out of the hands of juveniles, persons with a history of mental illness, and persons with criminal records. The 1993 Brady Bill, for example, requires a 5-day waiting period so that officials can check the records of all prospective gun buyers. This "bad person" strategy has quite clearly not kept guns out of the hands of the "bad guys." Between 500,000 and 750,000 illegal gun transactions occur every year,[56] and studies report that only one sixth of all gun-using felons acquired their guns through legal transactions.[57] Furthermore, restrictions on the sale and ownership of guns have not reduced overall gun ownership. Thus, even if gun regulations did keep guns out of the hands of the "bad guys," they would not do anything to prevent the many unplanned and unintended homicides committed by people without criminal records or histories of mental illness.

Some have responded to the obvious failure of existing gun regulations by arguing for more intensified enforcement of these regulations and more severe punishment of those who violate gun laws. Evaluations of such efforts report mixed findings. For example, the Kansas City Gun Experiment, which involved intensive police efforts to locate and seize illegal firearms, reportedly led to a decline is serious violence.[58] In other cities, however, it is not clear that similar efforts have reduced violence.[59]

Recognizing the limited effectiveness of gun restrictions and regulations, some cities have banned handguns altogether. In 1975, for example, the District of Columbia banned the purchase, sale, transfer, and possession of most handguns. The city of Chicago also bans the sale and ownership of handguns. The evidence from follow-up studies suggests that these citywide bans have not appreciably reduced lethal violence. Opponents of gun control use these findings to argue that bans on gun ownership do not work.[60] Another interpretation of the failure of the citywide gun bans is that to be effective, a ban would have to be federal (otherwise, people can simply buy their guns in neighboring jurisdictions).

But calls for a federal ban on handgun ownership are quite controversial. Opponents point out that even if a federal ban on handguns were adopted, there would still be nearly 200 million guns in circulation, and some gun owners would not turn in their weapons simply because a ban was passed. Both illegal gun ownership and the black market in guns would continue to exist. A federally funded gun "buy-back" campaign might be the most promising way to address these problems. City-sponsored buy-backs have been implemented and been somewhat successful in reducing the number of guns in circulation.[61] Although even a federally funded, enthusiastically promoted buy-back campaign would not get all guns out of circulation, it would significantly reduce their numbers and, we believe, the number of persons killed by firearms.[62]

On the other hand, public opinion polls suggest that only about 40% of Americans currently favor banning the possession of handguns. From our perspective, this fact highlights the need for more political and educational work aimed at countering the progun propaganda of the NRA and the gun industry itself.

COMMUNITY POLICING

In recent years, "community policing" has received a great deal of attention. Although not well defined, the label generally refers to efforts to increase interaction between officers and citizens, including foot patrols, community substations, and sponsorship of block clubs and neighborhood watches. The hope is that such interactions will increase the amount of information officers receive, which will in turn help them to locate and address criminal wrongdoing. To varying degrees, community policing also aims to increase the ability of citizens to direct police activity. In its most progressive versions, community policing aims at "coproduction," a situation in which citizens and officers are coequal partners in planning crime control and neighborhood improvement activities.[63]

Coproduction has proven to be an elusive goal. Even when community policing is officially adopted, officers prefer to view citizens as simply their "eyes and ears": sources of information about what occurs in neighborhoods when the patrol cars are not around. Citizens, in other words, are seen not as coequal partners, but as junior deputies in police-sponsored crime control efforts.[64] To the extent that this is the case, the potential for democratic oversight of the police is eliminated.

The emergence and popularity of three other developments in policing threaten to further reduce the potential democratizing impact of community policing. The first is known as "problem-solving policing." Here, the goal is to transform the police from a reactive force—one that simply responds to 911 calls after incidents have already occurred—to a proactive one. Proactive police officers attempt to discern patterns of criminal activity and to eliminate them. For example, if officers analyze crime data and learn that many cars are being stolen in a particular neighborhood, they might saturate the area with patrols to deter criminals and catch more suspects. Despite the popularity of this approach, research suggests that the number of patrol officers and proactive policing strategies have no effect on crime rates.[65]

The second major reform movement goes by several names—broken windows, order maintenance, quality of life, and zero tolerance. The origins of this movement can be traced to the influential argument that broken windows and other instances of disorder are important causes of crime. According to this view, signs of disorder—like unfixed broken windows—diminish residents' responsibility for their neighborhood, which in turn leads to a progressive growth of wrongdoing. This theory implies that policing should focus on maintaining order and preserving a high quality of life to reduce crime. In New York City, this emphasis led to "zero tolerance" for any behaviors and people classified as disorderly, such as the streetside "squeegie men" who clean windshields for cash.[66]

NYPD officials and New York City Mayor Rudolph Guliani argue that these tactics are responsible for declining crime rates in New York City. Although these declines have been significant, studies suggest that a number of factors have contributed to the drop in crime that has occurred in New York City and elsewhere. As noted in Chapter 9, these include demographic changes, declining unemployment levels, and an increased number of emergency trauma centers at major urban hospitals.[67] A study sponsored by the Justice Department suggests that the decline of the crack cocaine market has been especially important, a finding that helps to explain why the homicide rate has dropped in Los Angeles and other cities that have not adopted the zero-tolerance approach and increased in cities (such as Indianapolis) that have not experienced a decline in crack use.[68]

There are also political problems with problem-oriented and zero-tolerance policing. Unlike the more democratic versions of community policing, neither of these police strategies allows for citizen oversight of the police. In addition, these strategies continue to emphasize arrests and the threat of punishment as solutions to crime. This is most obvious with zero-tolerance policing, which sets officers loose on any number of (potential) "troublemakers." In New York City, "order maintenance" has meant a 50% increase in misdemeanor arrests. A disproportionate number of those arrested for petty crimes (such as vagrancy, disorderly conduct, and loitering) are Black and Latino.[69] And it is no surprise that complaints about overaggressive officers have increased significantly in zero-tolerance New York.[70]

Finally, one of the most significant changes in policing has been the addition of paramilitary (SWAT) teams in police departments around the country. Encouraged by federal grants and asset forfeiture laws, many police departments formed paramilitary units. The initial impetus for this development was the war on drugs. The deployment of paramilitary units has increased tenfold since the early 1980s. A recent survey found that 90% of police departments in cities of over 50,000 and 75% of those in cities under 50,000 now have paramilitary units. Many of these units are known to be particularly aggressive. In Albuquerque, New Mexico, for example, one researcher concluded that the SWAT team "had an organizational culture . . . that led them to escalate situations upward, rather than de-escalating." Critics also argue that the widespread use of paramilitary units for drug arrests, suicide threats, and even the serving of warrants symbolizes the fact that the "war on crime" is a war on our own citizens.[71]

In sum, despite all the talk about community policing, policing practices have become more aggressive and often keep the community in a very passive position vis-à-vis the police. The more democratic versions of community policing that enhance citizen oversight of the police, combined with independent, civilian-run police review boards, offer a more promising alternative than the aggressive tactics of the NYPD and the paramilitary units that now operate around the country.

CONCLUSION

The policies just described offer alternative ways of addressing crime in the United States. Ultimately, whether or not these and other policy alternatives are explored and implemented will depend on political action. In the current context, politicians across the ideological spectrum are reluctant to challenge "get tough" policies for fear of being labeled "soft on crime." This fear prevents any rational discussion or criticism of current anticrime policies and is a significant obstacle to change.

The only way politicians will reconsider the policies associated with the war on crime is if they are convinced that there is popular support for doing so. As was discussed in previous chapters, there are signs that this is the case. Groups and organizations across the country are beginning to challenge the policies and priorities of the war on crime, and a more careful analysis of public opinion polls shows that many Americans favor policies that address the social causes of crime. There are also signs that the elite consensus favoring current crime policies is breaking down. Many federal judges, for example, have registered their opposition to mandatory sentencing laws for drug offenders, and some prominent conservatives are openly critical of the war on drugs. These developments are quite promising, for it is only political opposition to the war on crime that will lead policy makers to rethink their conviction that punishment is the best solution to a whole range of social problems that have their origins in poverty and social inequality.

Notes

CHAPTER 1

1. Kaufman, "Prison Life Is All Around," p. 10. The quotations from Harold Richard and Derrick Ross are verbatim from this article; the rest of Sabrina's story is paraphrased.

2. Bureau of Justice Statistics, *Probation and Parole Populations, 1997*; Butterfield, "Inmates Serving More Time," p. A10.

3. Donziger, *The Real War on Crime*; Windelsham, *Politics, Punishment, and Populism*; Currie, *Crime and Punishment in America.*

4. Currie, *Crime and Punishment in America*, p. 14.

5. Schlosser, "The Prison Industrial Complex."

6. Bureau of Justice Statistics, *Prison Statistics, 1997.*

7. Currie, *Crime and Punishment in America*; Irwin and Austin, *It's About Time.*

8. Donziger, *The Real War on Crime.*

9. Maguire and Pastore, *Sourcebook of Criminal Justice Statistics 1997*, Table 1.1; Donziger, *The Real War on Crime.*

10. On this debate, see Miller and Holstein, *Constructionist Controversies.*

11. The terms "strict constructionism" and "contextual constructionism" are taken from Best, "But Seriously Folks." Best also offers a perspective that is very similar to our own.

12. Ibarra and Kitsuse, "Vernacular Constituents of Moral Discourse."

13. Ibid., p. 28.

14. See Troyer, "Some Consequences of Contextual Constructionism."

15. Boggess and Bound, *Did Criminal Activity Increase During the 1980's?*; Langan, "America's Soaring Prison Population."

16. Butterfield, "Inmates Serving More Time," p. A10.

17. Lynch, "Crime in International Perspective," p. 11.

18. Maguire and Pastore, *Sourcebook of Criminal Justice Statistics 1997*, Table 4.6; see also Miller, *Search and Destroy*, p. 13.

19. Bureau of Justice Statistics, *Correctional Populations in the United States, 1995*, Table 1.21.

20. Bureau of Justice Statistics, *Prisoners in 1996*, pp. 10-11; Bureau of Justice Statistics, *Prisoners in 1997*, pp. 11-12.

21. Donziger, *The Real War on Crime*; Tonry, *Malign Neglect*.

CHAPTER 2

1. Hagan, *Crime and Disrepute*, p. 20.

2. Gurr, *Violence in America*; Haller, "Bootlegging"; Monkkonen, *Police in Urban America, 1860-1920*.

3. Lane, "On the Social Meaning of Homicide Trends in America."

4. Neither the NCVS nor the UCR measure the kinds of crimes that are committed by the rich or powerful, such as embezzlement, fraud, violations of health and safety regulations, and so forth.

5. Boggess and Bound, "Did Criminal Activity Increase During the 1980's?"; O'Brien, "Police Productivity and Crime Rates."

6. The percentage of victims of violent crime who reported their victimization to the police increased from 44.2% in 1978 to 49.8% in 1992. See McCord, "Placing Violence in Its Context."

7. O'Brien, "Police Productivity and Crime Rates"; Orcutt and Faison, "Sex Role Attitude Change."

8. LaFree, *Rape and Criminal Justice*.

9. Donahue, "Some Perspectives on Crime and Criminal Justice Policy." See also Miller, *Search and Destroy*, p. 27.

10. Rand, Lynch, and Cantor, *Criminal Victimization, 1973-1995*, p. 3.

11. O'Brien, "Police Productivity and Crime Rates," p. 204.

12. For a review of this literature, see O'Brien, "Police Productivity and Crime Rates." Although most agree that homicide statistics are fairly reliable, there are a significant number of missing persons whose fate is never determined, and some unknown number of these persons are undoubtedly murder victims (Windelsham, *Politics, Punishment, and Populism*).

13. O'Brien, "Police Productivity and Crime Rates"; Donahue, "Some Perspectives on Crime." However, some scholars still use the UCR data to support their argument that crime—especially violent crime—is far more common today than in previous decades. See especially Currie, *Crime and Punishment in America*.

14. Butterfield, "Inmates Serving More Time."

15. Miller, *Search and Destroy*.

16. Van Dijk and Mayhew, *Experiences of Crime Across the World*, p. 199. See also Donziger, *The Real War on Crime*, and Tonry, *Malign Neglect*, p. 198.

17. See chap. 3 in Zimring and Hawkins, *Crime Is Not the Problem*.

18. See Kurki, "International Crime Survey," p. 4. Of the five countries that participated in all three surveys administered since 1988, only the United States shows consistent decreases in the crime rate.

19. Bureau of Justice Statistics, *Crime and Justice in the United States and in England and Wales, 1981-1996*.

20. Lynch, "Crime in International Perspective," p. 11. See also Zimring and Hawkins, *Crime Is Not the Problem.*

21. Zimring and Hawkins, *Crime Is Not the Problem.*

22. Maguire and Pastore, *Sourcebook of Criminal Justice Statistics 1994,* Table 6.32.

23. Bureau of Justice Statistics, *Prisoners in 1996,* Table 15.

24. Maguire and Pastore, *Sourcebook of Criminal Justice Statistics 1997,* Table 6.29.

25. See Currie, *Crime and Punishment in America,* for a critique of this argument.

26. Ibid, pp. 56-57.

CHAPTER 3

1. Reiman, *The Rich Get Richer;* Mokhiber, *Corporate Crime and Violence;* Smith, *Resisting Reagan.*

2. Lynch, "Crime in International Perspective," p. 11.

3. Irwin and Austin, *It's About Time*

4. Courtright, *Violent Land,* pp. 249-50.

5. Zimring and Hawkins, *Crime Is Not the Problem,* p. 126.

6. Zimring and Hawkins, *Crime Is Not the Problem.* See also Surette, *Media, Crime and Criminal Justice,* and Reiner, "Media Made Criminality."

7. Wilson, *When Work Disappears;* Currie, *Crime and Punishment in America.*

8. Zimring and Hawkins, *Crime Is Not the Problem,* pp. 124-37.

9. Zimring, "Is Gun Control Likely to Reduce Violent Killings?"

10. Zimring and Hawkins, *Crime Is Not the Problem,* p. 108.

11. Ibid.

12. Ibid.

13. Ibid., p. 114.

14. Wright and Rossi, *Armed and Considered Dangerous.*

15. Sloan et al., "Tale of Two Cities," quoted in Reiss and Roth, *Understanding and Preventing Violence,* p. 268.

16. Blumstein and Cork, "Linking Gun Availability to Youth Gun Violence."

17. Cook and Laub, "The Unprecedented Epidemic of Youth Violence."

18. Reiss and Roth, *Understanding and Preventing Violence,* p. 256.

19. Wallman, "Disarming Youth."

20. Wilkinson and Fagan, "The Role of Firearms in Violence 'Scripts,' " p. 73.

21. Gurr, *Violence in America.*

22. Krahn, Hartnagel, and Gartrell, "Income Inequality and Homicide Rates."

23. Messner, "Economic Discrimination and Societal Homicide Rates."

24. Hagan, *Crime and Disrepute.*

25. Walker, Spohn, and DeLone, *The Color of Justice,* p. 62.

26. Durkheim, *Suicide.*

27. Messner, "Economic Discrimination," p. 598. James Gilligan, however, provides a rather compelling account of the unmediated role of relative deprivation in the production of violence. See Gilligan, *Violence.*

28. Sherman et al., *Preventing Crime,* ch. 3, p. 1.

29. Ibid, p. v.

30. For an explication of this type of approach, see Sampson, "The Embeddedness of Child and Adolescent Development," pp. 31-77.

31. Shaw and McKay, *Juvenile Delinquency and Urban Areas*. For discussion of the relevance of Shaw and McKay's work for contemporary research, see Sampson and Wilson, "Race, Crime and Urban Inequality."

32. Messner and Tardiff, "Economic Inequality and Levels of Homicide"; Sampson, "Urban Black Violence," p. 366; Land, McCall, and Cohen, "Structural Co-Variates of Homicide Rates"; Zimring and Hawkins, *Crime Is Not the Problem.*

33. Wilson, *The Truly Disadvantaged*. The acronym AFDC refers to Aid to Families with Dependent Children.

34. Sampson, "The Embeddedness of Child and Adolescent Development."

35. Messner and Tardiff, "Economic Inequality."

36. Sullivan, *Getting Paid*. In this book, high poverty areas are defined as neighborhoods in which at least 30% of residents are poor.

37. Loic Waquant, cited in Sampson, "The Embeddedness of Child and Adolescent Development."

38. Wilson, *When Work Disappears*. In this book, high poverty areas are defined as census tracts in which at least 40% of residents are poor.

39. State Department of Labor, quoted in Perez-Pena, "New York's Income Gap Largest in the Nation," p. A14.

40. Wilson, *The Truly Disadvantaged.*

41. Sampson, "Urban Black Violence." Significantly, Sampson found that the percentage of households headed by a female was also significantly related to serious crime among Whites.

42. "Because segregation concentrates disadvantage, shifts in black poverty rates comparable with those observed during the 1970s have the power to transform the socioeconomic character of poor black neighborhoods very rapidly and dramatically, changing a low-income black community from a place where welfare-dependent, female-headed families are a minority to one where they are the norm, producing high rates of crime, property abandonment, mortality and educational failure." See Massey, "American Apartheid."

43. Logan and Molotch, *Urban Fortunes*, p. 114.

44. Wilson, *When Work Disappears*, p. 48. See also Levine and Harmon, *The Death of an American Jewish Community.*

45. Massey, "American Apartheid," p. 354.

46. Hagan, *Crime and Disrepute*, p. 97.

47. Bourgeois, *In Search of Respect.*

48. Goldstein et al., "Crack and Homicide in New York City, 1988."

49. Zimring and Hawkins, *Crime Is Not the Problem*, p. 248. The authors point out that New York City and Washington, DC, have larger than average drug industries. They estimate that, nationwide, drug-related homicides comprise 10% to 25% of all homicides (p. 144).

50. Goldstein et al., "Crack and Homicide in New York City."

51. Ibid, pp. 120-21.

52. Tonry, *Malign Neglect*, p. 109.

53. Hagan, *Crime and Disrepute*, p. 97.

54. See Chapter 9 for a more detailed discussion of the impact of the war on drugs on African American men.

55. Freeman, "Crime and the Employment of Disadvantaged Youths"; Petersilia and Turner, with Peterson, *Prison versus Probation in California*; Western and Beckett, "How Unregulated Is the U.S. Labor Market?"

56. Anderson, "The Code of the Streets," p. 82.

57. Wilson, *When Work Disappears*.
58. Anderson, "The Code of the Streets," p. 82.
59. Ibid., p. 88.
60. Bourgeois, "In Search of Horatio Alger, p. 66.
61. Anderson, "The Code of the Streets," p. 89.
62. Ibid., p. 92.
63. "Dissed" as in "disrespected." Anderson, "The Code of the Streets," p. 92.
64. Miller, *Search and Destroy*.
65. See Zimring and Hawkins, *The Scale of Imprisonment*.
66. Tonry, *Malign Neglect*.
67. See Butterfield, "Drop in Homicide Rates," p. A10.

CHAPTER 4

1. Kitsuse and Spector, "Toward a Sociology of Social Problems."
2. Edelman, *Constructing the Political Spectacle*; Gamson, *Talking Politics*; Gamson and Lasch, "The Political Culture of Social Welfare Policy"; Gamson and Modigliani, "The Changing Culture of Affirmative Action"; Gusfield, "Moral Passage"; Hilgartner and Bosk, "The Rise and Fall of Social Problems."
3. Garland, *Punishment and Modern Society*, p. 20.
4. Civil rights activists did break southern state laws, but they did so to draw attention to the unconstitutionality of those laws. Thus it is not clear that these civil rights tactics can be accurately described as "criminal" or even as "civil disobedience."
5. Cronin, Cronin, and Milakovich, *The U.S. Versus Crime in the Streets*.
6. Justice Whittaker, quoted in "Blamed in Crime Rise," p. 15.
7. Nixon, "If Mob Rule Takes Hold in the US," p. 64.
8. Quoted in Caplan, "Reflections on the Nationalization of Crime, 1964-8," p. 585.
9. "Goldwater's Acceptance Speech," p. A9.
10. "Goldwater at Illinois State Fair," p. A12.
11. Barkan and Cohn, "Racial Prejudice and Support for the Death Penalty for Whites"; Bennett and Tuchfarber, "The Social Structural Sources of Cleavage on Law and Order Policies"; Cohn and Halteman, "Punitive Attitudes Toward Criminals"; Corbett, "Public Support for 'Law and Order.' "
12. Omi, *We Shall Overturn*; Omi and Winant, *Racial Formation in the United States*.
13. Piven and Cloward, *Poor People's Movements*.
14. Johnson, "Remarks on the City Hall Steps," p. 1371.
15. Quoted in Edsall and Edsall, *Chain Reaction*, p. 51.
16. Quoted in Baker, *Miranda*, p. 245. On the stump, Wallace often concluded with the more baldly racist formulation: "[he] didn't get any watermelon to eat when he was 10 years old." Quoted in Carter, *The Politics of Rage*, p. 313.
17. Quoted in Ginsberg, *Race and the Media*.
18. Ibid, pp. 185-6. Katz and others show that the focus on the alleged misbehaviors of the poor has been central to their reconstruction as an undeserving underclass. See also Gans, *The War Against the Poor*; Morris, *Dangerous Classes*; and Schram, *Words of Welfare*.
19. Moynihan, *The Politics of a Guaranteed Income*, p. 42. On the "culture of poverty," see Lewis, *La Vida*.
20. Quoted in Matusow, *The Unraveling of America*, p. 143.
21. "President Forms Panel," p. A1.

22. Johnson, "Special Message to the Congress on Law Enforcement," p. 264.

23. Bayer, "Crime, Punishment and the Decline of Liberal Optimism."

24. Quoted in Marion, *A History of Federal Crime Control Initiatives*, p. 70.

25. Quoted in Matusow, *The Unraveling of America*, p. 401.

26. Republican National Party, "Republican Party Platform of 1968," p. 987.

27. Phillips, *The Emerging Republican Majority*, p. 39.

28. Jonathon Reider, "The Rise of the Silent Majority," p. 243.

29. Edsall and Edsall, *Chain Reaction*, p. 41.

30. Phillips, *The Emerging Republican Majority*.

31. Ehrlichmann, *Witness to Power*, p. 233.

32. Omi and Winant, *Racial Formation in the United States*.

33. Nixon, no less than his strategists, understood the significance of symbolic communication. Looking ahead to the 1972 campaign, he instructed his aides to "scrape away all the crap and just pick three issues that will give us a sharp image." The aides "shouldn't be concerned if it is something we will actually accomplish. . . . Rather, we should look in terms of how we create issues. We need an enemy." Quoted in Carter, *The Politics of Rage*, p. 398.

34. Edsall and Edsall, *Chain Reaction*, p. 150.

35. Epstein, *Agency of Fear*, p. 65.

36. Quoted in Epstein, *Agency of Fear*, p. 69.

37. Baum, *Smoke and Mirrors*, p. 41.

38. Milakovich and Weis, "Politics and Measures of Success." See also Wright, *The Great American Crime Myth*, pp. 35-37, for a discussion of other innovative techniques used by the Nixon administration to create the impression that the rate of crime was decreasing.

39. As Zimring and Hawkins point out, the traditional allocation of crime control responsibilities "is one in which the federal government plays a distant secondary role to that of the states and local governments." But because the Harrison Narcotics Act established federal responsibility for the enforcement of narcotics laws, the federal government has played an important role in drug control throughout the 20th century. See Zimring and Hawkins, *Search for Rational Drug Control Policy*, pp. 160-161. Heymann and Moore also note that the regulation of alcohol and other drugs has played an important role in expanding the scope of federal criminal jurisdiction (Heymann and Moore, "The Federal Role in Dealing With Violent Street Crime," p. 105).

40. The adoption of this line of reasoning helps to account for the Nixon administration's somewhat surprising support for methadone maintenance programs, aimed largely at reducing the likelihood that addicts would steal to finance their habit.

41. Baum, *Smoke and Mirrors*.

42. Ibid, p. 75.

43. Only when faced with "exigent circumstances"—a situation in which a suspect may have concealed a weapon or be able to easily destroy evidence—were law enforcement agents permitted to seize evidence without a warrant (Davey, *The New Social Contract*).

44. Quoted in Ibid., p. 106.

45. Bertram et al., *Drug War Politics*.

46. *United States v. Robinson*, quoted in Davey, *The New Social Contract*, p. 124.

47. Davey, *The New Social Contract*, p. 107.

48. Baker, *Miranda*.

49. Baum, *Smoke and Mirrors*, pp. 86-7, 93, 97.

50. As Bertram et al. point out, however, it is also true that although Presidents Ford, Carter, and (later) Clinton did not emphasize the crime and drug issues, neither did they attempt to reverse the expansion of the criminal justice system or issue any fundamental challenge to the logic of the wars on crime and drugs. Drug-law enforcement budgets, for example, continued to increase and reached $855 million by 1980 (Bertram et al., *Drug War Politics*, p. 110). The fact that criminal justice institutions continued to expand during these times of relative political quiet, they argue, reveals the ability of those bureaucracies with law enforcement responsibilities to influence the political agenda: "When Presidents such as Nixon, Reagan and Bush wanted to escalate drug enforcement, this drug control apparatus provided them with a firm basis and allies.... But even during times of relative calm ... the drug control bureaucracy has exerted pressures to sustain and even expand the drug war" (p. 126).

51. U.S. Department of Justice, *Attorney General's Task Force on Violent Crime*, p. v.

52. Davis, "The Production of Crime Policies," p. 127.

53. Reagan, "Remarks at the Conservative Political Action Conference Dinner," p. 252.

54. Reagan, "Remarks at the Annual Convention of the Texas State Bar Association in San Antonio," p. 1013.

55. Ibid., p. 886.

56. Reagan, "Remarks at a White House Ceremony Observing Crime Victims Week," p. 553.

57. Reagan, "Radio Address to the Nation on Proposed Crime Legislation," pp. 225-226.

58. For a review of this literature, see Hannon and DeFronzo, "The Truly Disadvantaged."

59. Reagan, "Remarks to Members of the National Governors Association," p. 238.

60. Reagan, "Remarks at a Fundraising Dinner," p. 672.

61. Flanagan, "Change and Influence in Popular Criminology."

62. "FBI Director Weighs War," p. A27.

63. Executive Office of the President, *Budget of the U.S. Government*.

64. Ibid.

65. Baum, *Smoke and Mirrors*, p. 145.

66. David Stockman, *The Triumph of Politics*, pp. 153-4.

67. Ibid., p. 154.

68. Bush, *Address to Students*.

69. See Baum, *Smoke and Mirrors*, p. 221.

70. Gallup, *The Gallup Poll*; see also Roberts, "Public Opinion, Crime and Criminal Justice."

71. For an extended discussion of the "crack panic" of 1986, see Reinarman and Levine, "Crack in Context"; and Beckett and Sasson, "The Media and the Construction of the Drug Crisis in America."

72. Stutman, *Dead on Delivery*, p. 148.

73. Ibid., p. 217.

74. Danielman and Reese, "Intermedia Influence and the Drug Issue."

75. Windelsham, *Politics, Punishment, and Populism*, p. 26.

76. Ibid.

77. Quoted in Karst, *Law's Promise, Law's Expression*, pp. 73-74.

78. Michelowski, "Some Thoughts Regarding the Impact of Clinton's Election," p. 6.

79. Democratic National Committee, "The 1992 Democratic Party Platform."

80. Bill Clinton, quoted in "Clinton Nurtures High Hopes."

81. Bill Clinton, quoted in Bertram et al., *Drug War Politics*, p. 117.

82. Baum, *Smoke and Mirrors*, p. 335.

83. Windelsham, *Politics, Punishment, and Populism*, p. 31; Idelson, "Democrat's New Proposal Seeks Consensus by Compromise."

84. According to one study, despite the fact that assault weapons are used in only a fraction of all gun murders, the Crime Bill's ban on these weapons contributed to an estimated 6.7% decline in total gun murders between 1994 and 1995 (The Urban Institute, cited in Windelsham, *Politics, Punishment, and Populism*, p. 123).

85. Windelsham, *Politics, Punishment, and Populism*, p. 50. Windelsham further argues that ultimately, the Congressional Black Caucus's main accomplishment was to sustain funding for prevention efforts, minimal as it was.

86. *Los Angeles Times, Public Opinion Survey*. A copy of this unpublished survey may be obtained from the authors.

87. Windelsham, *Politics, Punishment, and Populism*, p. 68.

88. For example, a *Washington Post*-ABC News Poll found that 39% of those polled trusted the Democrats to handle the crime problem; 32% had more faith in the Republicans. See Poveda, "Clinton, Crime and the Justice Department," p. 76.

89. Idelson, "Tough Anti-Crime Bill Faces Tougher Balancing Act." A small group of liberal Democrats in the Senate did propose an alternative package aimed at improving police training, abolishing mandatory sentencing statutes, and tightening gun restrictions. Members of the Congressional Black Caucus also criticized this proposed legislation, especially its rejection of the Racial Justice Act, which would have allowed defendants to use evidence of racial bias to challenge their death sentences. Neither of these efforts was ultimately successful.

90. Windelsham, *Politics, Punishment, and Populism*, p. 50.

91. Idelson, "Block Grants Replace Prevention, Police Hiring in House Bill."

92. Masci, "$30 Billion Anti-Crime Bill Heads to Clinton's Desk."

93. Windelsham, *Politics, Punishment, and Populism*.

94. Quoted in Kramer, "From Sarajevo to Needle Park," p. 29.

95. As we will see in Chapter 7, these sentiments co-exist with support for "tough" measures such as three-strikes laws and the death penalty.

96. See Currie, *Crime and Punishment in America*.

CHAPTER 5

1. Surette, *Media, Crime and Criminal Justice*, pp. 54-55.

2. Ibid.; Dominick, "Crime, Law Enforcement and the Mass Media."

3. Surette, *Media, Crime and Criminal Justice*, pp. 55-56.

4. Gorn, "The Wicked World," pp. 11-12.

5. Surette, *Media, Crime and Criminal Justice*, p. 55; Gorn, "The Wicked World," p. 9.

6. Surette, *Media, Crime and Criminal Justice*, p. 58.

7. Ibid., p. 159.

8. Ibid., p. 67.

9. Chiricos, Eschholz, and Gertz, "Crime, News and Fear of Crime."

10. "Living in Fear," p. B1.

11. On crime coverage in Denver, Colorado, see Colomy and Greiner, "Innocent Blood." On Boston, Massachusetts, see Sasson, "Beyond Agenda Setting."

12. "Living in Fear."

13. Cited in Surette, *Media, Crime and Criminal Justice*, p. 68.

14. Marsh, "A Comparative Analysis of Crime Coverage," p. 73.

15. Beckett, "Culture and the Politics of Signification"; Skidmore, "Telling Tales."

16. Reiner, "Media Made Criminality."

17. Surette, "Predator Criminals as Media Icons," pp. 134-5. See also Barak, "Between the Waves."

18. Soothhill and Walby, *Sex Crimes in the News*.

19. Beirne and Messerschmidt, *Criminology*.

20. Entman, "Representation and Reality."

21. The local news study examined three stations in Chicago, Illinois, between December 1989 and May 1990. See Entman, "Blacks in the News." The network news study examined 30 days of coverage on ABC, CBS, and NBC in 1990. See Entman, "Representation and Reality."

22. Reiner, "Media Made Criminality," p. 201; Chermak, *Victims in the News*; Elias, *Victims Still*.

23. Chiricos et al., "Crime, News and Fear of Crime," p. 354.

24. Yardley, "One Precinct," p. A1.

25. Reiner, "Media Made Criminality."

26. Iyengar, *Is Anyone Responsible?*

27. Reiner, "Media Made Criminality," p. 202; Nava, "Cleveland and the Press."

28. Nava, "Cleveland and the Press"; Iyengar, *Is Anyone Responsible?*

29. Sasson, *Crime Talk*; Elias, *Victims Still*; Barlow, "Race and the Problem of Crime."

30. For example, one study examined opinion columns published in six metropolitan newspapers from 1990 through 1991. The frame that attributed crime to failures of the criminal justice system was expressed in 55% of the columns. The frames that attributed crime to either poverty or family breakdown were each visible in about one third of the columns. See Sasson, *Crime Talk*. Studies of news weeklies report coverage that is even more one sided in favor of the "faulty system" perspective. See Elias, *Victims Still*, and Barlow, "Race and the Problem of Crime."

31. Ericson, Baranek, and Chan, *Representing Order*; Hall et al., *Policing the Crisis*. Indeed, Ericson et al. estimate that the proportion of news stories that focused on "deviance and control" was about 45% in newspapers, between 47% and 60% on television, and between 64% and 71% on the radio (pp. 239-42).

32. Garland, *Punishment and Modern Society*, chap. 2.

33. Best, *Random Violence*.

34. Fishman, "Crime Waves as Ideology"; Sherizen, "Social Creation of Crime News."

35. Beckett, "Media Depictions of Drug Abuse"; Beckett, *Making Crime Pay*; Chermack, "Crime in the News Media"; Elias, *Victims Still*; Fishman, "Crime Waves as Ideology."

36. Gans, *Deciding What's News*; Morgan, *The Flacks of Washington*; Nimmo, *Newsgathering in Washington*; Sigal, *Reporters and Officials*; Whitney et al., "Source and Geographic Bias in Television News 1982-4."

37. Becker, "Whose Side Are We On?"; Gans, *Deciding What's News*; Hall et al., *Policing the Crisis*; Herman and Chomsky, *Manufacturing Consent*; Schudson, *Discovering the News*.

38. Gans, *Deciding What's News*; Tuchman, *Making News*; Whitney et al., "Source and Geographic Bias."

39. Schlesinger and Tumber, *Reporting Crime*; Kasinsky, "Patrolling the Facts."

40. Reiner, "Media Made Criminality."

41. Lawrence, "Accidents, Icons and Indexing"; Herman and Chomsky, *Manufacturing Consent*; Schlesinger, "Rethinking the Sociology of Journalism"; Schlesinger, Tumber, and Murdock, "The Media Politics of Crime and Criminal Justice."

42. Erickson et al., *Representing Order*; Beckett, "Media Depictions of Drug Use"; Molotch and Lester, "News as Purposive Behavior."

43. Beckett, "Media Depictions of Drug Use"; Beckett, *Making Crime Pay*.

44. McCombs and Shaw, "The Agenda-Setting Function of the Mass Media," p. 177

45. Bennett, *Public Opinion in American Politics*; Iyengar and Kinder, *News That Matters*; Leff, Protess, and Brooks, "Crusading Journalism."

46. Gerbner and Gross, "Living With Television."

47. This study examined a random sample of residents of Tallahassee, Florida in 1994; see Chiricos et al., "Crime, News and Fear of Crime." For research demonstrating similar media effects for newspaper coverage of crime, see Liska and Baccaglini, "Feeling Safe by Comparison."

48. See, for example, Sparks, *Television and the Drama of Crime*.

49. Roberts and Edwards, "Contextual Effects in Judgements."

50. Ibid.; Roberts and Doob, "News Media Influence on Public Views on Sentencing"; Surette, *Media, Crime, and Criminal Justice*.

51. Iyengar, "Effects of Framing," p. 196.

52. For additional studies of the effects of media frames, see Beckett, "Media Depictions of Drug Use"; Gamson, *Talking Politics*; Iyengar, *Is Anyone Responsible?*; Roberts and Doob, "News Media Influence"; and Sasson, *Crime Talk*.

53. See Surette, *Media, Crime and Criminal Justice*, p. 205.

54. Leukefeld, "The Role of the National Institute."

55. Roberts, "Public Opinion, Crime and Criminal Justice."

56. Beckett, *Making Crime Pay*.

57. "Reagan: Drugs Are the 'No. 1' Problem," p. 18.

58. Speakes, "Press Briefing."

59. Ibid.

60. Fishman, "Crime Waves as Ideology."

61. See Chiricos et al., "Crime, News and Fear of Crime"; Colomy and Greiner, "Innocent Blood"; Best, *Random Violence*; Sasson, "Beyond Agenda Setting."

62. On media events, see Dayan and Katz, *Media Events*.

63. For a discussion of these studies, see Surette, *Media, Crime and Criminal Justice*, pp. 90-91.

64. Pritchard, "Homicide and Bargained Justice."

65. Surette, *Media, Crime and Criminal Justice*.

66. Beckett, *Making Crime Pay*; Brownstein, "The Media and the Construction of Random Drug Violence"; Reeves and Campbell, *Cracked Coverage*; Reinarman, "Crack Attack."

67. Morganthau, "Crack and Crime."Copyright 1986. Used with permission.

68. Merriam, "National Media Coverage of Drug Issues, 1983-7."

69. Reeves and Campbell, *Cracked Coverage*.

70. Reinarman, "Crack Attack."

71. Reeves and Campbell, *Cracked Coverage*.

72. Reinarman, "Crack Attack."

73. Jensen, Gerber, and Babcock, "The New War on Drugs"; Reinarman, "Crack Attack."

74. Orcutt and Turner, "Shocking Numbers and Graphic Accounts."

75. Baum, *Smoke and Mirrors,* pp. 219-20; Brownstein, "The Media and the Construction of Random Drug Violence"; Reinarman, "Crack Attack."

76. Reinarman, "Crack Attack"; Reinarman, Murphy, and Waldorf, "Pharmacology Is Not Destiny"; Waldorf, Reinarman, and Murphy, *Cocaine Changes.*

77. Brownstein, Ryan, and Goldstein, "Drug-Related Homicide in New York City"; Goldstein et al., "Crack and Homicide in New York City."

78. Brownstein, "The Media and the Construction of Random Drug Violence."

79. Goode, "The American Drug Panic of the 1980's"; Johnston, "America's Drug Problem."

80. Brownstein et al., "Drug-Related Homicide in New York City"; Goldstein et al., "Crack and Homicide in New York City."

81. Reinarman, "Unanticipated Consequences of Criminalization."

82. Forman and Lachter, "The National Institute on Drug Abuse Cocaine Prevention Campaign," chap. 3.

83. Beckett, *Making Crime Pay;* Reinarman, "Crack Attack."

84. Reeves and Campbell, *Cracked Coverage.*

85. Quoted in Baum, *Smoke and Mirrors,* p. 295.

86. Ibid., p. 323.

87. Brownstein, "The Media and the Construction of Random Drug Violence," p. 58.

88. U.S. Sentencing Commission, *Mandatory Minimum Penalties in the Federal Justice System.*

89. In this section, we report the findings of our own research. We examined all stories related to illegal drugs in three news weeklies (*U.S. News and World Report, Time, Newsweek*) and six metropolitan newspapers (*The Boston Globe, The New York Times, The Chicago Tribune, The Washington Post, The Los Angeles Times, The Atlanta Journal/ Constitution*) during two sampling periods. The sampling periods included April through May, 1995—following release of the U.S. Sentencing Commission's report—and September through November, 1995—the period during which Congress debated and rejected the Sentencing Commission's recommendations.

90. Jones, "Crack and Punishment."

91. Weikel, "War on Crack."

92. Flint, "Inside Views on Black Incarceration Issue," p. 29.

93. Selections from Flint, "Inside Views on Black Incarceration Issue," p. 29.

94. "Crime in America." See also Nadlemann et al., "The War on Drugs Is Lost," and Buckley, "Abolish the Drug Laws?"

CHAPTER 6

1. Donovan, "Armed with the Power of Television."

2. Lichter, Lichter, and Rothman, *Prime Time,* p. 276. Lichter and his colleagues base their findings on a random sample of 620 prime-time television shows broadcast between 1955 and 1986. Comparisons to "real world" crime draw upon the highly problematic Uniform Crime Reports of the F.B.I. (see Chapter 2). Estimates of "real world" crime that draw upon victimization surveys are higher, but even when these data were used as points of comparison the "television rate for violent crimes was fifteen times higher."

3. Lichter et al., *Prime Time,* p. 275.

4. Ibid., p. 299.

5. Reiner, "Media Made Criminality," p. 206.

6. Surette, *Media, Crime, and Criminal Justice*, p. 36.

7. Stark, "Perry Mason Meets Sonny Crockett," p. 244.

8. Carlson, *Prime Time Law Enforcement*, p. 29.

9. Lichter et al., *Prime Time*, p. 303.

10. Ibid., p. 303.

11. Ibid., p. 302.

12. Jeffrey Greenfield, quoted in Stark, "Perry Mason Meets Sonny Crockett," p. 252.

13. Gitlin, *Inside Prime Time*, p. 274.

14. Lichter et al., *Prime Time*, p. 31.

15. Ibid., p. 287.

16. Stark, "Perry Mason Meets Sonny Crockett," p. 262.

17. Carlson, *Prime Time Law Enforcement*, p. 43.

18. Haney and Manzolati, "Television Criminology," p. 128.

19. Pollan, "Can *Hill Street Blues* Save NBC?" Quoted in Stark, "Perry Mason Meets Sonny Crockett," p. 276.

20. Gitlin, *Inside Prime Time*, p. 317.

21. B. Keith Crew, "Acting Like Cops."

22. Sparks, *Television and the Drama of Crime*. See also Crew, "Acting Like Cops."

23. For example, roughly 1% of all felony arrests are rejected due to violations of the exclusionary rule. See Currie, *Confronting Crime*, pp. 66-67.

24. Reiner, "Media Made Criminality," p. 208. See also Surette, *Media, Crime and Criminal Justice*, pp. 39-40, and Lichter et al., *Prime Time*, pp. 290-300.

25. Lichter et al., *Prime Time*, p. 312.

26. Gitlin, *Inside Prime Time*, p. 286.

27. See University of California, Los Angeles, *U.C.L.A. Television Violence Monitoring Project*. Of the series *NYPD Blue*, *Homicide: Life on the Streets*, and *Law and Order*, the UCLA team comments as follows: "The three series . . . are commendable because they achieve a high level of grittiness and excitement without overemphasizing violence."

28. Fiske, *Television Culture*.

29. Powers, Rothman, and Rothman, *Hollywood's America*.

30. Ibid., p. 106.

31. Ibid., p. 108.

32. Ibid., p. 112.

33. Allen, Livingstone, and Reiner, "True Lies."

34. Ibid.

35. Ibid., p. 111.

36. Ibid., p. 67.

37. Ibid., p. 68.

38. Ibid. p. 102.

39. See Jenkins, *Using Murder*.

40. See Rapping, *Mediations*.

41. Reality-based police shows were popular in other countries before their introduction to the United States. See Cavender and Fishman, *Entertaining Crime*.

42. Fishman, "Ratings and Reality."

43. Ibid.

44. Ibid.

45. Doyle, " 'Cops.' " On voyeurism in relation to reality-based programs, see also Andersen, *Consumer Culture and TV Programming*, pp. 174-210, and Donovan, "Armed with the Power of Television."

46. Donovan, "Armed with the Power of Television."

47. Lichter et al., *Prime Time*, p. 294.

48. Kooistra, Mahoney, and Westervelt, "The World of Crime."

49. Cavender, "In the Shadow of Shadows."

50. Seagal, "Tales from the Cutting Room Floor."

51. Ibid.

52. *Cops*, 1 April 1997, KSTV, California.

53. Doyle, " 'Cops.' "

54. Donovan, "Armed with the Power of Television"; Seagal, "Tales from the Cutting Room Floor."

55. Jeffres and Perloff, *Mass Media Effects*, pp. 86-97.

56. Morgan and Signorielli, *Cultivation Analysis*.

57. Signorielli, "Television's Mean and Dangerous World," p. 88.

58. Potter, "Perceived Reality and the Cultivation Hypothesis."

59. Coleman, "The Influence of Mass Media and Interpersonal Communication"; Heath and Petraitis, "Television Viewing and Fear of Crime"; Heath and Gilbert, "Mass Media and Fear of Crime."

60. Gerbner et al., "The 'Mainstreaming' of America."

61. Carlson, *Prime Time Law Enforcement*. Several researchers have failed, in part or entirely, to replicate Carlson's findings. See Jeffres and Perloff, *Mass Media Effects*.

62. Oliver and Armstrong, "The Color of Crime."

63. Heath and Gilbert, "Mass Media and Fear of Crime"; Reiner, "Media Made Criminality."

64. In these studies, "light viewers" are those who watch up to 2 hours per day of television. See Morgan and Signorielli, *Cultivation Analysis*.

65. See especially Sparks, *Television and the Drama of Crime*, and Zillmann and Wakshlag, "Fear of Victimization."

CHAPTER 7

1. Lacayo, "Lock 'Em Up!" Copyright 1994, Time Inc. Reprinted by permission.

2. Ferraro, *Fear of Crime*.

3. Ibid. Ferraro and LaGrange, "The Measurement of the Fear of Crime"; Haghighi and Sorensen, "America's Fear of Crime."

4. Ferraro, *Fear of Crime*; Liska, Sanchirico, and Reed, "Fear of Crime and Constrained Behavior," p. 827; Skogan and Maxfield, *Coping with Crime*.

5. Ferraro, *Fear of Crime*, pp. 88 and 100. See also Gordon and Riger, *The Female Fear*; Stanko, *Intimate Intrusions*; and Stanko, *Everyday Violence*.

6. Ferraro, *Fear of Crime*, p. 64.

7. For a discussion of the "rationality" of fear of crime, see Sparks, "Reason and Unreason in 'Left Realism.' "

8. Ferraro, *Fear of Crime*; Lewis and Salem, *Fear of Crime*; Box, Hale, and Andrews, "Explaining Fear of Crime."

9. For general discussions of the public's propensity to name crime as the nation's most serious problem, see Chambliss, "Policing the Ghetto Underclass"; Warr, "Poll Trends"; and Roberts and Stalans, *Public Opinion, Crime and Criminal Justice*.

10. Because levels of public concern about crime and drugs vary with levels of elite political initiative on those issues, sorting out which side is leading and which is following is quite difficult. In this study, four case studies of month-by-month shifts in political initiative and public concern show that sudden drops in political attention to the crime and drug issues cannot be explained by prior shifts in levels of public concern but are followed by declining levels of public concern. See Beckett, "Setting the Public Agenda."

11. Bertram et al., *Drug War Politics*, pp. 113-114.

12. Ibid., p. 115

13. Alderman, "Leading the Public." On the crush of political and media attention to crime in 1993-1994, also see Poveda, "Clinton, Crime and the Justice Department."

14. Stinchcombe et al., *Crime and Punishment in America*, p. 31; Maguire and Pastore, *Sourcebook of Criminal Justice Statistics 1996*, Table 2.5.

15. Maguire and Pastore, *Sourcebook of Criminal Justice Statistics 1995*, Table 2.35; but see discussion in Roberts and Stalans, *Public Opinion*, pp. 207-8.

16. Maguire and Pastore, *Sourcebook of Criminal Justice Statistics 1994*, Table 2.39. See also discussion in Roberts and Stalans, *Public Opinion*, pp. 217-22.

17. Maguire and Pastore, *Sourcebook of Criminal Justice Statistics 1996*, Table 2.59. See also discussion in Roberts and Stalans, *Public Opinion*, pp. 265-76.

18. Maguire and Pastore, *Sourcebook of Criminal Justice Statistics 1994*, Table 2.48.

19. Roberts and Stalans, *Public Opinion*, p. 48.

20. Maguire and Pastore, *Sourcebook of Criminal Justice Statistics 1994*, Table 2.46, and 1996, Table 2.56; Gerber and Engelhardt-Greer, "Just and Painful: Attitudes Toward Sentencing Criminals."

21. Gerber and Engelhardt-Greer, "Just and Painful"; Gaubatz, *Crime in the Public Mind*; Roberts, "Public Opinion"; Bowers, "Capital Punishment and Contemporary Values"; Ellsworth and Gross, "Hardening of the Attitudes"; McCorkle, "Punish or Rehabilitate?"

22. Participants in the focus group discussions were drawn from neighborhood crime watch groups. For a description of the sample and research methodology, see Sasson, *Crime Talk*, especially Chapter 2.

23. Ibid., pp. 39-40.

24. Ibid., pp. 44-45.

25. On individualism and self-reliance as core values in American political culture, see Tocqueville, *Democracy in America*; Gans, *Middle American Individualism*; Bellah et al., *Habits of the Heart*; Gamson, *Talking Politics*; and Carbaugh, *Talking American*.

26. Roberts and Stalans, *Public Opinion*, pp. 207-9. See also Diamond and Stalans, "The Myth of Judicial Leniency in Sentencing," pp. 87-88.

27. Zimring and Hawkins, *Crime Is Not the Problem*, pp. 12-13. The authors describe the consequences of categorical contagion in this way: "The fear generated by the kidnap and murder of Polly Klaas in California provokes long sentences for residential burglars because the burglar in the citizen's scenario has acquired the characteristics of Polly Klaas's killer."

28. And in fact, this is precisely how members of the public tend to perceive typical offenses and offenders. In national surveys, respondents tend to overestimate the share of crime that is violent and the share of offenders who reoffend. They also tend to express the erroneous belief (see Chapter 2) that both the crime rate in general and the rate of violent crime are increasing. See Roberts, "Public Opinion," pp. 109-21; and Roberts and Stalans, *Public Opinion*, p. 33.

29. Roberts and Stalans, *Public Opinion*, p. 216.

30. See discussion in Chapter 5. News exposes on the failures of the justice system probably contribute to the public's tendency to overestimate rates of recidivism and underestimate the justice system's propensity to incarcerate. See Roberts, "Public Opinion," pp. 109-21.

31. Experimental evidence also points to this media effect: Researchers assigned subjects to read either news reports of criminal case or court documents; two thirds of those who read news accounts thought sentence was too light; more than half of those who read court documents thought sentence was too severe. See Roberts and Doob, "News Media Influences on Public Views of Sentencing."

32. Bowers, "Capital Punishment"; Roberts and Stalans, *Public Opinion*, p. 44.

33. In a comparison between sentencing preferences of jurors and judges in Chicago, researchers found jurors more willing than judges to assign probation alone, or probation and jail, as alternatives to prison time. See Diamond and Stalans, "The Myth of Judicial Leniency." For a thorough review of the evidence on the relative severity of the public versus the courts, see Roberts and Stalans, *Public Opinion*, pp. 210-12.

34. For a more detailed discussion of popular slogans and catch-phrases as instances of media discourse, see Gamson, *Talking Politics*; and Sasson, *Crime Talk*.

35. Barkan and Cohn, "Racial Prejudice and Support for the Death Penalty by Whites." See also Cohn, Barkan and Halteman, "Punitive Attitudes Toward Criminals: Racial Consensus or Racial Conflict?"

36. Rossi and Berk, *Just Punishments*. The researchers performed multiple regression analyses on the survey data to test the possibility that the correlation between punitiveness and opposition to civil rights might be spurious, that is, a consequence of some third variable (such as region or political orientation) associated with both racial prejudice and punitiveness. The correlation, however, survived all statistical controls.

37. See Chapter 4.

38. Gerber and Engelhardt-Greer, "Just and Painful," p. 71.

39. Maguire and Pastore, *Sourcebook of Criminal Justice Statistics 1995*, Table 2.37; Roberts and Stalans, *Public Opinion*, p. 123. "Crime prevention" in this case included "community education" and "youth programs."

40. Gallup, *The Gallup Poll*.

41. Flanagan, "Change and Influence in Popular Criminology," pp. 231-43; Maguire and Pastore, *Sourcebook of Criminal Justice Statistics 1995*, Tables 2.22 and 2.23.

42. Sasson, *Crime Talk*; Doble and Klein, *Punishing Criminals: The Public's View*, p. 38; Doble, Immerwahr, and Richardson, *Punishing Criminals: The People of Delaware Consider the Options*; Crime and Justice Foundation, *Shifting the Debate on Crime*. Interestingly, this "social breakdown" perspective is also widespread in England; see Loader, Girling, and Sparks, "Narratives of Decline."

43. Sasson, *Crime Talk*, p. 66.

44. Ibid., p. 73.

45. Ibid., p. 75.

46. McCorckle, "Punish or Rehabilitate?"; Gerber and Engelhardt-Greer, "Just and Painful"; Roberts and Stalans, *Public Opinion*, p. 200.

47. In response to the question, "Once people who commit crimes *are in prison*, which of the following do you think should be *the most important goal of prison*?" 48.4% chose "rehabilitation," 14.6% chose "punishment," and 33.1% chose "crime prevention/deterrence." See Maguire and Pastore, *Sourcebook of Criminal Justice Statistics 1996*, Table 2.6.

48. Cullen, Skovron, et al., "Public Support for Correctional Treatment."

49. Doble and Klein, *Punishing Criminals, The Public's View*, p. 38. See also Doble et al., *Punishing Criminals: The People of Delaware Consider the Options* and Crime and Justice Foundation, *Shifting the Debate on Crime*.

50. The national survey is cited in Ellsworth and Gross, "Hardening of the Attitudes." The statewide surveys, administered between 1985 and 1989, posed the following question: "Suppose convicted first-degree murderers in this state could be sentenced to life in prison without parole and also be required to work in prison for money that would go to the families of their victims. Would you prefer this as an alternative to the death penalty?" Evidence from these surveys also suggests that the public would be willing to accept parole of first-degree murderers after at least 25 years if an offender has fully met the restitution requirement. See Bowers, "Capital Punishment."

51. On the importance of symbolically communicating societal disapproval, see also Gaubatz, *Crime in the Public Mind*; and Kahan, "What Do Alternative Sanctions Mean?"

52. See Rossi and Berk, *Just Punishments*, pp. 181-82; Browning and Cao, "The Impact of Race on Criminal Justice Ideology"; Secret and Johnson, "Racial Differences in Attitudes Toward Crime Control."

53. See Maguire and Pastore, *Sourcebook of Criminal Justice Statistics 1996*, Table 2.69. Black and White punitiveness do not necessarily stem from the same sources. One statistical analysis finds that Black punitiveness correlates with fear of crime, whereas White punitiveness correlates with racial prejudice. See Cohn et al., "Punitive Attitudes Toward Criminals?" On the slight convergence of Black and White attitudes on crime control, see Secret and Johnson, "Racial Differences."

54. Chambliss, "Policing the Ghetto Underclass"; Davis, *City of Quartz*; Miller, *Search and Destroy*; Donziger, *The Real War on Crime*; Tonry, *Malign Neglect*.

55. Whitaker, "Decision and Division," p. 24.

56. Ibid.

57. Myers, "Bringing the Offender to Heel: Views of the Criminal Courts," p. 52. For similar findings, see Wortley, Macmillan, and Hagan, "Just Des(s)erts?"; and Hagan and Albonetti, "Race, Class and the Perception of Criminal Injustice," pp. 329-55.

58. See Turner, *I Heard It Through the Grape Vine*; Sasson, "African American Conspiracy Theories."

59. This is an expanded version of the transcript of the same session found in Sasson, "African American Conspiracy Theories," pp. 268, 271.

60. Turner, *I Heard It Through the Grape Vine*; Sasson, "African American Conspiracy Theories."

CHAPTER 8

1. Sasson, "Mobilizing For Change"; Tarrow, *Power in Movement*.

2. Rosenbaum, "Community Crime Prevention," p. 342.

3. Ibid., p. 347.

4. Podolefsky and Dubow, *Strategies for Community Crime Prevention*.

5. President's Commission on Law Enforcement and the Administration of Justice, *The Challenge of Crime in a Free Society*.

6. Hope, "Community Crime Prevention."

7. Rosenbaum, "Community Crime Prevention."

8. Ibid.; see also National Crime Prevention Council, *Working as Partners With Community Groups*; National Crime Prevention Council, *Partnerships to Prevent Youth*

Violence. By contrast, the Kennedy Administration's "War on Poverty" programs of the 1960s allocated federal funds to groups attempting to ameliorate the social conditions—especially "blocked opportunities"—that were believed to give rise to crime and delinquency. See Rosenbaum, "Community Crime Prevention," p. 352.

9. Cohen, *Visions of Social Control*; Crawford, "Appeals to Community and Crime Prevention"; Walklate, "Victims, Crime Prevention and Social Control."

10. Rosenbaum, "Community Crime Prevention"; Walklate, "Victims, Crime Prevention and Social Control."

11. Hope and Shaw, "Community Approaches to Reducing Crime."

12. See especially Crawford, "Appeals to Community and Crime Prevention," and Garland, "The Limits of the Sovereign State." Others argue that the ascendance of the crime issue on the local political agenda is a product of the increasing crime rate. To support this argument, researchers point out that the Uniform Crime Reports (UCR) data do indeed show an increase in crime at the same time that urbanites became more likely to identify crime as an important problem in their communities (see Jacob and Lineberry, "Crime, Politics and the Cities"). As was discussed in Chapter 2, however, this argument becomes more difficult to sustain if one looks at victimization survey data rather than the estimates provided by the UCR.

13. For slightly different versions of this argument, see Crawford, "Appeals to Community and Crime Prevention," and Garland, "The Limits of the Sovereign State."

14. Crawford, "Appeals to Community and Crime Prevention," p. 100.

15. For this reason, Garland refers to such appeals to community as part of the process of "responsibilization"—an effort to shift the responsibility for the crime problem away from the state (see Garland, "The Limits of the Sovereign State").

16. Currie, "Two Visions of Community Crime Prevention," pp. 280-81.

17. Ibid., pp. 282-3.

18. See Wilson and Kelling, "Broken Windows: The Police and Neighborhood Safety"; see also Skogan, *Disorder and Decline.*

19. A more recent iteration of this theory appears in Kelling and Coles, *Fixing Broken Windows.*

20. Walklate, "Victims, Crime Prevention and Social Control."

21. Kelling and Coles, *Fixing Broken Windows,* p. 42.

22. For an extended discussion of these and other criticisms of the "broken windows" approach, see Herbert, "Reassessing Police and Police Studies."

23. Sherman, "Thinking About Crime Prevention."

24. See Garofalo and McLeod, "The Structure and Operation of Neighborhood Watch Programs in the United States."

25. Garafalo and McLeod, "Structure and Operation"; Hope, "Community Crime Prevention"; Rosenbaum, "Community Crime Prevention"; Skogan, *Disorder and Decline.*

26. Sasson and Nelson, "Danger, Community and the Meaning of Crime Watch." This perception may be fairly accurate in the case of burglary, which is emphasized in the Neighborhood Watch literature, but it is a less accurate view for crimes such as homicide, domestic violence, and child abuse.

27. Ibid.

28. Hope, "Community Crime Prevention"; Rosenbaum, "Community Crime Prevention."

29. Research suggests that these perceptions are accurate: Because of increased unemployment, the expansion of the drug trade, and massive levels of incarceration in Black communities, kinship networks and community authority figures have been substantially weakened. See Anderson, *Streetwise,* and Wilson, *When Work Disappears.*

30. Sasson and Nelson, "Danger, Community and the Meaning of Crime Watch."

31. Garofalo and McLeod, "Neighborhood Watch Programs."

32. Skogan, *Disorder and Decline.*

33. Ibid., p. 362.

34. Harrington, "Popular Justice, Populist Politics: Law in Community Organizing."

35. Ibid., p. 181.

36. Rosenbaum, "Community Crime Prevention," p. 360.

37. Ibid; Podolefsky and Dubow, *Strategies for Community Crime Prevention.*

38. Podolefsky and Dubow, *Strategies for Community Crime Prevention.*

39. Ibid.

40. Ibid.; Sasson and Nelson, "Danger, Community and the Meaning of Crime Watch."

41. Hope, "Community Crime Prevention," p. 38.

42. Skogan, "Community Organizations and Crime," quoted in Tonry and Morris, *Communities and Crime.*

43. Rosenbaum, "Community Crime Prevention," p. 354.

44. Sherman, "Communities and Crime Prevention." See also Hope, "Community Crime Prevention."

45. Crawford, "Appeals to Community and Crime Prevention"; Walklate, "Victims, Crime Prevention and Social Control."

46. Crawford, "Appeals to Community and Crime Prevention"; Walklate, "Victims, Crime Prevention and Social Control."

47. Gusfield, "Moral Passage."

48. Davis, *City of Quartz,* p. 224.

49. Hope, "Community Crime Prevention," p. 49 (but see also p. 54).

50. Weed, *Certainty of Justice.*

51. Ibid.

52. Ibid., p. 9.

53. See Maguire, "The Needs and Rights of Victims of Crime," quoted in Tonry, *Crime and Justice*; Weed, *Certainty of Justice,* p. 10.

54. See Henderson, "The Wrongs of Victim's Rights," p. 944, and Mawby and Walklate, *Critical Victimology,* p. 77.

55. See Weed, *Certainty of Justice,* p. 10.

56. See Maguire, "The Needs and Rights of Victims," quoted in Tonry, *Crime and Justice*; Weed, *Certainty of Justice,* pp. 8-12.

57. Maguire, "The Needs and Rights of Victims," quoted in Tonry, *Crime and Justice*; Weed, *Certainty of Justice,* pp. 18-20.

58. Weed, *Certainty of Justice,* p. 21.

59. Henderson, "The Wrongs of Victim's Rights"; Mawby and Walklate, *Critical Victimology,* pp. 66-8.

60. As Shapiro points out, the existence of this alternative to the criminal justice system is often ignored by victim rights activists who seek to expand the rights of the victim in criminal proceedings. See Bruce Shapiro, "Victims and Vengeance: Why the Victims' Rights Amendment is a Bad Idea."

61. See, for example, Christie, "Conflicts as Property," pp. 1-15.

62. Many "restorative justice" programs, for example, seek to replace the current emphasis on punishment with the goal of compensating the victim for the harm done to them.

63. Weed, *Certainty of Justice,* pp. 13-14.

64. See Henderson, "The Wrongs of Victim's Rights," pp. 967-8; Weed, *Certainty of Justice*, pp. 24-26.

65. See, for example, Aynes, "Constitutional Considerations."

66. See Weed, *Certainty of Justice*, p. 14.

67. Shapiro, "Victims and Vengeance"; Elias, *Victims Still*, p. 32.

68. Elias, *Victims Still*, p. 32.

69. Shapiro, "Victims and Vengeance," p. 16.

70. Weed, *Certainty of Justice*, p. 18.

71. Smith, "Victims and Victim's Rights Activists."

72. Kleinknecht, "Victim's Rights Advocates on a Roll."

73. Shapiro, "Victims and Vengeance," p. 18.

74. Mawby and Walklate, *Critical Victimology*, p. 136.

75. Weed, *Certainty of Justice*, p. 137.

76. Maguire, "The Needs and Rights of Victims," quoted in Tonry, *Crime and Justice*.

77. Macleod, "Victim Participation at Sentencing."

78. Mawby and Walklate, *Critical Victimology*, p. 138.

79. Weed, *Certainty of Justice*, p. 136.

80. Elias, *Victims Still*, p. 31.

81. Shapiro, "Victims and Vengeance."

82. Ibid.; Prajean, *Dead Man Walking*.

83. Walker, Spohn, and DeLone, *The Color of Justice*.

84. Ibid.

85. Amnesty International, *United States of America: Rights for All*, chap. 3.

86. Williams, "Community Mobilization Against Urban Crime."

87. Walker and Kreisel, "Varieties of Citizen Review."

88. Dix, "Police Violence," pp. 59-63.

89. *Georgia v. Furman*, 408 U.S. 238 (1972).

90. Haines, *Against Capital Punishment*.

91. Ibid.

92. Anderson, "Organizing Against the Death Penalty," pp. 10-11.

93. "Capital Punishment Opposed," p. 625.

94. Quoted in Frankel and Weinstein, "Crusader."

95. Bertram and Sharpe, "War Ends, Drugs Win," p. 11.

96. Ibid.

97. Ibid.

98. This announcement came as something of a surprise. In February 1997, following the completion of a sixth federally funded study of needle exchange programs (NEPs) concluding that NEPs helped to prevent the spread of HIV and other blood-borne diseases and do not increase drug use, Health and Human Services Secretary Donna Shalala had announced her support for NEPs. Apparently, concerns about being labeled soft on drugs led the administration to refuse to lift the federal ban at the last minute. See "Inside the Beltway: Clinton Administration Endorses Needle Exchange Programs"; "Flat Earth AIDS Policy."

99. "Flat Earth AIDS Policy."

100. Donziger, *The Real War on Crime*.

101. Ibid.

102. Ibid.

103. Trebach, "Arizona and California Voters Seize Initiatives."

CHAPTER 9

1. Beckett, *Making Crime Pay*; Gray, *Drug Crazy*.

2. Jensen and Gerber, "The Civil Forfeiture of Assets"; McAnany, "Assets Forfeiture."

3. Rasmussen, *The Economic Anatomy of a Drug War*.

4. Egan, "The War on Drugs Retreats."

5. Maguire and Pastore, *Sourcebook of Criminal Justice Statistics 1998*, Tables 4.1 and 4.29.

6. Federal Bureau of Investigation, *Uniform Crime Reports, 1996*, p. 280.

7. Among high school seniors, more than 1 in 3 reported marijuana use and 1 in 10 use of either PCP (angel dust) or LSD. See Maguire and Pastore, *Sourcebook of Criminal Justice Statistics 1996*, Tables 3.69, 3.7, 3.6.

8. The NIDA surveys are of households and thus ignore institutionalized persons and the homeless, among whom are a disproportionate number of drug addicts. It may therefore be the case that during the 1980s drug dealing and using became more flagrant or destructive among the hard-core addict population. A rise in the number of "cocaine-related" emergency room visits coinciding with the 1980s crack epidemic suggests this possibility (See Tonry, *Malign Neglect*, and Currie, *Reckoning*). The drug war, however, was not a "surgical strike" aimed at this relatively small portion of the population of a handful of major cities. Instead, it was aimed more or less indiscriminately at all users and dealers, especially, as we shall see, at those who reside in minority inner city neighborhoods.

9. Tonry reviews a wider range of surveys and arrives at the same conclusions. See Tonry, *Malign Neglect*, chapter 3.

10. In recent survey years, for example, cocaine use during the last 30 days was reported by .8% of White, 1% of Black, and 1.1% of Hispanic respondents. Similarly, marijuana use during the last 30 days was reported by 3% of White, 3.5% of Black, and 2.8% of Hispanic respondents. Maguire and Pastore, *Sourcebook of Criminal Justice Statistics 1996*, Tables 3.72 and 3.76. Among high school students, ethnic differences are somewhat more pronounced, with Black students *less* likely than their White and Hispanic counterparts to be regular users of cocaine and several other illegal drugs. See, for example, Maguire and Pastore, *Sourcebook of Criminal Justice Statistics 1998*, Table 3.68.

11. Federal Bureau of Investigation, *Uniform Crime Reports, 1996*, p. 282.

12. Mauer and Huling, "Young Black Americans," p. 9.

13. See, for example, Gray, *Drug Crazy*, especially Chapter 2. See also Tonry, *Malign Neglect*, Chapter 3.

14. Chambliss, "Policing the Ghetto Underclass."

15. Notably, the conservatives and civil libertarians converged in their critiques of rehabilitation; Libertarians, however, believed a system of "just punishment" would imprison fewer people for shorter stretches, whereas conservatives viewed "just punishment" as a way to end what they perceived to be the permissiveness of a rehabilitation-oriented prison system. For a discussion of these issues, see Tonry, *Sentencing Matters*.

16. Ibid., p. 146.

17. Ibid., p. 146.

18. Donziger, *The Real War on Crime*, p. 27.

19. Massachusetts Sentencing Commission, "Report to the General Court."

20. "Overdosing on the Drug War," p. 1.

21. Ibid.

22. Tonry, *Sentencing Matters*, p. 152. Fifty federal judges, many of them conservative Reagan Administration appointees, have refused to hear drug cases; Elikann, *The Tough on Crime Myth*, p. 97.

23. Tonry, *Sentencing Matters*, pp. 139-42; Currie, *Reckoning*; Moore, "Supply Reduction"; Reuter and Kleiman, "Risks and Prices."

24. Beck and Brien, "Trends in U.S. Correctional Populations."

25. Bureau of Justice Statistics, *Prisoners in 1996*, p. 10.

26. Bureau of Justice Statistics, *Prisoners in 1996*, pp. 10-11; Bureau of Justice Statistics, *Prisoners in 1997*, pp. 11-12.

27. Reeves and Campbell, *Cracked Coverage*.

28. Donziger, *The Real War on Crime*, p. 119.

29. Defenders of the harsh penalties for crack argued that the substance was peculiarly destructive, as discussed in Chapter 4. As numerous scholars have pointed out, however, drug prohibition laws have historically derived their impetus from popular anxieties about racial minorities. See Bertram et al., *Drug War Politics*.

30. Federal Bureau of Investigation, *Uniform Crime Report, 1996*, p. 282; Sentencing Project, "National Inmate Population."

31. Sentencing Project, "National Inmate Population."

32. Calculated from Bureau of Justice Statistics, *Prisoners in 1997*, pp. 11-12.

33. Clark, Austin, and Henry, *Three Strikes and You're Out*.

34. "Washington Case."

35. To be convicted under the "second strike" provision, only the first felony need be "serious." See Clark et al., *Three Strikes and You're Out*.

36. Slater, "California's Pizza Bandit."

37. Donziger, *The Real War on Crime*, p. 19.

38. Elikann, *The Tough on Crime Myth*, pp. 112-13.

39. Dickey and Hollenhorst, *Three-Strikes Laws*.

40. Clark et al., *Three Strikes and You're Out*.

41. The California Department of Corrections estimated the cost of the law at $5.7 billion annually. See Greenwood et al., "Estimated Benefits," p. 69.

42. Dickey and Hollenhorst, *Three-Strikes Laws*, p. 6.

43. The court ruling opened the door to reconsideration of sentences for many persons convicted under the original law. Jerry Williams, the "pizza bandit" sentenced to life for stealing a slice of pepperoni pizza, was thus awarded a sentence reduction. See Stern, *A Sin Against the Future*.

44. Calculated from Table 11 in Beck, "Trends in U.S. Correctional Populations."

45. Beck, "Trends in U.S. Correctional Populations," p. 62.

46. Between 1977 and 1999, 12 persons who committed their crimes while they were children were executed in the United States. During the same period, at least 30 mentally retarded prisoners were put to death. Amnesty International, *USA: The Conveyor Belt of Death Continues*.

47. Dieter, *Innocence and the Death Penalty*; Death Penalty Information Center, *Additional Cases of Innocence and Possible Innocence*.

48. As Peterson and Bailey conclude in their comprehensive review of the literature, "the empirical evidence does not support the belief that capital punishment was an effective deterrent for murder in past years. Nor is there any indication that returning to our past execution practices [e.g., executing people more often and more quickly] would have any deterrent effect on the current homicide problem." See Peterson and Bailey, "Is Capital Punishment an Effective Deterrent for Murder?"

232 ◆ THE POLITICS OF INJUSTICE

49. See Walker, *Sense and Nonsense,* pp. 102-3.

50. For a review of the literature on deterrence and the death penalty, see Bailey and Peterson, "Murder, Capital Punishment, and Deterrence."

51. Baldus and Woodworth, "Race Discrimination and the Death Penalty."

52. Dieter, "The Death Penalty in Black and White."

53. Bohm, "The Economic Costs of Capital Punishment."

54. Sandys and McGarrell, "Attitudes Toward Capital Punishment."

55. Colomy and Greiner, "Innocent Blood."

56. See, for example, Bennett, DiIulio, and Walters, *Body Count.*

57. Cook and Laub, "The Unprecedented Epidemic of Youth Violence." Notably, as calculated by Cook and Laub, the homicide commission rate for teenage African American males more than tripled between 1985 and 1991. Cook and Laub further point out that, although the share of violent crimes "cleared" by arrest of a juvenile was only slightly higher in 1994 (13%) than in 1975 through 1979 (12%), the proportion of young people in the population was significantly smaller. This observation implies a higher rate of juvenile offending in the late 1980s and early 1990s.

58. "Law Permits Trial of Youths as Adults."

59. Cloud, Jon, "For they know not what they do?"

60. Schlosser, "The Prison-Industrial Complex."

61. Ibid.

62. Amnesty International, *United States of America—Rights for All,* p. 58; Butterfield, "Drug Treatment in Prisons Dips."

63. Schlosser, "The Prison-Industrial Complex."

64. See Feeley and Simon, "The New Penology."

65. Amnesty International, *United States of America—Rights for All,* p. 74. See also Porter, "Is Solitary Confinement Driving Charlie Chase Crazy?"; Stern, *A Crime Against the Future.*

66. Beilein and Krasnow, "Jail Prototype Leads to Faster Construction."

67. The female proportion of the state inmate population grew from 4% to 6%, the Hispanic proportion from 10% to 17%, and the Black proportion from 47% to 51%. The proportion of state inmates who are White dropped from 52% to 47%. See Beck, "Trends in U.S. Correctional Populations," pp. 47-48.

68. Miller, *Search and Destroy.* On annual prison census days, the percentage of state prisoners serving time for violent crimes dropped from 59% in 1980 to 47% in 1995. See Beck, "Trends in U.S. Correctional Populations," p. 49. The difference between these two measures of prison populations is due to the tendency of violent offenders to serve longer terms and hence accumulate within prisons.

69. "On any day, almost 200,000 people behind bars—more than 1 in 10 of the total—are known to suffer from schizophrenia, manic depression or major depression, the three most severe mental illnesses" (Butterfield, "Asylums Behind Bars"). Similarly, Elliott Currie notes that 7% to 15% of California jail inmates and 8% to 20% of prison inmates are seriously mentally ill. See Currie, *Crime and Punishment in America.*

70. Amnesty International, *United States of America—Rights for All,* p. 55.

71. See Staples, *The Culture of Surveillance.*

72. Applebome, "For the Ultimate Safe School."

73. Greene, "Educators Model Airport Security.

74. Bennett et al., *Body Count.*

75. Davey, *The New Social Contract.*

76. Lotke, *Hobbling a Generation;* Miller, *Hobbling a Generation.*

77. Reiss and Roth, *Understanding and Preventing Violence*. Comparable findings have been reported by government-sponsored panels of social scientists in both Canada and Great Britain; for details, see Tonry, *Sentencing Matters*, p. 137.

78. Tonry, *Malign Neglect*; Currie, *Crime and Punishment in America*; Zimring and Hawkins, *The Scale of Imprisonment*.

79. Mauer, "Americans Behind Bars: U.S. and International Use of Incarceration, 1995." On New York's prison and jail populations, see Bureau of Justice Statistics, "Prisoners in 1997," Table 4, and Bureau of Justice Statistics, "Correctional Populations in the United States, 1995," Table 2.8.

80. Schlosser, "The Prison-Industrial Complex."

81. Currie, *Confronting Crime*.

82. Ibid.

83. Quoted in Tonry, *Sentencing Matters*, p. 138.

84. Golub and Johnson, *Crack's Decline*.

85. Blumstein and Rosenfeld, "Assessing the Recent Ups and Downs in U.S. Homicide Rates," and Fagan et al., "Declining Homicide in New York City."

86. Miller, *Search and Destroy*, p. 9.

87. On the war on drugs, see Gray, *Drug Crazy*; Bertram et al., *Drug War Politics*; Currie, *Reckoning*; and Baum, *Smoke and Mirrors*.

88. Butterfield, "New Prisons Cast Shadow."

89. Stern, *A Crime Against the Future*, p. 51.

90. Western and Beckett, "How Unregulated Is the U.S. Labor Market?"

91. Currie, *Confronting Crime*.

92. Wilson, *When Work Disappears*; Wilson, *The Truly Disadvantaged*.

93. Egan, "The War on Drugs Retreats."

94. Butterfield, "As Inmate Population Grows, So Does a Focus on Children."

95. Kaufman, "Prison Life Is All Around."

96. "Voting Rights for Felons?"

97. Ibid.

98. Donziger, *The Real War on Crime*.

99. Eric Schlosser, "The Prison-Industrial Complex."

100. In the "prison-industrial complex" perspective, see Christie, *Crime Control as Industry*; Donziger, *The Real War on Crime*; and Chambliss, "Policing the Ghetto Underclass."

CHAPTER 10

1. Shaylor, "Organizing Resistance," p. 19.

2. This is true not just in the United States but in other industrialized countries as well. For further evidence of this association, see Currie, *Crime and Punishment in America*, pp. 125-30.

3. Hannon and DeFronzo, "The Truly Disadvantaged."

4. Currie, *Crime and Punishment in America*, pp. 125-6.

5. Ibid., p. 135.

6. Associated Press, "Citing Drop in Welfare Rolls, Clinton to Seek Further Cuts," p. A12.

7. Danziger and Gottschalk, *America Unequal*, p. 67.

8. Danziger and Weinberg, "The Historical Record," p. 33.

9. It is sometimes argued that poor children in the United States are poor compared to their middle and upper class counterparts, but not all that poor. In fact, poor children in the United States are considerably worse off than poor children in other industrialized countries. See Currie, *Crime and Punishment in America*, p. 121.

10. In California, an estimated 8% to 20% of prison inmates and 7% to 15% of jail inmates suffer from a serious mental illness. See Currie, *Crime and Punishment in America*, p. 33.

11. For example, research suggests that every dollar invested in Job Corps—a federal program aimed at helping high-risk youth obtain employment—returned $1.46 to society in reduced prison and income support costs and increased tax contributions. See Donziger, *The Real War on Crime*, p. 216.

12. Beckett, *Making Crime Pay*, p. 55; Reinarman and Levine, "Punitive Prohibition America."

13. See Chapters 15-17 in Reinarman and Levine, *Crack in America*.

14. By contrast, alcohol is involved in about ten thousand overdose deaths annually. See Nadlemann, "Drug Prohibition in the U.S.," p. 302.

15. Ibid. See also Zimmer and Morgan, *Exposing Marijuana Myths*.

16. According to the Uniform Crime Reports, state and local authorities made 695,201 marijuana arrests in 1997. (Of these arrests, over 87% were for possession.) Since 1965, state and local authorities have made over 11 million marijuana arrests. Federal authorities also make marijuana arrests, and although the exact number is unknown, there may be as many as 10,000 of these per year. The precise number of marijuana offenders who are currently incarcerated is also unknown. Estimates are that between 12% and 15% of the federal prison population—about 15,000 people—are serving time for marijuana violations and another 21,000 are serving time in state prisons or jails for such offenses. See Thomas, "Marijauna Arrests and Incarceration in the United States," and also Schlosser, "Reefer Madness."

17. Egan, "The War on Drugs Retreats."

18. See for example, Reinarman, "Unanticipated Consequences of Criminalization."

19. Waldorf, Reinarman, and Murphy, *Cocaine Changes*, mention the value of a "stake in conventional life." Also, a recent study published by the National Center on Addiction and Substance Abuse found that women from households with incomes greater than $75,000 were the most likely to try an illegal drug and women from households with incomes less than $15,000 were the least likely to do so. However, the study also found that although only 1 of 24 of the higher income women who tried a drug became "addicted," 1 in 6 of the poorer women were unable to control their use of illegal substances. Cited in Califano, "Welfare's Drug Connection," p. A19. See also Waldorf, Reinarman, and Murphy, *Cocaine Changes*.

20. Currie, *Reckoning*.

21. For example, the incidence of Fetal Alcohol Syndrome among children of chronically alcoholic mothers is strongly influenced by the social class of the mother: 4½% of the children of upper middle class alcoholics, versus 71% of those of poor alcoholic mothers, were diagnosed with FAS. See Bingol et al., "The Influence of Socioeconomic Factors."

22. The RAND Corporation study is reported in Sentencing Project, "Proposed Changes in Crack/Cocaine Sentencing Laws."

23. Shine and Mauer, "Does the Punishment Fit the Crime?"

24. See Nadlemann, "Drug Prohibition in the U.S.," p. 304.

25. Decriminalization is not the same thing as legalization. With the former, the state decides to reduce the official penalties for drug law violations and to deemphasize drug

law enforcement. By contrast, legalizing drugs would involve repealing the laws that prohibit the use or sale of controlled substances. Each of these options offers certain advantages and disadvantages. If a policy of decriminalization (combined with the legalization of marijuana) were adopted, the many people whose main problem is drug addiction would not be filling up our prisons and jails, and the money currently spent to imprison them could be spent on drug abuse prevention and treatment programs. However, under decriminalization, the drugs themselves would remain illegal, and their price would therefore remain artificially high. This means that the drug trade would continue to offer a high profit margin and therefore be regulated through the use of violence (although addressing the complex array of social and economic problems facing urban communities might reduce the numbers of people who are drawn into the drug trade.) Furthermore, because drugs other than marijuana would remain illegal, they would be impossible to regulate, and the "secondary" problems this causes—accidental overdoses, poisonings—would continue.

By contrast, the legalization of drugs would eradicate the black market for drugs and, presumably, the violence it spawns. By legalizing drugs the government would also make possible their regulation (just as alcohol is currently regulated by state and local governments). Furthermore, under legalization, drugs could be taxed, which would generate revenues that could be used to fund drug treatment and prevention. However, if these taxes were too high, they might lead to the creation of a black market. Furthermore, it is unclear what impact legalization would have on rates of drug abuse and how drugs might be distributed. See Nadelmann, "Drug Prohibition in the U.S"; Reinarman and Levine, *Crack in America*, pp. 214-24.

26. Nadelmann, "Drug Prohibition in the U.S.," p. 304.

27. Cohen, "Crack in the Netherlands"; Reinarman and Levine, *Crack in America*, pp. 288-315.

28. Cohen, "Crack in the Netherlands."

29. See, for example, Wilson, "Against the Legalization of Drugs."

30. Nadelmann, "Drug Prohibition in the U.S.," p. 304. See also Anderson, *Sensible Justice: Alternatives to Prison*.

31. Tonry, *Intermediate Sanctions in Sentencing Guidelines*.

32. Cullen, Wright, and Applegate, "Control in the Community: The Limits of Reform."

33. Umbreit, "Restorative Justice."

34. Ibid.

35. Ibid.

36. Sherman et al., "Experiments in Restorative Policing."

37. Umbreit, "Restorative Justice."

38. Garland, *Punishment and Welfare*; Rothman, *Conscience and Convenience*.

39. Garland, "Penal Modernism and Postmodernism," p. 187.

40. Donziger, *The Real War on Crime*, pp. 191-3; Irwin and Austin, *It's About Time*, chap. 5.

41. Irwin and Austin, *It's About Time*, pp. 118-25; Simon, *Poor Discipline*; Walker, *Sense and Nonsense About Crime and Drugs*, pp. 210-16.

42. Nationwide, parolees returned to prison comprised 12% of all total state prison admissions in 1974 but 29% of state prison admissions in 1989. See Simon, *Poor Discipline*, p. 210; also Irwin and Austin, *It's About Time*, Chapter 5.

43. Both experimental and statistical studies suggest that the employment prospects of job applicants with no criminal record are far better than those of persons who were convicted and incarcerated. See Western and Beckett, "How Unregulated is the U.S. Labor Market?" There is also evidence that offenders who are incarcerated are more likely to

reoffend than similar offenders who are convicted but sentenced to probation. See Petersilia and Peterson, *Prison versus Probation*.

44. Irwin and Austin, *It's About Time*.

45. Ibid., pp. 125-31.

46. Studies reporting that rehabilitation does not work often group all rehabilitation programs together and, as a result, do not differentiate between successful and unsuccessful programs. By contrast, studies that examine the impact of particular rehabilitation programs suggest that some of these are successful in reducing recidivism. See Cullen, Van Voorhis, and Sundt, "Prisons in Crisis."

47. Petersilia and Turner, "Comparing Intensive and Regular Supervision." This study also found no correlation between technical violations and new criminal offenses, a finding that challenges the widespread practice of incarcerating those who violate the technical conditions of probation.

48. This success was contingent on the program being fully implemented. See Currie, *Crime and Punishment in America*, p. 168.

49. In 1994, over half of all states reported that they had made cuts in or eliminated inmate education programs. The 1994 Crime Bill eliminated federal funding for prisoner education. As a result, the number of state prison inmates enrolled in postsecondary education declined from 38,000 to 21,000 (in a population of nearly 1 million). See Currie, *Crime and Punishment in America*, p. 169.

50. Between 1990 and 1997, the proportion of state prison inmates who received drug treatment declined from 24.5% to 9.7%. Over the same years, the proportion who had been drug users at the time of arrest increased from 50% to 57%. Butterfield, "Drug Treatment in Prisons Dips."

51. Indeed, there is evidence that the exconvicts' ability to find work or obtain economic assistance reduces rates of recidivism. See Berk and Rauma, "Remuneration and Recidivism."

52. About 70% of all homicide cases known to the police involve firearms. And although only about one third of all guns in circulation are handguns, handguns are used in about three fourths of all deaths caused by firearms. See Zimring and Hawkins, *Crime Is Not the Problem*, p. 199.

53. Although serious assaults with knives and other cutting instruments occur about as frequently as serious assaults with firearms, the latter are about five times as likely to result in death. See Zimring and Hawkins, *Crime Is Not the Problem*, p. 199.

54. Hornblower, "Have Guns Will Travel," p. 45.

55. On the importance of guns in the production of high homicide rates and the need for effective gun control, see Zimring and Hawkins, *Crime Is Not the Problem*. Of course, there are those who argue that widespread gun ownership reduces crime and violence by deterring would-be criminals. One study purporting to demonstrate this examined crime rates in 10 states that passed legislation allowing people to carry concealed weapons between 1977 and 1992. According to this study, the rate of murder, rape, and aggravated assault dropped in these 10 states after the passage of these laws. The author argues that these drops are a result of would-be criminals being deterred from committing crimes when the would-be victim just might have a pistol in her purse (see Lott, *More Guns, Less Crime*). However, critics point out that very few people actually carry concealed weapons in these states and that the deterrent effect of this practice would therefore be minimal. Furthermore, cross-cultural research suggests that rates of lethal violence are lower in societies characterized by few—not many—guns (see Zimring and Hawkins, *Crime Is Not the Problem*). Thus there is reason to suspect that the reported correlation between right-to-carry laws and declining levels of crime is a spurious one.

56. Walker, *Sense and Nonsense About Crime and Drugs,* p. 189. See also Zimring and Hawkins, *Crime Is Not the Problem,* pp. 200-1.

57. Walker, *Sense and Nonsense About Crime and Drugs.*

58. Sherman and Dennis P. Rogan, "Effects of Gun Seizure." In Boston, police efforts to seize guns were combined with community outreach programs aimed at enhancing opportunities for youth and diffusing gang violence. Shortly after this program was adopted, levels of violence declined significantly—although other cities in Massachusetts also experienced declining levels of violence. See Currie, *Crime and Punishment in America,* p. 179.

59. Walker, *Sense and Nonsense About Crime and Drugs,* p. 191-4.

60. Ibid, p. 185.

61. In 1974, the city of Baltimore offered $50 for handguns and eventually bought about 8,400 handguns—about one fourth of the number estimated to exist in the city. See Walker, *Sense and Nonsense About Crime and Drugs,* p. 187.

62. Skolnick and Bayley, *The New Blue Line.*

63. Ibid.

64. Sadd and Grinc, *Issues in Community Policing.*

65. See Walker, *Sense and Nonsense About Crime and Drugs,* p. 77.

66. Harcourt, "Reflecting on the Subject."

67. National Institute of Justice, "A Study of Homicide in Eight U.S. Cities."

68. Butterfield, "Drop in Homicide Rate."

69. Ibid.

70. Ibid. According to Harcourt, the number of complaints of police brutality received by the New York City Civilian Complaint Review Board rose from 3,580 in 1993 to 5,550 in 1997 (Harcourt, "Reflecting on the Subject").

71. Egan, "Soldiers of the Drug War."

References

Alderman, J. "Leading the Public: The Media's Focus on Crime Shaped Sentiment," *The Public Perspective* 5 (1994): 26-28.

Allen, Jessica, Sonia Livingstone, and Robert Reiner. "True Lies, Changing Images of Crime in British Postwar Cinema." *European Journal of Communication,* 13 (1998): 53-75.

Amnesty International. *United States of America—Rights for All.* New York: Amnesty International Publications, 1998.

_____. *USA: The Conveyor Belt of Death Continues* (press release), 3 December 1998.

Andersen, Robin. *Consumer Culture and TV Programming.* Boulder, CO: Westview, 1995.

Anderson, David. *Sensible Justice: Alternatives to Prison.* New York: New Press, 1998.

Anderson, Elijah. "The Code of the Streets." *Atlantic Monthly,* August 1994, 82.

_____. *Streetwise: Race, Class and Change in an Urban Community.* Chicago: University of Chicago Press, 1990.

Anderson, George. "Organizing Against the Death Penalty." *America* 178 (2 January 1998): 10-11.

Applebome, Peter. "For the Ultimate Safe School, Eyes Turn to Dallas." *New York Times,* 20 September 1995, B11.

Associated Press. "Citing Drop in Welfare Rolls, Clinton to Seek Further Cuts." *New York Times,* 25 January 1999, A12.

Atkinson, Anthony B., Lee Rainwater, and Timothy M. Smeeding. *Income Distribution in OECD Countries: Evidence From the Luxembourg Income Study.* Paris: Organization for Economic Cooperation and Development, 1995.

Aynes, Richard. "Constitutional Considerations: Government Responsibility and the Right Not to Be a Victim." *Pepperdine Law Review* 11 (1984): 63-116.

Bailey, William, and Ruth Peterson. "Murder, Capital Punishment, and Deterrence: A Review of the Literature." In *The Death Penalty in America,* edited by Hugo Adam Bedau. New York: Oxford University Press, 1997.

Baker, Liva. *Miranda: Crime, Law and Politics.* New York: Atheneum, 1983.

239

Baldus, David, and George Woodworth. "Race Discrimination and the Death Penalty: An Empirical and Legal Overview." In *America's Experiment with Capital Punishment: Reflections on the Past, Present and Future of the Ultimate Penal Sanction*, edited by James Acker, Robert Bohm, and Charles Lanier. Durham, NC: Carolina Academic, 1998.

Barak, Gregg. "Between the Waves: Mass-Mediated Themes of Crime and Justice." *Social Justice* 21 (1994): 133-47.

Barkan, Steven, and Steven Cohn. "Racial Prejudice and Support for the Death Penalty for Whites," *Journal of Research in Crime and Delinquency* 31 (May 1994): 202-9.

Barlow, Melissa Hickman. "Race and the Problem of Crime in Time and Newsweek Cover Stories, 1946-1995." *Social Justice* 25 (1998): 149-83.

Baum, Dan. *Smoke and Mirrors: The War on Drugs and the Politics of Failure.* New York: Little, Brown, 1996.

Bayer, Ronald. "Crime, Punishment and the Decline of Liberal Optimism." *Crime and Delinquency* 27 (April 1981): 169-190.

Beck, Allen. "Trends in U.S. Correctional Populations." In *The Dilemmas of Corrections*, edited by Kenneth Haas and Geoffrey Alpert. Prospect Heights, IL: Waveland, 1999.

Beck, Allen, and Peter Brien. "Trends in U.S. Correctional Populations." In *The Dilemmas of Corrections*, edited by Kenneth Haas and Geoffrey Alpert. Prospect Heights, IL: Waveland, 1995.

Becker, Howard. "Whose Side Are We On?" *Social Problems* 14 (1967): 239-47.

Beckett, Katherine. "Setting the Public Agenda: 'Street Crime' and Drug Use in American Politics," *Social Problems* 41 (1994): 425-47.

_____. "Culture and the Politics of Signification: The Case of Child Sexual Abuse," *Social Problems* 43 (February 1996): 57-76.

_____. *Making Crime Pay.* New York: Oxford University Press, 1997.

_____. "Media Depictions of Drug Use: The Impact of Official Sources," *Journal of Research in Political Sociology* 7 (1995): 161-82.

Beckett, Katherine, and Theodore Sasson, "The Media and the Construction of the Drug Crisis in America." In *The New War on Drugs*, edited by Eric Jensen and Jurg Gerber. Cincinnati: ACJS/Anderson, 1997.

Beilein, Thomas, and Peter Krasnow. "Jail Prototype Leads to Faster Construction, Lower Costs." *Corrections Today*, April 1996, 128-31.

Beirne, Piers, and James Messerschmidt. *Criminology.* New York: Harcourt Brace Jovanovich, 1991.

Bellah, Robert, Richard Madsen, William Sullivan, Ann Swidler, and Steven Tipton, *Habits of the Heart.* New York: Harper & Row, 1985.

Bennett, Lance. *Public Opinion in American Politics.* New York: Harcourt Brace Jovanovich, 1980.

Bennett, Stephan Earl, and Alfred Tuchfarber. "The Social Structural Sources of Cleavage on Law and Order Policies." *American Journal of Political Science* 19 (1975): 419-438.

Bennett, William, John DiIulio, and John Walters. *Body Count.* New York: Simon & Schuster, 1996.

Berk, Richard, and David Rauma. "Remuneration and Recidivism: the Long-Term Impact of Unemployment Compensation on Ex-Offenders." *Journal of Quantitative Criminology* 3 (1987): 3-27.

Bertram, Eva, Morris Blachman, Kenneth Sharpe, and Peter Andreas. *Drug War Politics: The Price of Denial.* Berkeley: University of California Press, 1996.

Bertram, Eva, and Kenneth Sharpe. "War Ends, Drugs Win." *The Nation* 264 (6 January 1997): 11.

Best, Joel. "But Seriously Folks: The Limitations of the Strict Constructionist Interpretation of Social Problems." In *Constructionist Controversies*, edited by Gale Miller and
James Holstein. Hawthorne, NY: Aldine de Gruyter, 1993.

_____. *Random Violence*. Berkeley: University of California Press, 1999.

Bingol, Nesrin, Carlotta Schuster, Magdalena Fuchs, Silvia Iosub, Gudrun Turner, Richard Stone, and Donald Gromisch. "The Influence of Socioeconomic Factors on the
Occurrence of Fetal Alcohol Syndrome." *Advances in Alcohol and Substance Abuse* 105
(1987): 105-18.

"Blamed in Crime Rise: Civil Rights Excesses." *U.S. News and World Report*, 27 February
1967, 15.

Blumstein, Alfred, and Daniel Cork. "Linking Gun Availability to Youth Gun Violence."
Law and Contemporary Problems 59 (1996): 5-24.

Blumstein, Alfred, and Richard Rosenfeld. "Assessing the Recent Ups and Downs in U.S.
Homicide Rates." *National Institute of Justice Journal* 237 (October 1998): 9-11.

Boggess, Scott, and John Bound. "Did Criminal Activity Increase During the 1980's?
Comparisons Across Data Sources." *Social Science Quarterly* 78 (1997): 725-36.

Bohm, Robert M. "The Economic Costs of Capital Punishment." In *America's Experiment
with Capital Punishment: Reflections on the Past, Present and Future of the Ultimate Penal
Sanction*, edited by James R. Acker, Robert M. Bohm, and Charles S. Lanier. Durham,
NC: Carolina Academic, 1998.

Bourgeois, Philippe. "In Search of Horatio Alger: Culture and Ideology in the Crack
Economy." In *Crack in America: Demon Drugs and Social Justice*, edited by Craig
Reinarman and Harry Levine. Berkeley: University of California Press, 1997.

_____. *In Search of Respect: Selling Crack in El Barrio*. New York: Cambridge University
Press, 1995.

Bowers, William. "Capital Punishment and Contemporary Values, People's Misgivings
and the Court's Misperceptions," *Law and Society Review* 27 (1993): 157-76.

Box, Steven, Chris Hale, and Glen Andrews. "Explaining Fear of Crime," *British Journal
of Criminology* 28 (1988): 340-56.

Browning, Sandra, and Liqun Cao. "The Impact of Race on Criminal Justice Ideology,"
Justice Quarterly 9 (1992): 685-701.

Brownstein, Henry H. "The Media and the Construction of Random Drug Violence."
Social Justice 18 (1991): 85-103.

Brownstein, Henry H., Patrick J. Ryan, and Paul Goldstein. "Drug-Related Homicide in
New York City: 1984 and 1988." *Crime and Delinquency* 38 (1992): 459-76.

Buckley, William F., ed. "Abolish the Drug Laws? 400 Readers Give Their Views."
National Review, 1 July 1996, 32-37.

Bureau of Justice Statistics. *Correctional Populations in the United States 1980."* Washington,
DC: Bureau of Justice Statistics, U.S. Department of Justice, 1981.

_____. *Correctional Populations in the United States 1990."* Washington, DC: Bureau of
Justice Statistics, U.S. Department of Justice, 1995.

_____. *Correctional Populations in the United States 1995."* Washington, DC: Bureau of
Justice Statistics, U.S. Department of Justice, 1997.

_____. *Correctional Populations in the United States 1996."* Washington, DC: Bureau of
Justice Statistics, U.S. Department of Justice, 1997.

_____. *Correctional Populations in the United States 1997."* Washington, DC: Bureau of
Justice Statistics, U.S. Department of Justice, 1998.

_____. *Crime and Justice in the United States and in England and Wales, 1981-1996:
Executive Summary*. Washington, DC: Bureau of Justice Statistics, U.S. Department of
Justice, 1998.

_____. *National Criminal Victimization Survey, Crime Trends, 1973-1997*. Washington, DC: Bureau of Justice Statistics, U.S. Department of Justice, 1998.

_____. *Probation and Parole Populations, 1997*. Washington, DC: Bureau of Justice Statistics, U.S. Department of Justice, 1998.

_____. *Prison Statistics, 1997*. (Washington, DC: Bureau of Justice Statistics, U.S. Department of Justice, 1998.

_____. *Prisoners in 1996*. Washington, DC: Bureau of Justice Statistics, U.S. Department of Justice, 1997.

_____. *Prisoners in 1997*. Washington, DC: Bureau of Justice Statistics, U.S. Department of Justice, 1998.

Bush, George. "Address to Students on Drug Abuse." *Public Papers of the President 1989*. Vol. 1: 746-9. Washington, DC: U.S. Government Printing Office, 1990.

Butterfield, Fox. "As Inmate Population Grows, So Does Focus on Children." New York Times, 7 April, 1997.

_____. "Asylums Behind Bars." *New York Times*, 5 March 1998, A1.

_____. "Drop in Homicide Rate Linked to Crack's Decline." *New York Times*, 27 October 1997, A10.

_____. "Drug Treatment in Prisons Dips as Use Rises, Study Finds." *New York Times*, 6 January 1999, A10.

_____. "Inmates Serving More Time, Justice Department Reports." *New York Times*, 11 January 1999, A10.

_____. "New Prisons Cast Shadow Over Higher Education." *New York Times*, 12 April 1995, A21.

Califano, Joseph. "Welfare's Drug Connection." *New York Times*, 24 August 1996, A19.

"Capital Punishment Opposed." *Christian Century* 110 (16 June 1993): 625.

Caplan, Gerald. "Reflections on the Nationalization of Crime, 1964-8." *Law and the Social Order* 3 (1973): 583-638.

Carbaugh, Donal. *Talking American*. Norwood, NJ: Ablex, 1988.

Carlson, James M. *Prime Time Law Enforcement: Crime Show Viewing and Attitudes Toward the Criminal Justice System*. New York: Praeger, 1985.

Carter, Dan. *The Politics of Rage*. New York: Simon & Schuster, 1995.

Cavender, Gray. "In the Shadow of Shadows: Television Reality Crime Programming." In *Entertaining Crime: Television Reality Programs*, edited by Gray Cavender and Mark Fishman. Hawthorne, NY: Aldine de Gruyter, 1998.

Cavender, Gray, and Mark Fishman. *Entertaining Crime: Television Reality Programs*. Hawthorne, NY: Aldine de Gruyter, 1998.

Chambliss, William. "Policing the Ghetto Underclass: The Politics of Law and Law Enforcement," *Social Problems* 41 (1994): 177-94.

Chermak, Steven. "Crime in the News Media: A Refined Understanding of How Crimes Become News." In *Media, Process and the Social Construction of Crime: Studies in Newsmaking Criminology*, edited by Gregg Barak. New York: Garland, 1994.

_____. *Victims in the News: Crime and the American News Media*. Boulder, CO: Westview, 1995.

Chiricos, Ted, Sarah Eschholz, and Marc Gertz. "Crime, News and Fear of Crime." *Social Problems* 44 (1997): 342-57.

Christie, Nils. "Conflicts as Property." *British Journal of Criminology* 17 (1977): 1-15.

_____. *Crime Control as Industry*. London: Routledge, 1993.

Clark, John, James Austin, and D. Alan Henry. *'Three Strikes and You're Out': A Review of State Legislation* (occasional paper). Washington, DC: National Institute of Justice, U.S. Department of Justice, September 1997.

"Clinton Nurtures High Hopes . . ." *National Journal,* 20 November 1993, 2794-5.

Cloud, Jon. "For They Know Not What They Do?" *Time,* 24 August 1998.

Cohen, Peter D. A. "Crack in the Netherlands: Effective Social Policy Is Effective Drug Policy." In *Crack in America: Demon Drugs and Social Justice,* edited by Craig Reinarman and Harry Levine. Berkeley: University of California Press, 1997.

Cohen, Stanley. *Visions of Social Control.* Cambridge: Polity Press, 1985.

Cohn, Steven, Steven Barkan, and William Halteman. "Punitive Attitudes Toward Criminals: Racial Consensus or Racial Conflict?" *Social Problems* 38 (1991): 287-96.

Coleman, C. "The Influence of Mass Media and Interpersonal Communication on Societal and Personal Risk Judgements." *Communication Research* 20 (1993): 611-28.

Colomy, Paul, and Laura Ross Greiner. "Innocent Blood: Ideal Victims and the Summer of Violence." *Social Problems* (in review).

Cook, Philip, and John Laub. "The Unprecedented Epidemic of Youth Violence." In *Crime and Justice: A Review of Research,* Vol. 24, edited by Mark H. Moore and Michael Tonry. Chicago: University of Chicago Press, 1998.

Corbett, Michael. "Public Support for 'Law and Order': Interrelationships With System Affirmation and Attitudes Toward Minorities." *Criminology* 19 (1981): 328-343.

Courtright, David. *Violent Land.* Cambridge, MA: Harvard University Press, 1996.

"Crack and Crime." *Newsweek,* 16 June 1986.

Crawford, Adam. "Appeals to Community and Crime Prevention," *Crime, Law and Social Change* 22 (1995): 97-126.

Crew, B. Keith. "Acting Like Cops: The Social Reality of Crime and Law on TV Police Dramas." In *Marginal Conventions,* edited by Clinton Sanders. Bowling Green, OH: Bowling Green State University Popular Press, 1990.

Crime and Justice Foundation. *Shifting the Debate on Crime: A Study of Public Opinion and New Approaches to Fighting Crime.* Boston, MA: Crime and Justice Foundation, 1991.

"Crime in America." *The Economist,* 8 June 1996, 17.

Cronin, Thomas E., Tania Z. Cronin and Michael Milakovich. *The U.S. Versus Crime in the Streets.* Bloomington: Indiana University Press, 1981.

Cullen, Frances, S. E. Skovron, J. E. Scott, and V. S. Burton, Jr. "Public Support for Correctional Treatment: The Tenacity of Rehabilitative Ideology." *Criminal Justice and Behavior* 17 (1990): 6-18.

Cullen, Frances, Patricia Van Voorhis, and Jody L. Sundt. "Prisons in Crisis: The American Experience." In *Prisons 2000: An International Perspective on the Current State and Future of Imprisonment,* edited by Roger Matthews and Peter Francis. London: Macmillan, 1996.

Cullen, Frances, John Paul Wright, and Brandon K. Applegate. "Control in the Community: The Limits of Reform?" In *Choosing Correctional Options,* edited by Alan Harland. Newbury Park, CA: Sage, 1996.

Currie, Elliott. *Confronting Crime: An American Challenge.* New York: Pantheon, 1985.

_____. *Crime and Punishment in America.* New York: Henry Holt, 1998.

_____. *Reckoning: Drugs, the Cities, and the American Future.* New York: Hill & Wang, 1993.

_____. "Two Visions of Community Crime Prevention." In *Communities and Crime Reduction,* edited by Tim Hope and Margaret Shaw. London: Her Majesty's Stationery Office, 1988.

Danielman, Lucig H., and Stephen D. Reese. "Intermedia Influence and the Drug Issue: Converging on Cocaine." In *Communication Campaigns About Drugs: Government, Media and the Public,* edited by Pamela Shoemaker. Hillsdale, NJ: Lawrence Erlbaum, 1989.

Danziger, Sheldon H., and Peter Gottschalk. *America Unequal.* Cambridge, MA: Harvard University Press, 1995.

Danziger, Sheldon H., and Daniel H. Weinberg. "The Historical Record: Trends in Family Income, Inequality and Poverty." In *Confronting Poverty: Prescriptions for Change*, edited by Sheldon H. Danziger, Gary D. Sandefur, and Daniel H. Weinberg. New York: Russell Sage, 1994.

Davey, Joseph D. *The New Social Contract: America's Journey from the Welfare State to Police State*. Westport, CT: Praeger, 1995.

Davis, David. "The Production of Crime Policies," *Crime and Social Justice* 20 (1983): 121-37.

Davis, Mike. *City of Quartz: Excavating the Future in Los Angeles*. New York: Vintage, 1992.

Dayan, Daniel, and Elihu Katz. *Media Events*. Cambridge, MA: Harvard University Press, 1992.

Death Penalty Information Center. *Additional Cases of Innocence and Possible Innocence*. Washington, DC: Death Penalty Information Center, 24 February 1998.

Democratic National Committee. *The 1992 Democratic Party Platform*. Washington, DC: Democratic National Committee, 1992.

Diamond, Shari, and Loretta Stalans. "The Myth of Judicial Leniency in Sentencing," *Behavioral Sciences and the Law* 7 (1989): 73-89.

Dickey, Walter, and Pam Stiebs Hollenhorst. "Three-Strikes Laws: Massive Impact in California and Georgia, Little Elsewhere." *Overcrowded Times* 9 (December 1998): 1-5.

Dieter, Richard. *The Death Penalty in Black and White: Who Lives, Who Dies, Who Decides*. Washington, DC: Death Penalty Information Center, June 1998.

_____. *Innocence and the Death Penalty: The Increasing Danger of Executing the Innocent*. Washington, DC: Death Penalty Information Center, July 1997.

Dix, Carl. "Police Violence: Rising Epidemic/Raising Resistance." *Black Scholar* 27 (spring 1997): 59-63.

Doble, John, Stephen Immerwahr, and Amy Richardson, *Punishing Criminals: The People of Delaware Consider the Options*. New York: Edna McConnell Clark Foundation, 1991.

Doble, John, and Josh Klein. *Punishing Criminals, The Public's View: An Alabama Survey*. New York: Edna McConnell Clark Foundation, 1989.

Dominick, Joseph R. "Crime, Law Enforcement and the Mass Media." In *Deviance and the Mass Media*, edited by Charles Winick. Beverly Hills, CA: Sage, 1978.

Donahue, John Jay. "Some Perspectives on Crime and Criminal Justice Policy." In *The Crime Conundrum*, edited by L. Friedman and G. Fisher. Boulder, CO: Westview, 1997.

Donovan, Pamela. "Armed with the Power of Television: Reality Crime Programming and the Reconstruction of Law and Order in the U.S." In *Entertaining Crime: Television Reality Programs*, edited by Gray Cavender and Mark Fishman. Hawthorne, NY: Aldine de Gruyter, 1998.

Donziger, Steven R., ed. *The Real War on Crime: The Report of the National Criminal Justice Commission*. New York: Harper Perennial, 1996.

Doyle, Aaron. " 'Cops': Television Policing as Policing Reality." In *Entertaining Crime: Television Reality Programs*, edited by Gray Cavender and Mark Fishman. Hawthorne, NY: Aldine de Gruyter, 1998.

Durkheim, Emile. *Suicide*. New York: Free Press, 1951.

Edelman, Murray. *Constructing the Political Spectacle*. Chicago: Chicago University Press, 1988.

Edsall, Thomas B., and Mary Edsall. *Chain Reaction: The Impact of Rights, Race and Taxes on American Politics*. New York: Norton, 1991.

Egan, Timothy. "Soldiers of the Drug War Remain on Duty." *New York Times*, 11 March 1999, A1, A16.

_____. "The War on Drugs Retreats, Still Taking Prisoners," *New York Times*, 28 February 1999, 1.

Ehrlichmann, John. *Witness to Power: The Nixon Years*. New York: Simon and Schuster, 1970.

Elias, Robert. *Victims Still: The Political Manipulation of Crime Victims*. London: Sage, 1993.

Elikann, Peter. *The Tough on Crime Myth*. New York: Insight, 1996.

Ellsworth, Phoebe, and Samuel Gross, "Hardening of the Attitudes: Americans' Views on the Death Penalty," *Journal of Social Issues* 50 (1994): 19-52.

Entman, Robert. "Blacks in the News: Television, Modern Racism and Cultural Change." *Journalism Quarterly* 69 (summer 1992): 341-61.

_____. "Representation and Reality in the Portrayal of Blacks on Network News." *Journalism Quarterly* 71 (1994): 509-20.

Epstein, Edward. *Agency of Fear: Opiates and Political Power in America*. New York: Random House, 1977.

Ericson, Richard, Patricia Baranek, and Janet Chan. *Representing Order*. Toronto: University of Toronto Press, 1991.

Executive Office of the President. *Budget of the U.S. Government*. Washington, DC: U.S. Government Printing Office, 1990.

Fagan, Jeffrey, Franklin Zimring, and June Kim. "Declining Homicide in New York City: A Tale of Two Trends." *National Institute of Justice Journal* 237 (October 1998): 12-13.

"FBI Director Weighs War on Drug Trafficking." *New York Times*, 26 February 1981, A27.

Federal Bureau of Investigation. *Uniform Crime Reports, 1964-1997*. Washington, DC: U.S. Department of Justice, 1965-1998.

Federal Bureau of Investigation. *Uniform Crime Report, 1996*. Washington, DC: U.S. Department of Justice.

Feeley, Malcolm, and Jonathan Simon. "The New Penology: Notes on the Emerging Strategy of Corrections and Its Implications." *Criminology* 30 (1992): 449-74.

Ferraro, Kenneth. *Fear of Crime: Interpreting Victimization Risk*. New York: State University of New York Press, 1995.

Ferraro, Kenneth, and Randy LaGrange. "The Measurement of the Fear of Crime." *Sociological Inquiry* 57 (1987): 70-101.

Fishman, Mark. "Crime Waves as Ideology," *Social Problems* 25 (1978): 531-43.

_____. "Ratings and Reality: The Persistence of the Reality Crime Genre." In *Entertaining Crime: Television Reality Programs*, edited by Gray Cavender and Mark Fishman. Hawthorne, NY: Aldine de Gruyter, 1998.

Fiske, John. *Television Culture*. New York: Routledge, 1987.

Flanagan, Timothy. "Change and Influence in Popular Criminology: Public Attributions of Crime Causation," *Journal of Criminal Justice* 15 (1987): 231-43.

Flanagan, Timothy, and Dennis Longmire, eds. *Americans View Crime and Justice*. Thousand Oaks, CA: Sage, 1996.

Flint, Anthony. "Inside Views on Black Incarceration Issue." *Washington Post*, 5 October 1995, 29.

Forman, Avraham, and Susan B. Lachter. "The National Institute on Drug Abuse Cocaine Prevention Campaign." In *Communication Campaigns About Drugs: Government, Media and the Public*, edited by Pamela Shoemaker. Hillsdale, NJ: Lawrence Erlbaum, 1989.

Frankel, Bruce, and Fannie Weinstein. "Crusader." *People Magazine* 48 (18 August 1997): 93.

Freeman, Richard B. "Crime and the Employment of Disadvantaged Youths." National Bureau of Economic Research Working Paper no. 3875, 1991.

Gallup, George, ed. *The Gallup Poll*. Wilmington, DE: Scholarly Resources, 1990.

Gamson, William, and Kathryn E. Lasch. "The Political Culture of Social Welfare Policy." In *Evaluating the Welfare State: Social and Political Perspectives*, edited by Shimon E. Spiro and Ephraim Yuchtman-Yaar. New York: Academic, 1983.

Gamson, William A. *Talking Politics*. Boston: Cambridge University Press, 1992.

Gamson, William A., and Andre Modigliani. "The Changing Culture of Affirmative Action." *Research in Political Sociology* 3 (1987): 137-77.

Gans, Herbert. *Deciding What's News*. New York: Vintage, 1979.

_____. *Middle American Individualism*. New York: Oxford, 1988.

_____. *The War Against the Poor*. New York: Basic Books, 1995.

Garland, David. "The Limits of the Sovereign State: Strategies of Crime Control in Contemporary Society," *British Journal of Criminology* 36 (1996): 445-71.

_____. "Penal Modernism and Postmodernism." In *Punishment and Social Control*, edited by Thomas G. Blomberg and Stanley Cohen. New York: Aldine de Gruyter, 1995.

_____. *Punishment and Modern Society: A Study in Social Theory*. Chicago: University of Chicago Press, 1990.

_____. *Punishment and Welfare: A History of Penal Strategies*. Aldershot, England: Gower, 1985.

Garofalo, James, and Maureen McLeod. "The Structure and Operation of Neighborhood Watch Programs in the United States." *Crime and Delinquency* 35 (July 1989): 326-44.

Gaubatz, Kathlyn Taylor. *Crime in the Public Mind*. Ann Arbor, MI: University of Michigan Press, 1995.

Gerber, Jurg, and Simone Engelhardt-Greer. "Just and Painful: Attitudes Toward Sentencing Criminals." In *Americans View Crime and Justice*, edited by Timothy Flanagan and Dennis Longmire. Newbury Park, CA: Sage, 1996.

Gerbner, George, and Larry Gross. "Living With Television: The Violence Profile." *Journal of Communication* 26 (1976): 173-99.

Gerbner, George, Larry Gross, Michael Morgan, and Nancy Signorielli. "The 'Mainstreaming' of America: Violence Profile No. 11." *Journal of Communication* 30 (summer 1980): 10-29.

Gilligan, James. *Violence*. New York: Vintage, 1996.

Ginsberg, Carl. *Race and the Media: The Enduring Life of the Moynihan Report*. Washington, DC: Institute for Media Analysis, 1996.

Gitlin, Todd. *Inside Prime Time*. New York: Pantheon, 1983.

Goldstein, Paul L., Henry H. Brownstein, Patrick J. Ryan, & Patricia A. Belluci. "Crack and Homicide in New York City, 1988: A Conceptually-Based Event Analysis." *Contemporary Drug Problems* 16 (1989): 651-87.

"Goldwater at Illinois State Fair." *Chicago Tribune*, 20 August 1964, A12.

"Goldwater's Acceptance Speech to GOP Convention." *New York Times*, 17 July 1964, A17.

Golub, Andrew Lang, and Bruce D. Johnson. *Crack's Decline: Some Surprises Across U.S. Cities*. Washington, DC: National Institute of Justice, U.S. Department of Justice, July 1997.

Goode, Erich. "The American Drug Panic of the 1980's: Social Construction or Objective Threat?" *Violence, Aggression and Terrorism* 3 (1989): 327-48.

Gordon, Margaret, and Stephanie Riger. *The Female Fear*. New York: Free Press, 1989.

Gorn, Elliott J. "The Wicked World: The National Police Gazette and Gilded-Age America." In *The Culture of Crime*, edited by Craig L. LaMay and Everette E. Dennis. New Brunswick, NJ: Transaction, 1995.

Gray, Mike. *Drug Crazy*. New York: Random House, 1998.

Greene, Robert. "Educators Model Airport Security to Prevent More Bloodshed. *Buffalo News*, 31 August 1998, 4A.

Greenwood, Peter, C. Peter Rydell, Allan F. Abrahamse, Jonathan P. Caulkins, James Chiesa, Karyn E. Model, and Stephen P. Klein. "Estimated Benefits and Costs of California's New Mandatory-Sentencing Law." In *Three Strikes and You're Out*, edited by David Sichor and Dale Sechrest. Newbury Park, CA: Sage, 1996.

Gurr, Ted R., ed. *Violence in America*. Vol. I. Newbury Park, CA: Sage, 1989.

Gusfield, Joseph. "Moral Passage: The Symbolic Process in Public Designations of Deviance." *Social Problems* 15 (1967): 175-88.

Hagan, John. *Crime and Disrepute*. Newbury Park, CA: Pine Forge, 1994.

Hagan, John, and Celesta Albonetti. "Race, Class and the Perception of Criminal Injustice in America," *American Journal of Sociology* 88 (1982): 329-55.

Haghighi, Bahram, and Jon Sorensen. "America's Fear of Crime." In *Americans View Crime and Justice*, edited by Timothy Flanagan and Dennis Longmire. Thousand Oaks, CA: Sage, 1996.

Haines, Herbert H. *Against Capital Punishment: The Anti-Death Penalty Movement in America, 1972-1994*. New York: Oxford University Press, 1996.

Hall, Stuart, Chas Critcher, Tony Jefferson, John Clarke, and Brian Roberts. *Policing the Crisis: Mugging, the State and Law and Order*. New York: Holmes and Meier, 1978.

Haller, M. H. "Bootlegging: The Business and Politics of Violence." In *Violence in America*, Vol. I, edited by Ted R. Gurr. Newbury Park, CA: Sage, 1989.

Haney, Craig, and Manzolati, John. "Television Criminology: Network Illusions of Criminal Justice Realities." In *Readings on the Social Animal*, edited by Elliot Aronson, 1983. San Francisco: W. H. Freeman.

Hannon, Lance, and James DeFronzo. "The Truly Disadvantaged, Public Assistance and Crime." *Social Problems* 45 (August 1998): 383-92.

Harcourt, Bernard E. "Reflecting on the Subject: A Critique of the Social Influence Conception of Deterrence, the Broken Windows Theory, and Order-Maintenance Policing, New York Style." *Michigan Law Review* 97 (1998): 292-389.

Harrington, Christine B. "Popular Justice, Populist Politics: Law in Community Organizing." *Social and Legal Studies* 1 (1992): 177-98.

Heath, Linda and Kevin Gilbert. "Mass Media and Fear of Crime." *American Behavioral Scientist* 39 (February 1996): 379-86.

Heath, Linda, and J. Petraitis. "Television Viewing and Fear of Crime: Where Is the Mean World?" *Basic and Applied Social Psychology* 8 (1987): 97-123.

Henderson, Lynne N. "The Wrongs of Victim's Rights." *Stanford Law Review* 37 (April 1985): 937-1021.

Herbert, Steve. "Reassessing Police and Police Studies." *Theoretical Criminology*, forthcoming.

Herman, Edward, and Noam Chomsky. *Manufacturing Consent*. New York: Pantheon, 1988.

Heymann, Philip B., and Mark H. Moore. "The Federal Role in Dealing With Violent Street Crime: Principles, Questions and Cautions." *Annals of the American Academy of Political and Social Science* 543 (January 1996): 103-15.

Hilgartner, Stephen A., and Charles L. Bosk. "The Rise and Fall of Social Problems: A Public Arenas Model." *American Journal of Sociology* 94 (July 1988): 53-78.

Hope, Tim. "Community Crime Prevention." In *Building a Safer Society: Strategic Approaches to Crime Prevention*, edited by Michael Tonry and David P. Farrington. Chicago: University of Chicago Press, 1995.

Hope, Tim, and M. Shaw, "Community Approaches to Reducing Crime." In *Communities and Crime Reduction*, edited by T. Hope and M. Shaw. London: Her Majesty's Stationery Office, 1988.

Hornblower, Margot. "Have Guns Will Travel." *Time*, 151 (6 July 1998).

Ibarra, Peter, and John Kitsuse. "Vernacular Constituents of Moral Discourse: An Interactionist Proposal for the Study of Social Problems." In *Constructionist Controversies*, edited by Gale Miller and James Holstein. Hawthorne, NY: Aldine de Gruyter, 1993.

Idelson, Holly. "Block Grants Replace Prevention, Police Hiring in House Bill." *Congressional Quarterly*, 18 February 1995, 530-32.

_____. "Democrat's New Proposal Seeks Consensus By Compromise." *Congressional Quarterly* 51 (14 August 1993): 2228-89.

_____. "Tough Anti-Crime Bill Faces Tougher Balancing Act." *Congressional Quarterly Weekly Reporter*, 29 January 1994, 171-73.

"Inside the Beltway: Clinton Administration Endorses Needle Exchange Programs." *Drug Policy Letter*, winter/spring 1997, 14.

"Inside Views on Black Incarceration Issue." *Boston Globe*, 20 October 1995, 29.

Irwin, John, and James Austin. *It's About Time*. Belmont, CA: Wadsworth, 1997.

Iyengar, Shanto. "Effects of Framing on Attributions of Responsibility for Crime and Terrorism." In *Crime and the Media*, edited by Richard V. Ericson. Aldershot, England: Dartmouth, 1995.

_____. *Is Anyone Responsible?* Chicago: University of Chicago Press, 1991.

Iyengar, Shanto, and Donald Kinder. *News That Matters*. Chicago: University of Chicago Press, 1987.

Jacob, Herbert, and Robert L. Lineberry. "Crime, Politics and the Cities." In *Crime in City Politics*, edited by Anne Heinz, Herbert Jacob, and Robert L. Lineberry. New York: Longman, 1983.

Jeffres, Leo W., and Richard M. Perloff. *Mass Media Effects*. Prospect Heights, IL: Waveland, 1997.

Jenkins, Philip. *Using Murder*. Hawthorne, NY: Aldine de Gruyter, 1994.

Jensen, Eric L., and Jurg Gerber. "The Civil Forfeiture of Assets and the War on Drugs: Expanding Criminal Sanctions While Reducing Due Process Protections." *Crime and Delinquency* 42 (1996): 421-34.

Jensen, Eric, Jurg Gerber, and Ginna Babcock. "The New War on Drugs: Grassroots Movement or Political Construction?" *Journal of Drug Issues* 21 (1991): 651-667.

Johnson, Lyndon B. "Remarks on the City Hall Steps, Dayton, Ohio." In *Public Papers of the Presidents 1964*. Vol. 2. Washington, DC: U.S. Government Printing Office, 1965.

_____. "Special Message to the Congress on Law Enforcement and the Administration of Justice." *Public Papers of the Presidents 1965*. Vol. 1. Washington, DC: U.S. Government Printing Office, 1966.

Johnston, Lloyd D. "America's Drug Problem: Is It Real or Is It Memorex?" In *Communication Campaigns About Drugs: Government, the Media and the Public*, edited by Pamela Shoemaker. Hillsdale, NJ: Lawrence Erlbaum, 1989.

Jones, Charisse. "Crack and Punishment: Is Race the Issue?" *New York Times*, 28 October 1995, A1.

Kahan, Dan. "What Do Alternative Sanctions Mean?" *University of Chicago Law Review* 63 (spring 1996): 591-653.

Karst, Kenneth L. *Law's Promise, Law's Expression: Visions of Power in the Politics of Race, Gender and Religion*. New Haven, CT: Yale University Press, 1993.

Kasinsky, Renee Goldsmith. "Patrolling the Facts: Media, Cops and Crime." In *Media, Process and the Social Construction of Crime: Studies in Newsmaking Criminology,* edited by Gregg Barak. New York: Garland, 1994.

Kaufman, Jonathan. "Prison Life Is All Around for a Girl Growing Up in Downtown Baltimore." *Wall Street Journal,* 27 October 1998, Interactive Edition (http://www.wsj.com).

Kelling, George, and Catherine Coles. *Fixing Broken Windows.* New York: Free Press, 1996.

Kitsuse, John, and Malcolm Spector. "Toward a Sociology of Social Problems: Social Conditions, Value-Judgements, and Social Problems." *Social Problems* 20 (1973): 407-19.

Kleinknecht, William G. "Victim's Rights Advocates on a Roll." *National Law Journal* 18 (1996): A1, A8.

Kooistra, Paul, John Mahoney, and Saundra Westervelt. "The World of Crime According to 'Cops.' " In *Entertaining Crime: Television Reality Programs,* edited by Gray Cavender and Mark Fishman. Hawthorne, NY: Aldine de Gruyter, 1998.

Krahn, Harvey, Timothy Hartnagel, and John Gartrell. "Income Inequality and Homicide Rates: Cross-National Data and Criminological Theories." *Criminology* 24 (1986): 269-93.

Kramer, Michael. "From Sarajevo to Needle Park." *Time,* 21 February 1994, 29.

Kurki, Leena. "International Crime Survey: American Rates About Average." *Overcrowded Times* 8 (October 1997): 4.

Lacayo, Richard. "Lock 'Em Up!" *Time,* 7 February 1994.

LaFree, Gary. *Rape and Criminal Justice: The Social Construction of Sexual Assault.* Belmont, CA: Wadsworth, 1989.

Land, Kenneth, P. McCall, and L. Cohen. "Structural Co-Variates of Homicide Rates: Are There Any Invariances Across Time and Space?" *American Journal of Sociology* 95 (1990): 922-63.

Lane, R. "On the Social Meaning of Homicide Trends in America." In *Violence in America,* Vol. I, edited by Ted R. Gurr. Newbury Park, CA: Sage, 1989.

Langan, Patrick A. "America's Soaring Prison Population." *Science* 251 (1991): 1568-73.

"Law Permits Trial of Youths as Adults for Guns at School." *New York Times,* 19 August 1998, B4.

Lawrence, Regina G. "Accidents, Icons and Indexing: The Dynamics of News Coverage of Police Use of Force." *Political Communication* 13 (1996): 437-54.

Leff, Donna R., David L. Protess, and Stephen C. Brooks. "Crusading Journalism: Changing Public Attitudes and Policy-Making Agendas." *Public Opinion Quarterly* 50 (1986): 300-15.

Leukefeld, C. "The Role of the National Institute on Drug Abuse in Drug Abuse Prevention Research." In *Persuasive Communication and Drug Abuse Prevention,* edited by L. Donohew, H. Sypher and W. Bukoski. Hillsdale, NJ: Lawrence Erlbaum, 1991.

Levine, Hillel, and Lawrence Harmon. *The Death of an American Jewish Community.* New York: Free Press, 1993.

Lewis, Dan, and Greta Salem. *Fear of Crime: Incivility and the Production of a Social Problem.* New Brunswick, NJ: Transaction, 1986.

Lewis, Oscar. *La Vida.*

Lichter, S. Robert, Linda S. Lichter, and Stanley Rothman. *Prime Time: How TV Portrays American Culture.* Washington, DC: Regnery, 1994.

Liska, Allen, and William Baccaglini. "Feeling Safe by Comparison." *Social Problems* 37 (1990): 360-74.

Liska, Allen, Andrew Sanchirico, and Mark Reed. "Fear of Crime and Constrained Behavior: Specifying and Estimating a Reciprocal Effects Model," *Social Forces* 66 (1988): 827-37.

"Living in Fear." *Los Angeles Times*, 23 August 1998, B1.

Loader, Ian, Evi Girling, and Richard Sparks, "Narratives of Decline: Youth, Dis/Order and Community in an English 'Middletown,' " *British Journal of Criminology* 38 (summer 1998): 388-403.

Logan, John, and Harvey Molotch. *Urban Fortunes*. Berkeley: University of California Press, 1987.

Los Angeles Times. *Public Opinion Survey: National Issues* (Survey #328) January 1994.

Lotke, Eric. *Hobbling a Generation: Young African American Men in D.C.'s Criminal Justice System Five Years Later*. Washington, DC: Sentencing Project, 1997.

Lott, John R. Jr. *More Guns, Less Crime: Understanding Crime and Gun Control Laws*. Chicago: University of Chicago Press, 1998.

Lynch, James. "Crime in International Perspective." In *Crime*, edited by James Q. Wilson and Joan Petersilia. San Francisco: Institute for Contemporary Studies, 1995.

Lynch, James P. and William J. Sabol, *Did Getting Tough on Crime Pay?* Washington, DC: The Urban Institute Crime Policy Report, August 1997.

Macleod, M. "Victim Participation at Sentencing." *Criminal Law Bulletin* 22 (1986): 501-17.

Maguire, Kathleen, and Ann L. Pastore, eds. *Sourcebook of Criminal Justice Statistics 1992*. Washington, DC: U.S. Department of Justice, Bureau of Justice Statistics, 1994.

Maguire, Kathleen, and Ann L. Pastore, eds. *Sourcebook of Criminal Justice Statistics 1994*. Washington, DC: U.S. Department of Justice, Bureau of Justice Statistics, 1995.

Maguire, Kathleen, and Ann L. Pastore, eds. *Sourcebook of Criminal Justice Statistics 1995*. Washington, DC: U.S. Department of Justice, Bureau of Justice Statistics, 1996.

Maguire, Kathleen, and Ann L. Pastore, eds. *Sourcebook of Criminal Justice Statistics 1996*. Washington, DC: U.S. Department of Justice, Bureau of Justice Statistics, 1997.

Maguire, Kathleen, and Ann L. Pastore, eds. *Sourcebook of Criminal Justice Statistics 1997*. Washington, DC: U.S. Department of Justice, Bureau of Justice Statistics, 1998 (retrieved from the World Wide Web 24 May 1999 at http://www.albany.edu/sourcebook).

Maguire, Kathleen, and Ann L. Pastore, eds. *Sourcebook of Criminal Justice Statistics 1998*. Retrieved from the World Wide Web 1 June 1999 at http://www.albany.edu/sourcebook.

Marion, Nancy E. *A History of Federal Crime Control Initiatives, 1960-1993*. Westport, CT: Praeger, 1994.

Marsh, H. L. "A Comparative Analysis of Crime Coverage in Newspapers in the United States and Other Countries From 1960-1989: A Review of the Literature." *Journal of Criminal Justice* 19 (1991): 67-80.

Masci, David. "$30 Billion Anti-Crime Bill Heads to Clinton's Desk." *Congressional Quarterly*, 27 August 1994, 2488-93.

Massachusetts Sentencing Commission. "Report to the General Court," Appendix A, 10 April 1996, Boston.

Massey, Douglas. "American Apartheid: Segregation and the Making of the Underclass." *American Journal of Sociology* 96 (1990): 329-57.

Matusow, Allen J. *The Unraveling of America: A History of Liberalism in the 1960's*. New York: Harper Torchbooks, 1984.

Mauer, Marc. *Americans Behind Bars: U.S. and International Use of Incarceration, 1995*. Washington, DC: Sentencing Project, 1997.

Mauer, Marc, and Tracy Huling. "Young Black Americans and the Criminal Justice System." Washington, DC: Sentencing Project, 1995.

Mawby, R. I., and S. Walklate. *Critical Victimology*. London: Sage, 1994.

Mayhew, Pat, and Jan J. M. Van Dijk. *Criminal Victimization in Eleven Industrialized Countries: Key Findings From the 1996 International Crime Victims Survey.* The Hague: Dutch Ministry of Justice, 1997.

McAnany, Patrick. "Assets Forfeiture as Drug Control Strategy." Paper presented at the annual meetings of the American Society of Criminology, New Orleans, Lousiana, November 1992.

McCombs, Maxwell, and Donald L. Shaw. "The Agenda-Setting Function of the Mass Media." *Public Opinion Quarterly* 36 (1972): 177.

McCord, Joan. "Placing Violence in Its Context." In *Violence and Childhood in the Inner City,* edited by J. McCord. New York: Cambridge University Press, 1997.

McCorkle, Richard. "Punish or Rehabilitate? Public Attitudes Toward Six Common Crimes," *Crime and Delinquency* 39 (1993): 240-52.

Merriam, John E. "National Media Coverage of Drug Issues, 1983-7." In *Communication Campaigns About Drugs: Government, the Media and the Public,* edited by Pamela Shoemaker. Hillsdale, NJ: Lawrence Erlbaum, 1989.

Messner, Steven. "Economic Discrimination and Societal Homicide Rates: Further Evidence on the Cost of Inequality." *American Sociological Review* 54 (1989): 597-611.

Messner, Steven, and Kenneth Tardiff. "Economic Inequality and Levels of Homicide: An Analysis of Urban Neighborhoods." *Criminology* 24 (1986): 297-316.

Michelowski, Raymond. "Some Thoughts Regarding the Impact of Clinton's Election on Crime and Justice Policy." *The Criminologist* 18 (May/June 1993).

Milakovich, Michael, and Kurt Weis. "Politics and Measures of Success in the War on Crime." *Crime and Delinquency* 21 (January 1975): 1-11.

Miller, Gale, and James Holstein. *Constructionist Controversies.* Hawthorne, NY: Aldine de Gruyter, 1993.

Miller, Jerome G. *Hobbling a Generation: Young African American Males in the Criminal Justice System of America's Cities: Baltimore, Maryland.* Washington, DC: Sentencing Project, 1992.

_____. *Search and Destroy: African-American Males in the Criminal Justice System.* New York: Cambridge University Press, 1996.

Mokhiber, Russell. *Corporate Crime and Violence.* San Francisco: Sierra Club Books, 1998.

Molotch, Harvey, and M. Lester. "News as Purposive Behavior: The Strategic Use of Routine Events, Accidents and Scandals." *American Sociological Review* 39 (1974): 101-112.

Monkkonen, Eric. *Police in Urban America, 1860-1920.* New York: Cambridge University Press, 1981.

Moore, Mark. "Supply Reduction and Drug Law Enforcement." In *Drugs and Crime,* edited by Michael Tonry and James Q. Wilson. Chicago: University of Chicago Press, 1990.

Morgan, D. *The Flacks of Washington: Government Information and the Public Agenda.* New York: Greenwood, 1986.

Morgan, Michael, and Nancy Signorielli, eds. *Cultivation Analysis: New Directions in Media Effects Research.* Newbury Park, CA: Sage, 1990.

Morganthau, Tom. "Crack and Crime." *Newsweek,* 16 June 1986, 16-22.

Morris, Lydia. *Dangerous Classes: The Underclass and Social Citizenship.* New York: Routledge, 1994.

Moynihan, Daniel P. *The Politics of a Guaranteed Income: The Nixon Administration and the Family Assistance Plan.* New York: Random House, 1973.

Myers, Laura. "Bringing the Offender to Heel: Views of the Criminal Courts." In *Americans View Crime and Justice*, edited by Timothy Flanagan and Dennis Longmire. Newbury Park, CA: Sage, 1996.

Nadlemann, Ethan. "Drug Prohibition in the U.S." In *Crack in America: Demon Drugs and Social Justice*, edited by Craig Reinarman and Harry Levine. Berkeley: University of California Press, 1997.

Nadlemann, Ethan A., Kurt Schmoke, Joseph D. McNamara, Robert W. Sweet, Thomas Szasz, and Steven B. Duke. "The War on Drugs Is Lost" (forum). *National Review*, 12 February 1996, 34-48.

National Corrections Reporting Program 1992. Washington, DC: U.S. Department of Justice, Office of Justice Programs, Bureau of Justice Statistics, 1994.

National Crime Prevention Council. *Partnerships to Prevent Youth Violence* (research brief). Washington, DC: Office of Justice Programs, U.S. Department of Justice, 1994.

National Crime Prevention Council. *Working as Partners With Community Groups* (research brief). Washington, DC: Office of Justice Programs, U.S. Department of Justice, 1994.

The National Drug Control Strategy, 1992: Budget Summary. Washington, DC: Office of the National Drug Control Policy, 1992.

The National Drug Control Strategy, 1998: Budget Summary. Washington, DC: Office of the National Drug Control Policy, 1998.

The National Drug Control Strategy, 1999: Budget Summary. Washington, DC: Office of the National Drug Control Policy, 1999.

National Institute of Drug Abuse. *Household Survey on Drug Abuse: Main Findings 1979*. Washington, DC: U.S. Department of Health and Human Services, 1980. 1982, 1985, 1988, 1990, 1993

National Institute of Drug Abuse. *Household Survey on Drug Abuse: Main Findings 1982*. Washington, DC: U.S. Department of Health and Human Services, 1983.

National Institute of Drug Abuse. *Household Survey on Drug Abuse: Main Findings 1985*. Washington, DC: U.S. Department of Health and Human Services, 1986.

National Institute of Drug Abuse. *Household Survey on Drug Abuse: Main Findings 1988*. Washington, DC: U.S. Department of Health and Human Services, 1989.

National Institute of Drug Abuse. *Household Survey on Drug Abuse: Main Findings 1990*. Washington, DC: U.S. Department of Health and Human Services, 1991.

National Institute of Drug Abuse. *Household Survey on Drug Abuse: Main Findings 1993*. Washington, DC: U.S. Department of Health and Human Services, 1994.

National Institute of Drug Abuse. *Preliminary Results From the 1996 National Household Survey on Drug Abuse*. Washington, DC: U.S. Department of Health and Human Services, 1997.

National Institute of Justice. "A Study of Homicide in Eight U.S. Cities: An NIJ Intramural Research Project" (research brief). Washington, DC: National Institute of Justice, U.S. Department of Justice, November, 1997.

National Institute on Drug Abuse. *Household Survey on Drug Abuse: Main Findings*. 1979, 1982, 1985, 1988, 1990, 1993.

National Institute on Drug Abuse. "Preliminary Results from the 1996 National Household Survey on Drug Abuse."Washington, DC: Department of Health and Human Services.

Nava, M. "Cleveland and the Press: Outrage and Anxiety in the Reporting of Child Sexual Abuse." *Feminist Review* 28 (1988): 103-21.

Nimmo, Dan. *Newsgathering in Washington: A Study in Political Communication*. New York: Atherton, 1964.

Nixon, Richard. "If Mob Rule Takes Hold in the US: A Warning from Richard Nixon." *U.S. News and World Report*, 15 August 1966, 64-65.

O'Brien, Robert M. "Police Productivity and Crime Rates: 1973-1992." *Criminology* 34 (1996): 183-207.

Oliver, Mary Beth, and G. Blake Armstrong. "The Color of Crime: Perceptions of Caucasians' and African Americans' Involvement in Crime." In *Entertaining Crime: Television Reality Programs*, edited by Gray Cavender and Mark Fishman. Hawthorne, NY: Aldine de Gruyter, 1998.

Omi, Michael. *We Shall Overturn: Race and the Contemporary American Right*. Ph.D. dissertation, University of California, Santa Cruz, 1987.

Omi, Michael, and Howard Winant. *Racial Formation in the United States*. New York: Routledge and Kegan Paul, 1986.

Orcutt, James, and Rebecca Faison. "Sex Role Attitude Change and Reporting of Rape Victimization, 1978-1985." In *Criminal Behavior: Text and Readings*, edited by Delos H. Kelly. New York: St. Martin's, 1994.

Orcutt, James D., and J. Blake Turner. "Shocking Numbers and Graphic Accounts: Quantified Images of Drug Problems in the Print Media." *Social Problems* 40 (1993): 190-206.

"Overdosing on the Drug War." *Boston Globe*, 24 September 1995, 1.

Perez-Pena, Richard. "New York's Income Gap Largest in the Nation." *New York Times*, 17 December 1997, A14.

Petersilia, Joan, and Ruth Peterson. *Prison versus Probation*. Santa Monica, CA: RAND, 1986.

Petersilia, Joan, and Susan Turner. "Comparing Intensive and Regular Supervision for High-Risk Probationers." *Crime and Delinquency* 36 (January 1990): 87-111.

Petersilia, Joan, and Susan Turner, with Joyce Peterson. *Prison versus Probation in California: Implications for Crime and Offender Recidivism*. Santa Monica, CA: RAND, 1986.

Peterson, Ruth D., and Bailey, William C. "Is Capital Punishment an Effective Deterrent for Murder? An Examination of the Social Science Research." In *America's Experiment with Capital Punishment: Reflections on the Past, Present and Future of the Ultimate Penal Sanction*, edited by James R. Acker, Robert M. Bohm, and Charles S. Lanier. Durham, NC: Carolina Academic, 1998.

Phillips, Kevin. *The Emerging Republican Majority*. New York: Arlington House, 1969.

Piven, Francis, and Richard Cloward. *Poor People's Movements: Why They Succeed, How They Fail*. New York: Arlington House, 1969.

Podolefsky, Aaron, and Frederic Dubow. *Strategies for Community Crime Prevention: Collective Responses to Crime in Urban America*. Springfield, IL: Charles C Thomas, 1981.

Porter, Bruce. "Is Solitary Confinement Driving Charlie Chase Crazy?" *New York Times Magazine*, 8 November 1998, 52-58.

Potter, W. "Perceived Reality and the Cultivation Hypothesis." *Journal of Broadcasting and Electronic Media* 30(1986): 159-74.

Poveda, Tony G. "Clinton, Crime and the Justice Department," *Social Justice* 21 (fall 1994): 73-84.

Powers, Stephen, David J. Rothman, and Stanley Rothman. *Hollywood's America*. Boulder, CO: Westview, 1996.

Prajean, Sister Helen. *Dead Man Walking*. New York: Random House, 1993.

"President Forms Panel to Study Crime Problems." *New York Times*, 27 July 1965, A1.

President's Commission on Law Enforcement and the Administration of Justice. *The Challenge of Crime in a Free Society*. Washington, DC: U.S. Government Printing Office, 1967.

Pritchard, David. "Homicide and Bargained Justice." In *The Media and Criminal Justice Policy: Recent Research and Social Effects*, edited by Ray Surette. Springfield, IL: Charles C Thomas, 1990.

Rand, Michael, James P. Lynch, and David Cantor. *Criminal Victimization, 1973-1995.* Washington, DC: Bureau of Justice Statistics, U.S. Department of Justice, 1997.

Rapping, Elayne. *Mediations.* Boston: South End, 1994.

Rasmussen, David W. *The Economic Anatomy of a Drug War: Criminal Justice in the Commons.* Lanham, MD: Rowman and Littlefield, 1994.

"Reagan: Drugs Are the 'No. 1' Problem." *Newsweek,* 18 August 1986, 18.

Reagan, Ronald. "Radio Address to the Nation on Proposed Crime Legislation." In *Public Papers of the Presidents 1984.* Vol. 2. Washington, DC: U.S. Government Printing Office, 1985.

_____. "Remarks at the Annual Conference of the National Sheriff's Association in Hartford, Conn." In *Public Papers of the Presidents 1984.* Vol. 2. Washington, DC: U.S. Government Printing Office, 1985.

_____. "Remarks at the Annual Convention of the Texas State Bar Association in San Antonio." In *Public Papers of the Presidents 1984.* Vol. 2. Washington, DC: U.S. Government Printing Office, 1984.

_____. "Remarks at the Conservative Political Action Conference Dinner." In *Public Papers of the Presidents 1983.* Vol. 1. Washington, DC: U.S. Government Printing Office, 1984.

_____. "Remarks at a Fundraising Dinner Honoring Former Representative John M. Ashbrook in Ashland, Ohio." In *Public Papers of the Presidents 1983.* Vol. 1. Washington, DC: U.S. Government Printing Office, 1984.

_____. "Remarks to Members of the National Governors Association." In *Public Papers of the Presidents 1988.* Vol. 1. Washington, DC: U.S. Government Printing Office, 1989.

_____. "Remarks at a White House Ceremony Observing Crime Victims Week." In *Public Papers of the Presidents 1983.* Vol. 1. Washington, DC: U.S. Government Printing Office, 1984.

Reeves, Jimmie L., and Richard Campbell. *Cracked Coverage: Television News, the Anti-cocaine Crusade, and the Reagan Legacy.* Durham, NC: Duke University Press, 1994.

Reider, Jonathon. "The Rise of the Silent Majority." In *The Rise and Fall of the New Deal Order, 1930-1980,* edited by Steve Fraser and Gary Gerstle. Princeton, NJ: Princeton University Press, 1989.

Reiman, Jeffrey. *The Rich Get Richer and the Poor Get Prison.* New York: Macmillan, 1990.

Reinarman, Craig. "Crack Attack: America's Latest Drug Scare, 1986-92." In *Images of Issues,* edited by Joel Best. New York: Aldine de Gruyter, 1995.

_____. "Unanticipated Consequences of Criminalization: Hypotheses on How Drug Laws Exacerbate Drug Problems." *Perspectives on Social Problems* 6 (1994): 217-32.

Reinarman, Craig and Harry Levine. "Crack in Context: Politics and Media in the Making of a Drug Scare." *Contemporary Drug Problems* 16 (1989): 535-577.

_____. "Punitive Prohibition America." In *Crack in America: Demon Drugs and Social Justice,* edited by Craig Reinarman and Harry Levine. Berkeley: University of California Press, 1997.

Reinarman, Craig, Sheigla Murphy, and Dan Waldorf. "Pharmacology Is Not Destiny: The Contingent Character of Cocaine Abuse and Addiction." *Addiction Research* 2 (1994): 1-16.

Reiner, Rob. "Media Made Criminality: The Representation of Crime in the Mass Media." In *The Oxford Handbook of Criminology,* 2nd ed., edited by Mike Maguire, Rod Morgan, and Robert Reiner. Oxford, England: Clarendon, 1997.

Reiss, Jr., Albert, and Jeffrey Roth, eds. *Understanding and Preventing Violence.* Washington, DC: National Academy Press, 1993.

Republican National Party. "Republican Party Platform of 1968." In *CQ Almanac*. Washington, DC: Congressional Quarterly, Inc., 1968.

Reuter, Peter, and Mark Kleiman. "Risks and Prices: An Economic Analysis of Drug Prices." In *Crime and Justice: A Review of Research*, edited by Michael Tonry and Norval Morris. Chicago: University of Chicago Press, 1986.

Roberts, Julian V. "Public Opinion, Crime and Criminal Justice." In *Crime and Justice: A Review of Research*, Vol. 16, edited by Michael Tonry. Chicago: University of Chicago Press, 1992.

Roberts, Julian, and A. Doob. "News Media Influence on Public Views on Sentencing," *Law and Human Behavior* 14 (1990): 451-68.

Roberts, Julian, and Don Edwards. "Contextual Effects in Judgements of Crimes, Criminals and the Purpose of Sentencing." *Journal of Applied Social Psychology* 19 (1992): 902-917.

Roberts, Julian, and Loretta Stalans. *Public Opinion, Crime and Criminal Justice*. Boulder, CO: Westview, 1997.

Rosenbaum, Dennis. "Community Crime Prevention: A Review and Synthesis of the Literature," *Justice Quarterly* 5 (September 1988): 323-95.

Rossi, Peter, and Richard Berk. *Just Punishments: Federal Guidelines and Public Views Compared*. Hawthorne, NY: Aldine de Gruyter, 1997.

Rothman, David. *Conscience and Convenience: The Asylum and Its Alternatives in Progressive America*. New York: HarperCollins, 1980.

Sadd, Susan, and Randolph Grinc. *Issues in Community Policing: Problems in the Implementation of Eight Innovative Neighborhood-Oriented Policing Projects*. Washington, DC: National Institute of Justice, 1994.

Sampson, Robert J. "The Embeddedness of Child and Adolescent Development: A Community-Level Perspective on Urban Violence." In *Violence and Childhood in the Inner City*, edited by Joan McCord. Cambridge, England: Cambridge University Press, 1997.

_____. "Urban Black Violence: The Effect of Male Joblessness and Family Disruption." *American Journal of Sociology* 93 (1987): 348-82.

Sampson, Robert, and William J. Wilson. "Race, Crime and Urban Inequality." In *Crime and Inequality*, edited by John Hagan and Ruth Peterson. Stanford, CA: Stanford University Press, 1995.

Sandys, Marla, and Edmund F. McGarrell. "Attitudes Toward Capital Punishment: Preference For the Penalty or Mere Acceptance?" *Journal of Research in Crime and Delinquency* 32 (May 1995): 191-213.

Sasson, Theodore. "African American Conspiracy Theories and the Social Construction of Crime," *Sociological Inquiry* 65 (1995): 265-85.

_____. "Beyond Agenda Setting: The Framing Effects of 'Nannygate' on a Death Penalty Debate." Paper presented at the annual meeting of the American Society of Criminology, Washington, DC, November, 1998.

_____. *Crime Talk: How Citizens Construct a Social Problem*. New York: Aldine de Gruyter, 1995.

_____. "Mobilizing For Change: Social Movements in Modern Society." In *Understanding Society*. Thousand Oaks, CA: Pine Forge Press, 2000.

Sasson, Theodore, and Margaret K. Nelson. "Danger, Community and the Meaning of Crime Watch: An Analysis of the Discourses of African-American and White Participants." *Journal of Contemporary Ethnography* 25 (July 1996): 171-200.

Schlesinger, Philip. "Rethinking the Sociology of Journalism." In *Public Communication: The New Imperatives*, edited by Marjorie Ferguson. London: Sage, 1990.

Schlesinger, Philip, and Howard Tumber. *Reporting Crime: The Media Politics of Criminal Justice*. Oxford: Clarendon, 1994.

Schlesinger, Philip, Howard Tumber, and Graham Murdock. "The Media Politics of Crime and Criminal Justice." *British Journal of Sociology* 42 (1991): 397-420.

Schlosser, Eric. "The Prison Industrial Complex." *Atlantic Monthly*, December 1998, 51-77.

_____. "Reefer Madness." *Atlantic Monthly*, August 1994, 45-63.

Schram, Sanford. *Words of Welfare: The Poverty of Social Science and the Social Science of Poverty*. Minneapolis: University of Minnesota Press, 1995.

Schudson, Howard. *Discovering the News: A Social History of American Newspapers*. New York: Basic Books, 1978.

Seagal, Debra. "Tales from the Cutting Room Floor." *Harpers Magazine*, November 1993, 50-57.

Secret, Philip, and James Johnson. "Racial Differences in Attitudes Toward Crime Control," *Journal of Criminal Justice* 17 (1989): 361-75.

Sentencing Project. "National Inmate Population of Two Million Projected by 2000." Washington, DC: Sentencing Project. Retrieved from the World Wide Web 3 June 1999 at http://www.sentencingproject.org/pubs/tsppubs/prison1.htm

_____. "Proposed Changes in Crack/Cocaine Sentencing Laws Would Increase Number Minorities in Prison, Have Little Impact on Drug Abuse." Washington, DC: Sentencing Project, 1997.

Shapiro, Bruce. "Victims and Vengeance: Why the Victims' Rights Amendment Is a Bad Idea." *The Nation* 264 (10 February 1997): 11-19.

Shaw, Clifford, and Henry McKay. *Juvenile Delinquency and Urban Areas*. Chicago: University of Chicago Press, 1942.

Shaylor, Cassandra. "Organizing Resistance: Building a Movement Against the Prison Industrial Complex," *Colorlines* 1 (fall 1998).

Sherizen, Steven. "Social Creation of Crime News: All the News That's Fitted to Print." In *Deviance and the Mass Media*, edited by Charles Winick. Beverley Hills, CA: Sage, 1978.

Sherman, Lawrence. "Communities and Crime Prevention." In *Preventing Crime: What Works, What Doesn't, and What's Promising*, edited by Lawrence W. Sherman, Denise C. Gottfredwon, Doris L. MacKenzie, John Eck, Peter Reuter, and Shawn D. Bushway. Washington, DC: Department of Justice, Office of Justice Programs, National Institute of Justice, 1997.

_____. "Thinking About Crime Prevention." In *Preventing Crime: What Works, What Doesn't, What's Promising*, edited by Lawrence W. Sherman, Denise C. Gottfredwon, Doris L. MacKenzie, John Eck, Peter Reuter, and Shawn D. Bushway. Washington, DC: Department of Justice, Office of Justice Programs, National Institute of Justice, 1997.

Sherman, Lawrence. "Experiments in Restorative Policing: A Progress Report on the Canberra Reintegrative Shaming Experiments (RISE)." 30 June 1998. Canberra, Australia: Australian National University and Australian Federal Police.

Sherman, Lawrence, and Dennis P. Rogan. "Effects of Gun Seizure on Gun Violence." *Justice Quarterly* 12 (December 1995): 673-93.

Shine, Cathy, and Marc Mauer. "Does the Punishment Fit the Crime?" Washington, DC: Sentencing Project, 1993.

Sigal, Leon. *Reporters and Officials: The Organization and Politics of Newsmaking*. London: D. C. Heath, 1973.

Signorielli, Nancy. "Television's Mean and Dangerous World: A Continuation of the Cultural Indicators Perspective." In *Cultivation Analysis: New Directions in Media Effects*

Research, edited by Michael Morgan and Nancy Signorielli. Newbury Park, CA: Sage, 1990.

Simon, Jonathan. *Poor Discipline: Parole and the Social Control of the Underclass.* Chicago: University of Chicago Press, 1993.

Skidmore, P. "Telling Tales: Media, Power, Ideology and the Reporting of Child Sexual Abuse in Britain." In *Crime and the Media,* edited by D. Kidd-Hewitt and R. Osborne. London: Pluto, 1995.

Skogan, Wesley. *Disorder and Decline.* Berkeley: University of California Press, 1990.

Skogan, Wesley, and Michael Maxfield. *Coping with Crime.* Beverley Hills, CA: Sage, 1981.

Skolnick, Jerome, and David Bayley. *The New Blue Line.* New York: Free Press, 1986.

Slater, Eric. "California's Pizza Bandit Facing Life in Prison." *Philadelphia Inquirer,* 22 January 1995.

Smith, Brent L. "Victims and Victim's Rights Activists: Attitudes Toward Criminal Justice Officials and Victim-Related Issues." *Criminal Justice Review* 13 (Spring 1988): 21-28.

Smith, Christian. *Resisting Reagan: The U.S. Central America Peace Movement.* Chicago: University of Chicago Press, 1996.

Soothhill, Keith, and Sylvia Walby. *Sex Crimes in the News.* New York: Routledge, 1991.

Sparks, Richard. "Reason and Unreason in 'Left Realism': Some Problems in the Constitution of the Fear of Crime." In *Issues in Realist Criminology,* edited by Roger Matthews and Jock Young. London: Sage, 1992.

_____. *Television and the Drama of Crime: Moral Tales and the Place of Crime in Public Life.* Buckingham, UK: Open Unversity Press, 1992.

Speakes, Larry. *Press Briefing by Larry Speakes, The White House, Office of the Press Secretary, July 30, 1986.* Doc. no. 1847-07/30, Ronald Reagan Library, Simi Valley, CA.

Stanko, Elizabeth. *Everyday Violence: How Women and Men Experience Sexual and Physical Danger.* London: Pandora, 1990.

_____. *Intimate Intrusions: Women's Experience of Male Violence.* London: Routledge, 1985.

Staples, William. *The Culture of Surveillance.* New York: St. Martin's, 1997.

Stark, Steven. "Perry Mason Meets Sonny Crockett: The History of Lawyers and the Police as Television Heroes." *University of Miami Law Review* 42 (1987): 244.

Statistical Abstract of the United States. Washington, DC: U.S. Department of Commerce, Bureau of the Census, 1998. Retrieved from the World Wide Web 4 June 1999 at http://www.census.gov/statab/www/

Stern, Vivian. *A Sin against the Future.* Boston: Northeastern University Press, 1998.

Stinchcombe, Arthur, Rebecca Adams, Carol Heimer, Kim Lane Scheppele, Tome Smith, and D. Garth Taylor. *Crime and Punishment in America: Changing Attitudes in America.* San Francisco, CA: Jossey-Bass, 1980.

Stockman, David. *The Triumph of Politics.* New York: Avon, 1986.

Stutman, Robert. *Dead on Delivery: Inside the Drug Wars, Straight From the Street.* Boston: Little, Brown, 1992.

Sullivan, Mercer. *Getting Paid.* Ithaca, NY: Cornell University Press, 1989.

Surette, Ray. *Media, Crime and Criminal Justice: Images and Realities,* 2nd ed. Belmont, CA: Wadsworth, 1998.

_____. "Predator Criminals as Media Icons." In *Media, Process and the Social Construction of Crime: Studies in Newsmaking Criminology,* edited by Gregg Barak. New York: Garland, 1994.

Tarrow, Sidney. *Power in Movement.* New York: Cambridge University Press, 1994.

Thomas, Chuck. "Marijauna Arrests and Incarceration in the United States: Preliminary Report." Washington, DC: Marijuana Policy Project, November 1998.

Tocqueville, Alexis de. *Democracy in America*. New York: Random House, 1981.

Tonry, Michael, ed. *Crime and Justice: A Review of Research*. Vol. 14. Chicago: University of Chicago Press, 1991.

————. *Intermediate Sanctions in Sentencing Guidelines*. Washington, DC: National Institute of Justice, U.S. Department of Justice, 1997.

————. *Malign Neglect: Race, Crime and Punishment in America*. Oxford, England: Oxford University Press, 1995.

————. *Sentencing Matters*. New York: Oxford University Press, 1996.

Tonry, Michael, and Norval Morris, eds. *Communities and Crime, Crime and Justice: A Review of Research*. Vol. 10. Chicago: University of Chicago Press, 1987.

Trebach, Arnold. "Arizona and California Voters Seize Initiatives." *Drug Policy Letter*, winter/spring 1997, 23-24.

Troyer, Ronald. "Some Consequences of Contextual Constructionism." *Social Problems* 39 (1992): 35-37.

Tuchman, Gayle. *Making News: A Study in the Construction of Reality*. New York: Free Press, 1978.

Turner, Patricia. *I Heard it Through the Grape Vine*. Berkeley: University of California Press, 1993.

Umbreit, Mark S. "Restorative Justice Through Victim-Offender Mediation: A Multi-Site Assessment." *Western Criminological Review* 1 (1998). Available: http://wcr.sonma.edu/v1n1/umbreit.html

University of California, Los Angeles. *U.C.L.A. Television Violence Monitoring Project*. Retrieved from the World Wide Web 19 May 1999, http://media-awareness.ca/eng/med/home/resource/ucla.htm

University of Michigan. *Monitoring the Future Study*, 1998. Retrieved from the World Wide Web 1 June 1999, http://www.isr.umich.edu/src/mtf/pr98t3.html

U.S. Department of Commerce. *State Government Finances, 1973-1994*. Washington, DC: U.S. Government Printing Office, 1974-1995.

U.S. Department of Justice. *Attorney General's Task Force on Violent Crime: Final Report*. Washington, DC: U.S. Government Printing Office, 1981.

U.S. Sentencing Commission. *Mandatory Minimum Penalties in the Federal Justice System: Special Report to Congress*. Washington, DC: Government Printing Office, 1991.

Van Dijk, Jan J. M., and Pat Mayhew. *Experiences of Crime Across the World: Key Findings of the 1989 International Crime Survey*, 2nd ed. Boston: Kluwer Law and Taxation, 1991.

"Voting Rights for Felons?" (editorial). *New York Post*, 27 February 1999.

Waldorf, Dan, Craig Reinarman, and Sheigla Murphy. *Cocaine Changes: The Experience of Using and Quitting*. Philadelphia: Temple University Press, 1991.

Walker, Samuel. *Sense and Nonsense About Crime and Drugs*. Belmont, CA: Wadsworth, 1994.

Walker, Samuel, and Betsy Wright Kreisel. "Varieties of Citizen Review: The Implications of Organizational Features of Complaint Review Procedures for Accountability of the Police." *American Journal of the Police* 15 (1996): 65-88.

Walker, Samuel, Cassia Spohn, and Miriam DeLone. *The Color of Justice: Race, Ethnicity and Crime in America*. Belmont, CA: Wadsworth, 1996.

Walklate, Sandra. "Victims, Crime Prevention and Social Control." In *Beyond Law and Order: Criminal Justice Policy and Politics Into the 1990s*, edited by Robert Reiner and Malcolm Cross. Hampshire, CT: Macmillan Academic and Professional, 1991.

Wallman, Joel. "Disarming Youth." *The HFG Review* 2 (fall 1997).

Warr, Mark. "Poll Trends: Public Opinion on Crime and Punishment," *Public Opinion Quarterly* 59 (1995): 296-310.

"Washington Case Is a Test for '3 Strikes' Law." *Boston Globe*, 21 June 1994.

Weed, Frank. *Certainty of Justice*. Hawthorne, NY: Aldine de Gruyter, 1995.

Weikel, Dan. "War on Crack Targets Minorities Over Whites." *Los Angeles Times*, 21 May 1995, A1.

Western, Bruce, and Katherine Beckett. "How Unregulated Is the U.S. Labor Market? The Dynamics of Jobs and Jails, 1980-1995." *American Journal of Sociology* 104 (January 1999): 1030-60.

Whitaker, Mark. "Decision and Division: Whites v. Blacks," *Newsweek*, 16 October 1995, 24.

Whitney, Charles D., M. Fritzer, S. Jones, S. Mazzarella, and L. Rakow. "Source and Geographic Bias in Television News 1982-4." *Journal of Electronic Broadcasting and Electronic Media* 33 (1989): 159-74.

Wilkinson, Deanna and Jeffrey Fagan. "The Role of Firearms in Violence 'Scripts': The Dynamics of Gun Events Among Adolescent Males." *Law and Contemporary Problems* 59 (winter 1996).

Williams, A. Kevin. "Community Mobilization Against Urban Crime: Guiding Orientations and Strategic Choices in Grassroots Politics." *Urban Affairs Review* 30 (January 1995): 407-31.

Wilson, James Q. "Against the Legalization of Drugs." In *Taking Sides: Clashing Views on Controversial Issues in Drugs and Society*, edited by Raymond Goldberg. Guildford, CT: Dushkin, 1993.

Wilson, James Q., and George Kelling. "Broken Windows: The Police and Neighborhood Safety." *The Atlantic Monthly*, March 1982, 29-38.

Wilson, William J. *The Truly Disadvantaged*. Chicago: University of Chicago Press, 1987.

_____. *When Work Disappears: The World of the New Urban Poor*. New York: Alfred A. Knopf, 1996.

Windelsham, David James George Hennessy (Lord). *Politics, Punishment, and Populism*. New York: Oxford University Press, 1998.

Wolff, Edward N. "Recent Trends in the Size Distribution of Household Wealth." *Journal of Economic Perspectives* 12 (summer 1998): 131-50.

Wortley, Scot, Ross Macmillan, and John Hagan. "Just Des(s)erts? The Racial Polarization of Perceptions of Criminal Injustice," *Law and Society Review* 31 (1997): 637-76.

Wright, James, and Peter Rossi. *Armed and Considered Dangerous: A Survey of Felons and Their Firearms*. Hawthorne, NY: Aldine de Gruyter, 1994.

Wright, Kevin. *The Great American Crime Myth*. Westport, CT: Greenwood, 1985.

Yardley, Jim. "One Precinct, 2 Very Different Murder Cases." *New York Times*, 18 March 1999, A1, A23.

Zillmann, D., and Wakshlag, J. "Fear of Victimization and the Appeal of Crime Drama." In *Selective Exposure to Communication*, edited by D. Zillmann and Jennings Bryant. Hillsdale, NJ: Lawrence Erlbaum, 1985.

Zimmer, Lynn, and John P. Morgan. *Exposing Marijuana Myths: An Objective Review of the Scientific Literature*. New York: Lindesmith Center, 1995.

Zimring, Franklin. "Is Gun Control Likely to Reduce Violent Killings?" *University of Chicago Law Review* 35 (1968): 721-37.

Zimring, Franklin, and Gordon Hawkins. *Crime Is Not the Problem: Lethal Violence in America*. New York: Oxford University Press, 1997.

_____. *The Scale of Imprisonment*. Chicago: University of Chicago Press, 1995.

_____. *Search for Rational Drug Control Policy*. New York: Cambridge University Press, 1992.

Index

whites and, 79
Violent Crime Control and Law
    Enforcement Act of 1994, 71-72, 73
Violent Juvenile Offender program, 205
Voters, 55, 56, 57
    African American males, 192
    felons, 192

Wages, declining, 197
War on crime, 47, 51-54
    consequences of, 196
    crime rate and, 190-191
    federal, 50
    media and, 11
    victims rights movement and, 164
War on drugs, 47, 126, 172-175, 209
    activist groups and, 167-169
    cop shows depicting, 111
    criticism of, 70, 93, 95-98, 167-169
    emergence of, 66
    escalation of, 67-68
    failure of, 68-69, 191
    federal government and, 64-70
    fictional television shows and, 105
    media and, 88-98
    Republicans and, 10
    sentencing and, 168
War on poverty, 51-54, 62
Warren Court, 59
Washington, DC:
    African American males under
        correctional supervision in, 2, 189
    African American drug dealers, 41
    handgun control, 206
    homicide rate, 40
Washington State, three strikes law in, 180
Wealth, distribution of, 33, 150
Welfare, 51, 62, 197
    conservatives attacking, 62

spending on, 192
Welfare culture, 48, 53
Welfare reform, 136, 139, 197
Welfare state, 63
White(s):
    block-watch programs, 151-152
    civil rights causes and, 56
    crack use by, 95-96
    crime news coverage and, 79
    family income, 34
    in state prisons, 187
    incarceration for drug crimes, 179-180
    media crime depictions and, 84
    violent crime and, 79
White cops, racism and, 141
White voters, 56, 57
White women, fear of crime and, 83
Wilson, William Julius, 36-37, 42
Women:
    fear of crime and, 83, 120, 122-123
    heading households, 51, 52
    in state prisons, 187
    incarcerated, 192

Youth:
    boot camps for offenders, 70
    control over, 36, 37
    death penalty and, 183
    drug use by, 173
    gun use, 32, 184, 185
    opportunities for, 54
    supervision of, 152
    violent crime by, 184
Youth offenders:
    reintegrating into society, 205
    See also Juvenile offenders

Zero tolerance policing, 208, 209